SAGGISTICA 24

Intimate History of the Great War

Letters, Diaries, and Memoirs
from Soldiers on the Front

Intimate History of the Great War
Letters, Diaries, and Memoirs from Soldiers on the Front

Quinto Antonelli

Translated by
Siân Elaine Gibby

BORDIGHERA PRESS

Library of Congress Control Number: 2016953054

Originally published in Italian as

Storia intima della grande guerra:
lettere, diari e memorie dei soldati dal fronte
Donzelli Editore, 2014

© 2016 English translation by Siân Elaine Gibby
© 2014 by Donzelli Editore

All rights reserved. Parts of this book may be reprinted only by written permission from the author, and may not be reproduced for publication in book, magazine, or electronic media of any kind, expect for purposes of literary review by critics.

Printed in the United States.

Published by
BORDIGHERA PRESS
John D. Calandra Italian American Institute
25 West 43rd Street, 17th Floor
New York, NY 10036

SAGGISTICA 24
ISBN 978-1-59954-111-2

Table of Contents

Translator's Note	ix
Preface	xi
Chronology	xv
Introduction Great War and People: Representations, voices, writings	1
Italians on the Russian Front	69
The Blessing	91
Beyond the Border of Irredentist Lands	97
The Deadly Rumbling	111
Machines Against Diggers	125
The Enormous Olive Press	147
The Assault	173
Killing the Enemy	195
The Grand Hotel of Fear	209
On the Front of the Endless Winter	217
Giuseppe and Maria	237
A Painful and Heartfelt Nostalgia	247
The Moral Revolt	269
Impossible Flights	289
Sources	307
Index of Place Names	319

Translator's Note

Quinto Antonelli thoughtfully "pre-translated" into standard Italian a number of the soldiers' entries that were written in dialects or with irregular syntax and spelling, it having been determined that approximating these unique facets of their communication in English would be impossible.

Readers of the original Italian publication, then, have exclusive access to some of the subtle aspects of the soldiers' "voices" that can be discerned only via their native tongues.

However, the personalities of these men still shine brightly through the words on the page, even in English: in their choices of what to write about, their vivid descriptions and emotions, their humor and creativity, and their confessions and philosophical musings.

Preface

This volume, which brings together letters, diaristic notes, and autobiographical memoirs of the Great War, is an anthology of very distinct qualities: The texts here selected are the works of ordinary soldiers, very rarely officers, they are texts that have a social meaning (referred to as the "populist" category of workers: peasants, laborers, artisans),[1] they are situated in the channel of popular or populist writings, and they distance themselves, almost invariably, from syntactic and orthographic norms (and for that reason may seem unmanageable).

The letters and diaries of these common soldiers (memoirs are a different case) weren't written for those of us reading them now; they were part of an intimate communication, inside the circle of family, as a part of the continuing oral colloquia characterized by filial and conjugal confidences. We posthumous readers were not imagined, with the result that when faced with the fragility of this writing our presence now has a kind of intrusive, indecent quality. Cultured officers, on the other hand (to say nothing of officer-writers or officer-journalists) even when writing to their families or drawing out apparently classified notes are writing a bit for posterity, and even a bit for us. That little or great "literary" and formal quality that governs their writing includes us, who, as their model readers, need not worry so much about the scruples of such reading.[2]

---

[1] The category of "people's" [or "populist," as we have translated it here] even while fashioning itself mostly as an exclusive term, nevertheless has its use, it defines the subject we are talking about in a way rather clearly contrasting itself to the people it is not (the elites). On this question the bibliography is enormous: cfr. P. Burke, *La storia culturale*, Italian edition edited by P. Capuzzo. Bologna: Il Mulino, 2006, pp. 40-42.

[2] We refer naturally to the figure brought to the fore by Umberto Eco in *Lector in fabula. La cooperazione interprativa nei testi narrative*. Milan: Bompiani; 1983.

The second distinctive trait that sets this anthology apart from others (which have been more numerous in the past) is a very broad concept of "Italian." The texts included here mean to recount the war experiences of "all" the Italians who live in our land, including those who a hundred years ago were Austrian subjects, such as those from Trentino, from Venezia Giulia, and from Trieste. This seems to us to be a choice that, without being too emphatic, might also assume an ethical aspect inasmuch as it places in circulation memoirs that for a long time had been excluded from the national story, considered for too long to be marginal and lived as separate, when not actually conflicting.³ Clearly all this complicates the narrative and puts into crisis unities of time and place: For the Austrian Italians the war began a year earlier with the general conscription of August 1, 1914, their destination being the eastern front, Polish Galizia, Bucovina, Volinia, and the enemy the Russian army. In 1915, with the entrance of Italy into the war and the consequent opening up of the Italo-Austrian front (an arc of about 500 kilometers that traversed the eastern Alps from Ortles to the gulf of Trieste) some thousands of Italian-speaking soldiers, despite the decisions of the Austro-Hungarian hierarchies and because of the nature of that army, ended up fighting in the mountains of Trentino and Karst against the Italian army.⁴ The reader will find therefore memoirs that come out of opposing fronts, which in the end create a tale of Italians that is not only richer but also freer.⁵

Having established this collection, it remains only to describe the new "dispositio," the method of combination or, to put it in cinematographic terms, the editing of the texts.

---

3 Cfr. R. Bodei, *Libro della memoria e della speranza*. Bologna: Il Mulino, 1995.

4 The decision made by the Austrian General Viktor Dankl, commander of the Tirolese territorial defense, has to do, though not exclusively, with the Trentinos believed to be totally "untrustworthy." Cfr. O. Uberegger, *L'altra guerra. La giurisdizione militare in Tirolo durante la prima guerra mondiale*. Trento: Società di studi trentini di scienze storiche, 2004, pp. 326-329.

5 It is reassuring to know that Marco Mondini too, in his most recent work, adopts an inclusive approach similar to ours: cfr., M. Mondini, *La guerra italiana. Partire, raccontare, tornare 1914-18*. Bologna: Il Mulino, 2014.

As one will be able to read in the introductory chapter, the organization of anthologies dedicated to the Great War for the most part obey a formal criterion whereby the texts follow an alphabetical order by writer or else a chronological order, or are grouped by type (letters, testaments, songs, war correspondence). There are however also more elaborate systems, efforts to compose thematic chapters, almost always prescribed or of a nationalistic rhetoric or else those devoted to a nationalistic pedagogy that aspires to raise up ideals of exemplary behavior (the ideals, faith, and will, but also the crises, suffering, and mortality of the combatants).

Our anthology adheres to a different criterion: It presents the texts in such a way as to create a collective account, where the chapters signal stages of a journey of the soldiers into the depth of that separate universe, into that real and true "elsewhere" that is the "war zone." Unloaded from the military trains, the soldiers delve into an unknown territory, and step by step they discover the march, the trench, the front line, the bombardment, the advance watch, the assault, as they become more and more conscious of the frailty of their own bodies and of their own minds.

The theme of this anthology therefore is the experience of the common soldier in war, a journey of the initiate, told "live" in real time to their families or recollected years later to the generation of their children and grandchildren. We have deliberately omitted texts written from prison, which tell of a completely different experience and which by their significance and their numbers merit their own volume.

Chronology

1914

June 28   Assassination in Sarajevo of Austrian Archduke Francis Ferdinand and of his wife, Countess Sofia Chotek.

July 23   Austria's ultimatum to Serbia.

July 28   Austria-Hungary declares war on Serbia.

July 31   Emporer Franz Joseph gives the order for general deployment of troops and of national conscription: Men between ages twenty-one and forty-two years are called up.

August 1   Germany declares war on Russia.

August 3   Germany declares war on France.

August 5   Austria-Hungary declares war on Russia.

August 6   Serbia declares war on Germany.

August 12   Great Britain and France declare war on the Austro-Hungarian Empire.

August 23   Japan declares war on Germany.

September 9   The French stop the Germans on the Marne.

September 6-12   The Battle of Lemberg. The Russians defeat the Austrians and undertake the occupation of Galizia as far as the field trenches of Krakow.

October 29   The Turkish Empire enters the war on the German side.

November 2-5   The Allies declare war on Turkey.

December 29   Italy occupies the port of Valona.

1915

April 22 Germany for the first time uses poison gas on the Western Front.

April 25 Allies land at Gallipoli: a bloodbath.

May 1 Austro-German counteroffensive begins in Galizia: In two months the entirety of Galizia is reconquered.

May 3 Italy nullifies the Triple Alliance of 1882.

May 3-23 The "glorious days of May": interventionist protests in many Italian cities.

May 20 The Italian Parliament affords extraordinary powers to the government in case of war. The Socialists vote against it.

May 23 Italy declares war on Austria-Hungary, and the following day the Italian army crosses the border.

May 24 At Ypres, on the western front, there is a heavy attack by Germany with poison gas.

June 22 Troops of the Central Powers retake Galizia and enter Leopoli.

June 23 First Battle of Isonzo. The offensive ends on July 7 with 15,000 Italian casualties and 10,400 Austrian.

July 18 Second Battle of Isonzo, which lasts until August 3.

August 5 The Austro-Germans occupy Warsaw.

August 21 Italy declares war on Turkey.

September 6 Bulgaria enters the war on the side of the Central Powers.

October 7 New offensive against Serbia. Belgrade falls and the Serbian army begins its retreat.

October 18 Third Battle of Isonzo, which lasts until November 3: 67,000 Italian casualties, 42,000 Austrian.

October 19   Italy and Russia declare war on Bulgaria.

November 10   Fourth Battle of Isonzo. It is suspended until December 5: 49,000 Italian casualties, 25,000 Austrian.

1916

January 8   Austria invades Montenegro.

February 21   German offensive at Verdun begins with a hail of bombs.

February 27   The French resist: At Verdun a soldier dies every forty-five seconds.

March 9   Germany declares war on Portugal.

March 11   Fifth Battle of Isonzo: It is interrupted after five days.

March 15   Austria-Hungary declares war on Portugal.

April 17   An Italian mine blows up the peak of Col di Lana.

May 15   The Austrian offensive in Trentino begins.

June 4   Russian Gen. Alexei Brusilov launches a general offensive against the Austro-Germans on the eastern front.

June 24   The high-plains battle (Strafexpedition) fails; the Austrians fall back.

June 29   The Austrians use poison gas for the first time at Karst.

July 1   The Battle of the Somme begins between the English and German armies. It will end "officially" only on November 18, leaving a million dead on the field.

July 12   Cesare Battisti and Fabio Filzi, volunteers from Trento in the Italian army, captured, tried, and condemned for high treason, are locked up in the cellar of the castle of Buonconsiglio, in Trento.

August 6 Sixth Battle of Isonzo: It lasts until the 16th of August.

September 14-17 War of attrition resumes with the seventh Battle of Isonzo.

October 10-13 Eighth Battle of Isonzo.

November 1-4 Ninth Battle of Isonzo. In the three autumn battles, the Italians lose 77,300 men, the Austrians 74,300.

November 21 Emperor Franz Joseph dies. He is succeeded by his great-nephew Carl.

December 6 German troops enter Bucharest.

1917

March 10 General strike in Petrograd.

March 15 Tzar Nicholas is forced to abdicate; it is the end of the Romanovs.

April 6 The United States declares war on Germany.

May 12-28 Tenth Battle of Isonzo. Heavy losses: 112,000 Italian and 76,000 Austrian.

June 3 Albania becomes an Italian protectorate.

June 10-25 Italian offensive on the Asiago plain. The Battle of Ortigara will mean the loss of 25,000 Italian soldiers.

July 1 General Brusilov launches the last desperate Russian offensive against the Austro-German lines.

July 2 Greece declares war on the Central Powers, against Turkey and against Bulgaria.

August 1 Pope Benedict the 15th appeals for peace; war is a "useless massacre."

August 14 China enters the war on the side of the Allies.

August 17 - September 15 Eleventh Battle of Isonzo: 160,000 Italians lost, 85,000 Austrians.

October 23-25 In Russia, the Bolsheviks, led by Lenin, take power.

October 24 The Austro-Germans attack near Caporetto. The Italian front is demolished at the Isonzo.

November 10 The Italian army is deployed on the Piave River.

November 22 (Julian calendar) Soviet Russia signs an armistice with the Central Powers.

December 7 The United States declares war on Austria-Hungary.

December 9 Romania yields and signs the armistice with the Central Powers.

1918

January 8 U.S. President Woodrow Wilson enunciates the fourteen points necessary for world peace.

March 3 Soviet Russia signs the peace treaty of Brest-Litovsk.

May Civil war begins in Russia: The Red Army pits itself against the counter-revolutionary "White" movement.

June 15-23 The Austrian offensive fails, which had extended from Asiago to the mouth of the Piave.

July 16 The Bolsheviks of Yekaterinburg execute Tsar Nicholas II and his entire family.

August Allied troops arrive in Siberia to combat the Bolsheviks.

September 29 Bulgaria surrenders to Allied troops.

October 24 - November 3 Italian offensive that ends in the victory of Vittorio Veneto and the armistice of Villa Giusti.

November 3 Italian troops enter Trento and Trieste.

November 4   At 3P.M. the war in Italy ends.

November 9   Revolution breaks out in Berlin. William II abdicates and the country is declared the German Republic.

November 11   At 11A.M. the war on the western front ceases.

November 12   Abdication of Carl I of Austria. It is proclaimed the Austrian Republic.

November 16   The Hungarian Republic is born.

December 1   In Belgrade Yugoslavia is born: the kingdom of the Serbs, the Croats, and the Slovenes.

December 31   Spanish flu, the largest pandemic in history, kills, in the course of one year, 450,000 Americans, 400,000 Germans, 375,000 Italians, 150,000 Britons, and 6 million Indians.

A mia moglie Marisa

Great War and People: Representations, Voices, Writings

THE SEMANTICS OF SACRIFICE

Initially, and for some time, it was only members of the upper middle class who publicly recounted tales of the war, who documented the stories of their sons fallen in the course of the conflict and were resurrected via the publication of their private correspondence. If the commemoration of the deaths of individual young officers began during the war, it is in the years immediately following that it took the form of monument campaigns ("an incoming tide of stone")[1] by which hundreds of pamphlets, produced by their relatives, feed a worship that situates itself, as Oliver Janz writes, "at the intersection point between public and private spheres, halfway between individual mourning and patriotic meaning, between family and nation, an existential overcoming of the crisis and political instrumentalization."[2] Along with biographical profiles, funeral elegies, and commemorative texts from friends and family, in many cases the pamphlets contain also a selection of letters from the fallen soldier, addressed to parents, to siblings, or to their closest friends, comprising in their totality a first grand epistolary corpus with both celebrative

---

1 M. Isenghi, *Le Guerre degli italiani. Parole, immagini, ricordi, 1848-1945*. Milan: Mondadori, 1989, p. 346.
2 O. Janz, *Monumenti di carta. Le pubblicazioni in memoria dei caduti della prima Guerra mondiale*, in *Mom omnis moriar. Gli Opuscoli di necrologio per I caduti italiani nella Grande Guerra*. Rome: Bibliografia analitica, Edizioni di Storia e Letteratura, 2003, pp. 11-44; cit. a p. 14. Cfr. The same author *Lutto, famiglia e nazione net culto dei caduti della prima Guerra mondiale in Italian*, in *La morte per la patria. La celebrazione dei caduti dal Risorgimento alla Repubblica*, edited by O. Janz and L. Klinkhammer. Rome: Donzelli, 2008, pp. 63-79. The library counts 2,300 memorial pamphlets for 1,500 dead; 82 percent officers; 3 percent sub-officers; 14 percent ordinary soldiers (who, however, don't come from the lower classes); more than 95 percent of the fallen come from the upper-middle class and have a college degree.

and testamentary uses. The letters of the deceased are called upon to witness death as a "conscious, if not actually joyous, sacrifice," "a heroic victory over oneself," "a dedication," an expression of the highest morality.[3] Certainly the publication of the letters "recalls the dead to life and provides from the beyond a voice of consolation for the living and, in all probability, relieves them also from a sense of guilt."[4] From these publications—which put into circulation thousands of letters and entries of diaristic, intellectual, historical, and official pieces from the period—some exemplary texts stand out that will form true and proper "monuments in paper."

The collection put together by Giuseppe Prezzolini, a highly regarded intellectual, nationalist, and interventionist, concludes at the end of 1917 and was published over the course of 1918 (but subsequently completely rewritten in 1921).[5] Not only is it one of the first anthologies, but also one that creates and consecrates a canon made up of works by officer-writers and of "final" letters (letters as wills, one might say) written by the hands of officers, young and not so young, passionate interventionists and volunteers, who died in the course of the conflict. We find already here many notable pages of literature from the war, those of Fernando Agnoletti, Corrado Alvaro, Antonio Baldini, Armando Bartolini, Giovanni Bellini, Giosue Borsi, Franco Ciarlantini, Piero Jahier, Arturo Onofri, Alfredo Panzini, Mario Puccini, Umberto Saba, Renato Serra, Scipio Slataper, Ardegno Soffici, Carlo e Gianni Stuparich, Giuseppe Ungaretti (and, of a different type, we also find texts of Emilio Cecchi and of Renato Simoni).[6] Excluded from the canon

---

[3] Ibid., pp. 30-31.

[4] Ibid., p. 31.

[5] G. Prezzolini, *Tutta la Guerra. Antologia del poplo italiano sul fronte e nel paese*, 2nd edition, completely redone and amplified. Florence: Bemporad, 1921.

[6] A sub-canon will come to be created later by the writers who died during the conflict; cfr. C. Padovani (edited by) *Antologia degli scrittori morti in guerra*. Florence: Vallechi, 1929. The cited authors and their works we be analyzed by Mario Isnenghi in the now classic work *Il mito della grande Guerra. Da Marinetti a Malaparte*. Rome-Bari: Laterza, 1973(2) (1st edition 1970) to which we will refer later. Amplifying and continuing Isnenghi's volume is the anthology put together by

for various reasons are more extreme writers, D'Annunzio, Marinetti, Malaparte: omissions one can understand in the context of an anthology to be used in schools. "I was looking for the most sober writers," writes Prezzolini, "the ones hewing most closely to reality, the freshest; and from them the most serious, closest, and freshest pieces."[7]

Educational intent won't allow for rhetoric, emphasis, over-excitement, imprecision, or abuse of words. To young people, this direction of the anthology teaches them the "sad necessity" of the war that is, Prezzolini affirms, neither barbarity, nor a primitive wildness, but "the capability of risking one's life for a higher ideal." War is a school for life: "The courage of war becomes a courage of peace, the risk of the battle in the height of a soul that dares venture into life. The fights for the regimental flag become the fight for the flag of one's own self."[8]

The stories and poems of war, continues Prezzolini, these selections, those from the canon, can also transmit in a precise way the "prosaic" character of modern war. "The teacher insists on the character of the new heroism, no longer made up of insolent stunts, of individual adventures, of sly improvisations. The teacher makes them see the heroism of constancy and of work, the strength of the soldier holding firm under bombardment, the calculations of the commander in combining actions of artillery, infantry, and aircraft."[9] Prezzolini's war is sensible, rational, moral: "In this the enemy removes his character of contingent individuality in exchange for one as the ideal obstacle to the realizing of a better end."[10]

To youth (Fascist youth) is dedicated also the large collection of letters curated by Antonio Monti and published in 1935.[11] Selected from those preserved at the War Archives

---

Andrea Cortellessa, *Le notti chiare erano tutte un'alba. Antologia dei poeti italiani nella Prima Guerra mondiale*. Milan: Bruno Mondadori, 1998.
7 G. Prezzolini, Prefazione alla prima edizione, in Id., *Tutta la Guerra*, cit. p. x.
8 Ibid., p. xii.
9 Ibid., pp. xiv-xv.
10 Ibid., p. xvi.
11 A. Monti (editor), *Lettere di combattenti italiani nelle grande guerra*, 2 vol. Florence:

in Milan (of which Monti was the director), the letters give voice to just under three hundred officers, mostly between seventeen and twenty-four years old and of low rank (many aspiring sub-lieutenants and lieutenants, a few captains), all killed in the course of the conflict. The celebratory context of the operation can't hide the dimensions of a "generational massacre"[12] that had struck in particular the limited corps of reserve/adjunct officers. About this Marco Mondini writes, "Destined principally for regiments of infantry in virtue of being platoon or company commanders [...] the middle-class soldiers with epaulets were in effect the main victims of the difficult daily life in the trenches and were massacred during the regular assaults against the enemy trenches, adding up to a death toll consistently higher than that of ordinary soldiers and significantly higher than those of career colleagues or those from other armies."[13]

We find ourselves therefore with, as Monti does not fail to repeat in his brief preface, letters of will and testament, aimed at maintaining the necessity and the goodness, or rather the nobility of the Italian cause. The marching orders that sent these young officers to their deaths are repetitive and interchangeable among various interventionists: the nation, the national awakening, the ancient right, the right of nations, Greater Italy, the real Unified Italy, the martyrs of the Reunification, the completion of our votes, the holy ideal, German barbarity, barbarians who oppress our brothers, the German propensity to brutality, the German masters of the world, the secular enemy.[14]

Edizione Roma, May 24, 1935. The two volumes are part of a series "La Guerra e la milizia negli scrittori italiani d'ogni tempo" directed by Francesco Grazioli, general and senator, and by Gioacchino Volpe, historian and scholar of Italy.

12 "That's how it was," writes Marco Mondini, "that the dead who were younger than twenty-five, an age group that represented less than a fifth of the population according to the census of 1911, were 260,000 (and these, at least 7,500 between seventeen and eighteen years old), which is to say half of the dead in the army operative between 1915 and 1918." Mondini, *La guerra italiana*. Cit., p. 66.

13 Ibid., pp. 66-68.

14 On the interchangeability of the movements cfr. Isnenghi, *Il mito della grande guerra* cit., pp. 249-250.

And yet notwithstanding the strict selection process and the modification of texts (most of them have been edited) with the end result of bringing them back into a corpus that has an unvarying tone, not all the letters tell the same story or offer a homogenous vision of the war. It's understood that next to the war-festival (all the heroic rage, a bragging and audacious affair, a spontaneous and generous event of patriotism) there is nevertheless also the war-horror of the trenches and the no-mans-land strewn with corpses. "These mountains," writes Captain Alberto Cucchi, "are now scattered with crosses and bloody clothes, and it's not unusual to see a blackened hand appear or a head with the eyes partly eaten by crows. And the crosses keep coming, and the air becomes putrid; every corner of it is a painful memory. Every one of us has a greatly resigned spirit and keeps himself ready at any moment to be killed."[15]

Dismal and agonizing, too, the passage described by Lieutenant Aldo Ravasini: "A sudden racket breaks like lightning through the dreary moonlight and trembles in the sky like a shining snake searching through space. Everything for a moment is lit by a single light, white and probing, that seems to arouse and reanimate them. The corpses that the burial detail hadn't managed to collect seemed to rise in protest toward the bothersome light that disturbed the stupor of their eternal rest, and from the enormous basins that seemed like amphitheaters the white bones of imaginary sepulchers appear like a crowd of phantasms."[16]

We find the discomfort and disorientation of someone who had dreamed of a "beautiful" war ("We are inside a kind of hole or cave, made of rocks, stones, sacks of earth, tree trunks"),[17] the difficult test of waging war in the high mountains ("Swearing, words of grief and encouragement mixed in

---
15 Monti (editor), *Lettere di combattenti italiani* cit., I, p.134. Cucchi dies at Falcade on October 31, 1916.
16 Ibid., p. 136. Ravasini dies on San Michele October 25, 1915.
17 Ibid., pp. 121-122. These are the words of Pietro Boeri Cascino who dies on the Karst plateau on November 2, 1915.

with the furious whistles of the blizzard and became lost far, far away . . ."),[18] the burning nostalgia for lost family.

But this epistolary monument erected, we repeat, for celebratory ends makes evident above all a disquieting, obsessive passion for death (for one's own death): What was considered the "real" war, filled with understanding of existence, becomes an occasion for a death that can give meaning to life itself.[19]

Lieutenant Pietro Bartoletti writes: "My ultimate dream is that a bullet will engrave me in the burning flesh of the fire of my soul, for the desire of the holy stigmata: Life is sacrifice; war is life, therefore death is freedom, therefore war and sacrifice together are freedom. If you return unharmed from war, it means you haven't suffered enough to be worthy of happiness."[20] Giosue Borsi, celebrated poet, saint, and hero,[21] writes similarly: "Therefore everything is favorable for me, everything is set for me to make an auspicious and beautiful death, the time, the place, the season, the occasion, the age. I couldn't do better to crown my life; I feel all the satisfaction of doing what is good and generous. Don't cry for me, Mamma, if it is written up there that I must die. Don't cry, because you

---

18 Ibid., p. 125. The story comes from Anacleto Raimondi, who dies on the Italian Dente of Pasubio October 10, 1916.

19 A. d'Orsi, *I chierici alla guerra. La seduzione bellica sugli intellettuali da Adua a Baghdad*. Turin: Bollati Boringhieri, 2005, p. 22.

20 Monti (editor), *Lettere di combattenti italiani* cit., II, p. 31. Bartoletti dies at Karst on May 24, 1917.

21 Giosue Borsi, Catholic intellectual, journalist, and poet, dies at Plava on November 10, 1915, becoming immediately "the martyr" of the Catholics. Cfr. G. Cavagnini, *Poeta, santo, eroe. It mito di Giosue Borsi nella grande guerra (1915-1918)*, in "Memoria e ricerca," 2013, 44, pp. 107-122. Adolfo Omodeo has an extremely hard judgment of him: "Giosue Borsi, the journalist who converted to Catholicism just before the war, seems a soul in a state of chaos. He is obsessed, maybe by the influx of his converts, by an insistent and obstinate mania for apology, first for Catholicism and then for the war. The homiletic effusions go beyond the person they pertain to. His letters are written to be published; this includes those that should have been private and intimate. The letters he writes to his mother were meant to be passed on to the newspaper." A. Omodeo, *Momenti della vita di guerra. Dai diari e dale lettere dei caduti, 1915-1918*, edited by A. Galante Garrone. Turin: Einaudi, 1968, p.256.

would be grieving my happiness. I shouldn't be mourned, but envied."[22]

Nationalist ideals and religious faith are founded in an interrelationship of codes. "Bless, my dear ones, this war," writes Lieutenant Annibale Calini in his last testament letter. "Without her, I would probably end up miserably sick in mind and body. War has destroyed me like fire, but has also crowned my death in light, it has purified me."[23]

Many of the letters published by Antonio Monti can be found in the work, of an entirely different scope and depth, of Adolfo Omodeo, *Movimenti della vita di Guerra* (*Movements of Wartime Life*).[24] Removed from the celebratory and nationalist framework in which they were placed, together with others they make up a different picture of the war, more reunifying, more Mazzinist: "a war completely opposed to the ignoble rhetoric of the gazetteers and also somewhat different from the pure negativity of the realist novel, a civic war, without songs, tiring but overcome by means of tenacity and virility and relying on a pure sense of duty that is the dominant theme in the correspondence of the best of them." So writes Vittorio Foa to his family when he read in prison "the very beautiful book" of Omodeo, concluding that the Italian war seems to him "really like a middle-class war, but not in the usual sense of that term from the historical materialists, but rather as a war supported by those patriotic and nationalistic ideals that were part of the intellectual bourgeoisie that maintains heirs in the generation of the Reunification and is capable of promulgating indefinitely national-liberal principles without turning them into their opposite, imperialism." An illusion naturally "paid for dearly."[25]

---

[22] Monti (editor), *Lettere di combattenti italiani* cit., II, p. 36.
[23] He dies at Pasubio on September 10, 1916. Ibid., p. 60.
[24] Published serially in "La Critica," from June 20, 1929 to November 20, 1933, *Momenti della vita di guerra* comes out in book form by Laertza in 1943.
[25] Vittorio Foa, letter to relatives, September 16, 1938, in Id. *Lettere della giovinezza. Dal Carcere 1935-1943*, edited by F. Montevecchi. Turin: Einaudi, 2010, pp. 483-487.

In other words, Omodeo asserts (in a polemic with fascism) that a liberal Reunification preparation for war, like a fourth war of independence characterized by the Mazzini-Garibaldian tradition, nevertheless at the same time reduces the movements that lead to war, dissolves the multiple contradictory tensions, marginalizes nationalistic attitudes, and, even more seriously, ignores (with an annoyed gesture) extraneousness, indifference, the dissent of the popular masses.[26]

And yet, once one understands that Omodeo's investigation "parades throughout the world the patriotic consensus of the officials and actually of a certain type of officer,"[27] *Momenti della vita di Guerra* remains, even with its limitations, an original book that's also occasionally powerful. If we read it as a dictionary, a non-alphabetical list of voices, we will find there all the aspects (even those most horrific) of the experience of war, starting from the times and places of memories of the Reunification: the high-school curriculum that established the national patriotic rhetoric and semantics and the family tradition that spurred young men to emulate their grandfathers. And so, little by little, we come to the enthusiastic discovery of the Alps, the sense of the poetry of nature and of frugal living[28]; the no-less-surprising encounter with peasant peoples who to the young officers always seemed to be patient and healthy; the descent into the mud of the trenches ("For three days I am sleeping in mud, among the mud, with the mud, I eat and drink a mixture of mud, I breathe mud, my skin and my bones are muddy")[29]; the fascination with war ("I've become like an addict")[30]; the act of killing the enemy ("in a

---

26 Cfr. Isnenghi, *Il mito della grande guerra*, cit. pp. 248-249.
27 Ibid., p. 284, note 8.
28 "It may seem absurd or paradoxical, but the Great War did have the merit of making the Italians discover their own mountains. Even more paradoxical is the fact that that discovery, right in the middle of a bloody war, should be expressed in the alienating language of a bucolic landscape." M. Armiero, *Le montagne della patria. Natura e nazione nella storia d'Italia. Secoli XIX e XX*. Turin: Einaudi, 2013, p. 99.
29 Omodeo, *Momenti della vita di guerra* cit., p. 146. The writer is Carlo Stuparich.
30 Ibid., p. 100. The author is Leopoldo Aguiari, volunteer, who dies at age nine-

furious bayonet attack, I cut a man's throat ...")[31]; the dissolution of hope; the loss and the fatigue; horror ("You cannot imagine the horror and the slaughter of hand-to-hand combat. It's a horrible thing, and I hope it will never be tested again among civilized people")[32]; the chaos of nighttime ("and cannon fire all night long [...] and all night long people passing by, weeping, calling for help in the darkness of the deluge. Lost people, frightened, left behind during the battle, who now can't get back to the others. And now they are crying, weeping, falling down in the mud, soaked through, demoralized, frightened of getting in trouble, aware that they already are in serious trouble. And all night these people come and go through the valley, in the dark, under water, through the shooting from the lookouts, thrashing around and getting stuck in the barbed wire fence. What hell!").[33]

The dictionary could then continue with the anger toward soldiers who shirked their orders or townsmen and elegant women accused of ignoring the suffering at the front; or with disgust for journalists who systematically misrepresented the realities of the war.[34] And it could end with indifference supplanting horror, the oblivion that replaces pity for fallen comrades, the primordial egoism of life that takes the place of mourning.

---

teen at San Michele.
31 Ibid., p. 116. The author is Giorgio Lo Cascio.
32 Ibid., p. 184. The author is Rocco Stassano.
33 Ibid., p. 190. The author is Teodoro Capocci.
34 Omodeo cites Claudio Calandra's protest. "What really is disgusting is their obstinate desire to describe the war as a poetic thing, made out of poetry and sentiment rather than out of blood, horror, and inconceivable suffering. I am a terribly failed painter, however, in my soul as much an artist as a chronicler, and I can assure you that in the war I found nothing nothing excessively poetic: maybe because I was always in the trenches, and the gentlemen 'reporters' were far away in their observation areas. It depends on one's point of view. When a grenade explodes in a cemetery Barzini says, 'that the crosses bowed to its passing' but he doesn't say that the cadavers in advanced states of putrefaction fly into the air in shreds and curse the trenches with their stench from God knows how many kilometers away. Where he was, he couldn't smell the stink; where we were, we couldn't breathe." Ibid., p. 4, note 1.

Omodeo writes: "The combatants were the proof of a hypothesis brought up by a poetic fantasy of Chateaubriand's: that the rising of the dead, even of those beloved dead, would be a terrifying encumbrance, because pain is healed and new loves and new dreams occupy one's heart. These soldiers were a little bit dead themselves, even before dying: At home, life went on and, like grass on old battlefields, little by little scars formed over the wounds in emotions and in memories in the hearts of fathers and mothers."[35]

THE DISCOVERY OF THE PEOPLE

The Italian soldier, the one who made war not by choice but by force, is a man, writes Marco Mondini, "around twenty-five years old, on average, a peasant, in one out of two cases (or else a day laborer or manual laborer), hailing mostly from the South, and would be led into combat by an even younger reserve officer, possibly a student, a clerk, or a professional of some kind, who was destined to die sooner than and more often than his men."[36]

For these young officers, coming into contact with and then living alongside these troops of common soldiers took on the dimensions of a surprising discovery; but it must be said, rarely does an encounter of coming together with men of different social classes and a moving away from one's own people become a valued experience or an opportunity for actual learning. The social asymmetry translates into a paternal gaze, often friendly and beneficent but that nonetheless reaffirms the diversity of human essence.

Apart from more complex reflections on the social virtues of the peasantry, we find right away the first impressions of these young middle-class boys affected by the psychological "minority" status of these people: good, naïve, impulsive, capricious; they have the "natural" characteristics of children.

---

35 Omodeo, *Momenti della vita di guerra* cit., p. 213.
36 Mondini, *La guerra italiana* cit., p. 86.

For example, Lieutenant Augusto Vivante, a law student from Pavia, writes: "These men of an uncertain future — who from discomfort and fatigue are made tough, ripped up, and dirty, often brutal in their actions and speech, violent and vengeful against the enemy — these men who really are making war, have, rather, the souls of children, souls that, while sometimes capricious, are at their core good, mild, generous. And we carry in our wandering this outward shape and this substance, and often those who see the one don't believe in the other. It is necessary to understand these fighting men in their peculiarities, in their weaknesses, in their distractions; their desires should be given some respect — in fact they should be anticipated and indulged the way one does with children recuperating from some long illness.

"They're so good! If they can confront the enemy with the cruelest hatred, when they turn around one hears from them nothing but expressions of affection and love for one another, even among those unknown to them. Imagine how they must be with their own families."[37]

We find similar considerations also in the correspondence of Lieutenant Giovanni Battista Pecorella, of Palermo, a student of literature. "All my soldiers are peasants. But such goodness! Such innocence! . . . They look at me candidly, through their eyelashes. They are kids. When I told them I was nineteen, one burst out, 'But how much you've studied!' I couldn't punish any of them. It would be disrespectful, wicked, unjust."[38]

"They are like lost ones in a new place," writes Giuseppe Garrone. "They look at you with the sweetest eyes and deep."[39]

One might add to this also the exultation of the common nature in the army, the role of peasants as infinitely resigned,

---
37 Letter to his mother, May 10, 1918, in *Scrivini piu che poui. L'epistolario familiar di Augusto Vivanti in guerra (1915-1919)*, edited by C. Guani. Milan: Unicopoli ("Annali di storia pavese. Fonti e ricerche storiche. Nuova serie"), 2011, p. 34.
38 Letter to relatives, November 29, 1916, in G. B. Pecorella, *Amo quell che ero e non saro piu. Lettere dal fronte (1916-1919)*. Milan: Unicopli, 2012, p. 58.
39 Letter to family, March 19, 1916, in Omodeo, *Momenti della vita di guerra* cit., p. 69.

patient, disposed to obedience. "They are a resigned people. They are a patient, sound, country people," writes Scipio Slataper.[40] And with him other intellectuals and writers would learn from a "school of patience and simple humanity of the peasant soldiers" only later to instruct them and illuminate for them the necessity of adapting to wartime.[41]

Piero Jahier is the officer-writer who, more or less than others, takes it upon himself to turn upside-down a condition of objective economic poverty, of underdevelopment, of social alienation, of subordination resulting in moral superiority. In his major work, *Con me e con gli alpine* (*With Me and with the Alpine Troops*), published serially in January of 1918,[42] a book by turns noble and tormented, Jahier traces and celebrates "the ethic of the mountain man" as opposed to the impoverished humanity of the city worker who doesn't know what it's like to work hard in creating anything, who "drowns in the boredom of repetition," who labors for the salary, lives for the love of money, who goes on strike for the power to make things better, and if he has any belief at all, it is in politics. In contrast, the mountain man is ready "to recreate civilization every moment," has a passion for work well done, has many skills, is the caretaker of what he creates, he is disciplined and resigned (because he considers "the evils of society to be like the evils of nature," evils that are eternal and unpredictable), he sacrifices himself willingly ("because the law of the mountains is sacrifice"), and finally, despite exertion, he is always happy.[43] For these reasons, mountain men and by extension peasants are or can become the best soldiers; in fact, as Mario Isnenghi writes: "The peasant represents the prototypical soldier, seeing as how all of his existence—it is practically guaranteed—predisposes him and guarantees him

---

40 Letter to family, October 12, 1915, ibid., p. 155.
41 Indispensible on the theme is the cited volume by Isnenghi, *Il mito della grande guerra*, pp. 274-281; pp. 305-310.
42 Quote from the Vallechi edition of Firenze, 1967, third volume of the works of Jahier comprising, in addition to the text in question, the autobiography *Ragazzo*.
43 Ibid., p. 217-232.

an attitude of quiet, absolute, and fatalistic subordination. In no other kind of man — it's understood — is to be found to such a degree inculcated the duty for others to command and for him to obey."[44]

THE VOICE OF THE PEASANT SOLDIER

The representation of common soldiers has long been filtered through the ideological gaze of the officer-writers (be they paternalistic or diffident or authoritarian).[45] Gianni Stuparich's sketch of the silent peasant on the train en route to the front can serve as the emblem of an entire social class: "In a corner shine the uncovered teeth of a silent peasant, with fixed and lustrous eyes; he isn't listening, he isn't talking, amid all the wasted and woeful chatter of the others, he alone is absorbed in an unconscious preoccupation, but it is one that turns his gaze feverish and that freezes his body, making his soul rigid with an intense stupor."[46]

Restoring a voice (the personal identity, subjectivity, presence, dignity, historical protagonism) to those who were common soldiers becomes the objective, starting in the early 1960s,

---

[44] Isnenghi, *Il mito della grande guerra* cit., p. 307.

[45] Rather noted, for example, are the angry expressions of Carlo Emilio Gadda distributed in truth fairly equally between officials and soldiers, incapable of adjusting to the roles they are given: to some to order and to others to submit with discipline. One representative note, that of June 22, 1916. "Our infantry is good: The Italian soldier is weak, especially the southerner; he's necessarily dishonest, like the enemy, but also through neglect. He takes care of his bodily needs close to the trenches, filling the terrain with shit. He doesn't even try to make a single bathroom, he instead makes the whole line a bathroom. He's bad at shooting his gun, which is anyway dirty and rusty. He loses bullets and tools for digging (it took me quite a bit of time and effort to get my picks and spades together!); he snoozes during the day when he could be reinforcing the line. In compensation for all this he is patient, sober, generous, good, helpful, courageous, and impetuous on the attack." Unlike other officers, who want to be loved by their men, Gadda has a realistic sense of his function and has no intention of winning their hearts. Cfr. C.E. Gadda, *Giornale di guerra e prigionia*. Turin: Einaudi, 1980 (1st edition 1955), pp. 131-132.

[46] G. Stuparich, *Guerra del '15 (Dal taccuino d'un volontario)*. Milan: Garzanti, 1940, pp. 4-5.

of non-academic historians, political militants, and cultural organizers in the context of more complex research into the history and culture of the subaltern classes. The objective of bringing together the voices was understood literally, because if the hegemonic culture is limited to literature, writes Gianni Bosio, political militant of the libertarian Left and precursor of a social history based on oral sources, only the tape recorder can restore "to the culture tied to the means of oral communication the instrument of emergence, of becoming conscious. . . . The possibility of capturing with a tape recorder ways of being, relating, communicating . . . gives back to the culture of the oppressed classes the possibility of preserving the modes of their own awareness, that is, their own culture."[47] Regarding the theme of the war, what Bosio sought (and with him Cesare Bermani and the group Nuovo Canzoniere Italiano) is popular dissent, the opposition, gestures of disobedience and of rebellion intended to overturn that image of the good and patient people passed down in the literature of war. And therefore from the outset that vast repertory of protest and anti-militaristic songs that, censored and suppressed, express a radical subversion of values was brought to light. Borrowing from tunes of songs in vogue or typical themes from storytellers, the songs retrace real and symbolic places of the conflict (from Ortigara to Doberdo, from Monte Nero to Podgora, to Cortina, to Gorizia, to Pasubio, to Grappa, to Piave), mocking the king, the government, the generals (above all Generalissimo Cadorna, about whom there are an unknown number of satirical verses); they subvert the celebratory rhetoric ("It's the 24th of May/ when Italy declares war/ she commits a crime/ the earth can't tolerate anymore"), cursing the interventionists ("cursed be the young students/ who studied and wanted the war/ they hurled Italy into the fray/ for a hundred years they'll feel the pain"). It is in this

---

47 G. Bosio, *Elogio del magnetofono*, in *L'intellettuale rovesciato*, Edizioni Bella Ciao, Milano 1975, p. 171. The book that brings together, as the subtitle states, *Interventi e ricerche sulla emergenza d'interesse verso le forme di espressione e di organizzazione spontanee nel mondo popolare e proletario* (gennaio 1963-agosto 1971), has come out in a new edition edited by Cesare Bermani. Milan: Jaca Book, 1998.

first large investigation, conducted mostly in Lombardy and Piedmont, that one of the most famous anti-militaristic songs emerges, "O Gorizia tu sei maledetta," where the affront to the city symbol comes via a subversive desire: "Treacherous gentlemen officers/ that wanted the war/ slaughterers of sold meat/ and youth destroyed."[48]

The testimony, the telling of one's own experience in the war, follows the song and also in this case brings to light the soul of the people's soldier in revolt. In the interviews of Cesare Bermani, conducted in Novara between 1963 and 1966, the testimonies tell of officers murdered by their own men ("those officers who were evil were gotten rid of"), of socialist leaflets passed around at the front that incited desertion, of small but frequent arguments between soldiers and officers.[49] The lengthy tales of Belochio told by Gianni Bosio to Acquanegra sul Chiese go back over the coersive nature of the military system, over the trials, the firing squads — employed also in cases of little importance, such as being late coming back from leave.[50] But Bosio, in his monograph on Acquanegra begun at the end of the 1950s and never completed, tells us something about making stories, about the necessity of going

---

[48] It was because of "Gorizia" and this line in particular, sung in 1964 in Spoleto during the Festival dei due Mondi, il Nuovo Canzoniere Italiano was denounced for contempt of the armed forces. On the activity of the NCI cfr. *Per una storia de il Nuovo Canzoniere Italiano*, in "*In Nuovo Canzoniere Italiano,*" s. III, 1976, 3. On the repertory of war songs, see the essay by Cersare Bermani, "*La trasmissione della memoria della guerra attraverso il canto popolare,*" in "*Nessuno potra tenersi in disparate.*" *La Grande Guerra: memoria, territorio, documentazione*, edited by A. Mignemi. Novara: Interlinea Edizioni, 2009, pp. 133-157. Cesare Bermini was one of the first and the best equipped collectors of popular songs; the foundation of the Nuovo Canzoniere Italiano and the Istituto Ernesto De Martino are due to him and to Gianni Bosio. On Bermani see also the essay "Il canto sociale," in *Gli Italiani in guerra*, III, t.2, *La Grande Guerra. Dall'intervento alla "vittoria mutilate,"* edited by M. Isnenghi e D. Ceschin. Turin: Utet, 2008, pp. 838-856. Notable for philological dimension and interest is the two-volume anthology edited by Virgilio Savona and Michele Straniero, *Canti della Grande Guerra*. Milan: Garzanti, 1981.

[49] C. Bermani, *L'Altra cultura. Interventi, rassegne, ricerchi. Riflessi culturali di una milizia politica (1962-1969)*. Milan: Edizioni del Gallo, 1970, pp. 47-51.

[50] G. Bosio, *Il trattore ad Acquanegra. Piccola e grande storia in una comunita contadina*, edited by C. Bermani. Bari: De Donato, 1981, pp. 43-56.

back over stories, about the modalities of communication, about the audience that listens, and about the social spaces of orality.

"For the entire postwar period, and finishing at the second conflict, children, after dinner, a la Funtana, sitting close to la Sorba [at the place where the water emerges] or there on the Pesa [on the platform of the weigh station], they used to pass the summer evenings listening to the interminable stories: not facts, episodes, chronicles, but rather long tales, as though to bring us close to them in the arc of their suffering. Mud and lice, ice and water, and hunger, an immense hunger, and fear of snipers and terror of the Germans. Again, in the telling, one understood that they felt like a giant herd of sheep, of poor devils sent to the slaughter. For those who rebelled there was the firing squad or the court martial that, for no good reason, could mean years in jail."[51] Belochio and the other veterans, Bosio also records, would repeat their stories, dozens, maybe hundreds of times, "epically," as though talking about things that didn't pertain any longer to them.

If with the use of the tape recorder Bosio and Bermani meant to retrace the historical and cultural roots of the socialist movement and to trace an alternative history of the oppressed, in the 1970s "oral history" broadens its horizons, interacts with European (specifically British) experiences, sharpens its own instruments, and expands exponentially the historical field and the techniques used to study it. "The innovation it introduces to history" writes Luisa Passerini in one of the clearest reflections, "are discourses whose referent to reality can be multiple and should be deciphered. Moreover, oral history doesn't use chosen discourses, but has the ambition of engaging the language in its totality, not only that of illustrious men, but also that of the common person, not only cultivated languages but also dialects, not only explicit expressions, but the inarticulated codices of those who don't have an official voice and who are constrained to speak and to leave testimony of

---

51 Ibid., p. 45.

themselves and their own lives."[52] Furthermore, specifically via these discourses, Passerini adds, "the exigency is that of tackling the study of human beings not just with respect to political power, to economic structures, and to social organizations, but also with respect to interpersonal behaviors, to psychological and cognitive mechanisms, and to interests, ideas, images, that reside in the head of individuals."[53]

The repertory of themes brought up and developed by "oral history" in these last decades has little by little become greater: the history of women; of immigration; the history of small local communities; the world wars (more the second than the first on account of the disappearing witnesses); the Resistance, culture, and work of the peasant world; the workers' movement and its clashes; and the more comprehensive histories of life.[54]

The Great War with its already old testimonies doesn't become the principal theme of the "oral history," and it's already been the focus of two important collections. The first, *Il mondo dei vinti* (*The World of the Defeated*), is the work of Nuto Revelli, officer in the Russian campaign, partisan commander, and independent researcher, devoted to "rebuilding and preserving a military past and a peasant past, archeologist of the memory of something and of someone who no longer exists or is about to disappear."[55]

---

[52] L. Passerini, *Conoscenza storica e storia orale. Sull'utilita e il danno delle fronti orali per la storia*, introductory essay to *Storia orale. Vita quotidiana e cultura material delle classi subaltern*, edited by L. Passerini. Turin: Rosenberg & Seiler, 1978, p. VIII.

[53] Ibid., pp. VIII-IX. On Luisa Passerini see also *Storia e soggettivita. Le fonti orali, la memoria*, La Nuova Italia, Firenze, 1988, and the later *Memoria e Utopia. Il primate dell'intersoggettivita*. Turin: Bollati Boringhieri, 2003.

[54] Cfr. G. Barrera, A. Martini, A. Mule, editors, *Fonti orali. Censimento degli istituti di conservazione*. Rome: Ministero per I beni culturali e ambientali-Ufficio central per I beni archivistici, 1993. The cases of Veneto and Toscana are exemplars: see the monograph "Venetica," s. III, 2004, 9 (in particular G. De Sandre, *Storia Orale: il case Veneto. Bibliografia e primo bilancio, 1978-2003*, pp. 89-106) and the volume edited by Alessandro Andreini and Pietro Clemente, *I custodi delle voci. Archivi orali in Toscana. Primo censimento*. Florence: Regione Toscana, 2007.

[55] M. Isnenghi, *Parabola dell'autobiografia. Dagli archive della classe agli archive dell'io*, in "Rivista di storia contemporanea," 1992, 2-3, pp. 382-401. Nuto Revelli is the

The World of the Defeated brings together 270 testimonials recorded on a tape recorder. The theme of Revelli's research is (or aims to be) the impoverished countryside of Cuneo, the earthquake provoked by industrialization, and the depopulation of the mountain. But the memory of the Great War, more than a half a century past, interrupts every interview with an obsessive and painful urgency, like a wound, like an illness.

"I don't want to hear any more about the war," says Revelli in the margins of his research. "My interviewees however wanted to talk only about war, the very old ones about the war of 1915-18, and the old ones about the Second World War. I need to defend myself because if they begin the interview with tales from the war, they won't talk about anything else. The beginning of the stories in *The World of the Defeated* has stayed with me. If the testimonials begin with them telling me about the peak of the Rombon or of the Ortigara, I would say to myself, "I'm screwed." Because they were reliving the battles, and the life in the trenches, and the bullets whistling by and the dead friend.... Then I would try to stop them, but it wasn't easy to interrupt those stories. I was interested in other themes: the peasant family, work, emigration, the distant past, the life of yesterday and of today. They had the war on their brains, and they judged other topics to be marginal, things of little importance. The day it was proposed to me to speak with Minetu 'l Minor, I said to myself, "This time I will get to listen to a complete discourse on emigration." Minetu is the diminutive of Bartolomeo, and minor means miner. I knew that this Minetu nicknamed the Miner had worked in many mines in Europe. But it wasn't to be. Minetu had the Tonale on his mind, the battles of the Tonale, and he acted out the life in the trenches and the bullets that whistled.... He

---

author, among others, of La strada del davai. Turin: Einaudi, 1966, which collects the statements of forty soldiers returned from the Russian front; *L'ultimo fronte. Lettere di soldati caduti o disperse nella seconda guerra mondiale.* Turin: Einaudi, 1971; *L'anello forte. La donna: storie di vita Contadina.* Turin: Einaudi, 1985. *Il mondo dei vinti*, which has the subtitle *Testimonianze di vita Contadina*, is published in 1977 divided into two volumes: the first dedicated to the plateau and to the hill of Cuneese, the second to the mountain and to the Langhe.

did eventually speak to me about his emigration, but it took a while to get to it."[56]

The war memory of the farmers from Cuneo, so many years on, privileges the fragment, is subject to sudden illuminations, it descends toward woeful reflections on what it used to be: too young, too ignorant, too obedient ("We were never rebellious; we weren't even capable of being rebellious").[57] Out of this comes a scene characterized by a generalized dissent, but as Mario Disnenghi has observed, it doesn't have to do with a dissent that was "politically organized and completely aware, but rather with an indirect dissent, of indifference and unconnected to the values that sustain that war: a dissent that one may characterize as on this side rather than on that of war as historical fact."[58]

The fragmented narratives fixed in memory are such that one can make of them, if one so desires, a small anthology.

Self-inflicted wounds: "A brother of mine extracted his teeth, a few of them from Margarita had their teeth pulled; they were already ruined! One guy from Fossano poisoned himself with lead; he died. Another, he was from the South, injected himself with oil in his spinal cord; he became crippled, he ended up in jail."[59]

---

[56] N. Revelli, *Una esperienza di ricerca nel mondo contadinno*, in *Storia orale e storie di vita*, edited by L. Lanzardo. Milan: Franco Angeli, 1989, pp. 43-51; cit., to pp. 47-48. Cfr. Also N. Revelli, *La memoria della guerra nelle champagne cuneesi*, in *La grande guerra. Esperienza, memoria, immagini*, edited by D. Leoni and C. Zadra. Bologna: Il Mulino, 1986, pp. 605-609.

[57] Revelli, *Il mondo dei vinti* cit., I, p. 39. Statement of Giuseppe Daniele.

[58] Isnenghi, *Valori poplari e valori ufficiali nella mentalita del soldato fra le due guerre mondiali*, in *Quaderni storici*, 1978, 38, pp. 701-709; cit., to p. 703; this deals with an intervention in the presentation of *Il mondo dei vinti*. Isnenghi's assessment is probably right, even if the radical nature of some of the statements indicated attitudes that bore similarities to insubordination. On the other hand, Isnenghi himself, some years prior, in relation to the non-involvement of the public, put forth a different opinion: "It remains to be seen if [...] the ideological coopting, in letting itself get involved with the social ethics of the upper classes, doesn't represent, rather than the lingering of the proletariat beyond history and middle-class society, instead the first step in a spontaneous opposition that, on the other extreme and in appropriate circumstances, is insubordinate." Id., *Il mito della grande guerra* cit., p. 311.

[59] Revelli, *Il mondo dei vinti* cit., I, p. 16. Testimony of Giacomo Martinengo.

An assault on Ortigara: "Then in the morning, at 7, the order came down to begin the assault. 'Out!' yelled the captain. 'You go first, and then we'll follow,' his soldiers said to him."[60]

Informal gestures of truce: "On Rombon the Germans are ten meters away; they give us Cognac, and we give them loaves of bread. They yell: Italian good; no shoot. They come into our trenches; they taste their Cognac to show us it's not poisoned; they talk, we're blood brothers, they speak the way we're speaking now, we make ourselves understood. They're sick of it all too."[61]

The suppressing of a lieutenant: "We have a terrible lieutenant, guy from Lombardy. A pal of mine says to me, 'Tonight, I'm getting my revenge. I'm gonna kill him.' He lay in wait for him, he knocked him down with a blow from his musket, he killed him. He justified it like this: 'He didn't give me the order; I fired.' Nothing happened to him."[62]

Unburied corpses: "In the trenches [of San Michele] the dead were standing up, they held one another up. And everything made of iron on them turned green from the mustard gas, military stars, shoe nails, jacket buttons..."[63]

Wounds: "We were making the assault, we didn't understand anything, the wounds were poisoning us, we were like rabid dogs. We went through the dead without taking a breath. The wounds 'n balurdiu 'l servel [they stupefied the brain] we were going forward like drunkards and stabbing people with our bayonettes."[64]

---

[60] Ibid., p. 39. Testament of Giuseppe Daniele.

[61] Revelli, *Il mondo dei vinti* cit., p. 103. Testimony of Giovanni Allinio. "Prove di non violenza" Anna Bravo calls it in her book *La conta dei salvati. Dalla Grande Guerra al Tibet: storie di sangue risparmiato*. Rome-Bari: Laterza, 2013, p. 51.

[62] Revelli, *Il mondo dei vinti*, cit., II, p. 33. Testimony of Pietro Bruno.

[63] Ibid., p. 69. Testimony of Giovanni Battista Ponzo.

[64] Ibid., p. 74. Testimony of Giacomo Andreis. This element of the injections that made the combatant lose his lucidity temporarily returns in the story of Giovanni Montanaro: "We were all rendered like infants; they had to inject us to make us stronger, you're no longer a person or nothing. [...] We had those injections that

The military chaplain: "There was a military chaplain there who said only: 'Hope in God . . . ' What God?, my captain yelled at him. 'Your God who has no compassion for 14 million mothers who toss and turn at night, calling for their sons? Your God . . . You should be ashamed.' The chaplain ran away."[65]

The second collection of testimonies, all of them dedicated to the Great War (thirty-five interviews), comes out a bit after the work of Revelli, in 1980, as the ninth volume of the "Working Class World of Lombardy"[66] series. Published without adequate commentary and historical contextualization, the oral texts, among them those supported by old notes and diary comments, often reveal themselves to be sparse, disorganized, filled with holes, and contradictory as regards chronology and military events. And yet none of them is without interest. Almost all of them take place among the corps of the Alpinists and combatants in the Alps; the thirty-five testimonials, bearing the insignia of the horsemen of Vittorio Veneto, are portals to a memory distant if not in contradiction to the Alpinists' and mountaineers' mythology. The same esprit de corps shows itself rarely, and it doesn't always keep the Alpine "war dream" fresh.[67] Luigi Baccolo recounts that at Grappa their unit came to an understanding with the Germans: "We gave them something to eat, and they threw back to us tobacco and cigarettes." And they came up with signals to warn one another so as to limit the damages from bombing missions. But then, recounts Baccolo, "the riflemen went up, and between them and the Germans there

---

left us like idiots." Ibid., pp. 174-175.
65 Ibid., p. 136. Testimony of Angelo Fantino.
66 S. Fontana-M. Pieretti (editors), *La Grande Guerra. Operai e contadini Lombardi nel primo conflitto mondiale*, Silvana Editoriale-Regione Lombardia ("*Mondo popolare in Lombardia*," IX), Milano 1980. The testimonies are collected by Sandra and Mimmo Boninelli (Bergamo province), Giorgio Sbaraini (Brescia province), and Floriano Soldi (Cremona province).
67 On this see M. Mondini, *Alpini. Parole e immagini di un mito guerriero*. Rome-Bari: Laterza, 2008.

were abuses immediately: shots fired, artillery launched, flamethrowers . . . " If it had been just the Alpini left up there, everything would have been different, he concludes.[68]

Of the honor of war, which would live together in popular memory with the horror of war, it seems that here there is no trace. That pride that coexists with repulsion, the pride of holding one's ground, "of having done one's part, of having stuck it out to the end," that Antonio Gibelli glimpses in his autobiography of the Piemontese farmer Giovanni Pistone and that he seems to be able to find also in the stories of other veterans,[69] that pride is replaced, in this repertoire of remembrances, by a nameless condemnation, by incredulity at deeds that were committed that now seem desperate and senseless, often at the cry that accompanies the recounting of slaughter.

If this is the general tone, the basso continuo, nonetheless every experience is different from the others. It depends on the date of deployment, on the corps assigned, on the destination. Giacomo Colombo, for example, who ended up at the second front of Val di Ledro, in Trentino, talks not so much about himself as he does about the trial of rehabilitation of his buddy Amerigo Rizzardini, executed at Ala in Val Lagarina on Easter of 1918, because he came back from an approved leave twenty minutes late.[70] Lorenzo Fanetti sull Adamello recounts that "more than a battle against the Germans it was a battle against the weather, going out in -30 to -40 degrees."[71] Luigi Giovanetti, still obsessed with the assaults on Ortigara,

---

68 Fontana-Pieretti (editors), *La Grande Guerra. Operai e contadini Lombardi* cit., p. 160. Testament of Luigi Baccolo. We find the same judgment about the rifle corps also in the testament of Giovanni Brodini: "When the infantry went down at Isonzo, they were on respectful terms with the enemies; they even talked back and forth. With the riflemen, on the other hand, it was a huge gunfight; machine guns here and machine guns there, nonstop firing . . . the riflemen were like that: a bit over-excited." Ibid., p. 183.

69 A. Gibelli, *La grande Guerra degli italiani, 1915-1918*. Milan: Sansoni, 1998, pp. 384-388.

70 Fontana-Pieretti (editors), *La Grande Guerra. Operai e contadini Lombardi* cit., pp. 240-245. Testament of Giacomo Colombo.

71 Ibid., p. 259.

sees "dozens and dozens of soldiers insane and tied to the gurneys; they were driven out of their minds by fear." But then he offers an instant so profane from the Karst front that it scatologically outdoes even Gadda: "There in Karst, you know, there were thousands of soldiers, they made a latrine as wide as this table and about twenty meters long; they put boards over it so people could go and do their business. . . . Everyone had hemorrhoids, with the gross stuff we ate and the heat that there was, that killed you. Imagine to yourself: in there was the ugliest stuff beasts make, a whole host of flies, bluebottles, mosquitoes, God knows what else all was down there, Jesus and Mary . . . There was the danger of illness, of some infection, I'm talking about thousands of people at that part of the front. Sure, they threw down there a bit of lime mortar, a good thing we had it there. This was the war; not always grand and beautiful words!"[72]

It is a journey into degradation and abjection. Giuseppe Micheletti: "I remember that, there in Karst, there was an ugly case: One day all the soldiers were ill, all infected, to tell you the truth, and they didn't know why or how, because there were never women in the trenches, so how could it be? Not even in the second line did you see a woman; however there were nearby some houses with people in them, and they dared one another to go over and they found a girl there: they take her, they tie her to a tree, they put a stick of dynamite inside her and they blew her up: It's a savage thing, not human. There was nothing left of her, not even her shadow, it was all bits and pieces. When I passed that place, my skin crawled and my blood churned; but in wartime one becomes used to thinking that human life was worthless."[73]

---

72 Ibid., p. 336.
73 Ibid., p. 364.

The people and the alphabet

The voice that in war literature states "I" is invariably that of a lower-class officer, selected, often interviewed, and one that over the course of the war matures into a more suffering sense of awareness. The troop of simple soldiers is destined to remain at the bottom, in an anonymity out of which emerge from time to time brief profiles, among a wide range of types. The only exception is Cola, the soldier Cola, the protagonist of the novel of Mario Puccini of the same name, which was announced in 1918 but not issued until 1927. A "reality novel," as Alberto Asor Rosa defines it, in which Puccini "traces with efficacy the figure of a simple soldier, a humble Tuscan peasant, already the father of four, as the true hero of that war, whose own ideal motivations were lost very quickly along the way leaving behind just the modest, stubborn obedience to a duty only recently recognized."[74]

Now, it isn't the case that this Cola, who in an earlier time had to appear, in the subtitle of the book, as a portrait of an Italian—this "digger" soldier always so sensible, something of a know-it-all, devoted to his local poet Vencini (because Vencini loves the common person and writes beautiful poems and "in Tuscany those who recite poetry in public places, people love them because the one who has a poetic soul deserves every companionship")[75]—it's not the case, we repeat, that the peasant-soldier Cola is illiterate and can't even write his own name.

From the imaginary to the real, from novel to journal, it's a short step. Sorrentino, the Neapolitan attendant of Captain Levi, in the profile offered by Silvio D'Amico, another officer-intellectual, is one of the most well-liked soldiers: "He knows how to do everything, tailor, carpenter, barber to the

---

[74] A. Asor Rosa, *L'epopea tragica di un popolo non guerriero*, in *Storia d'Italia*, "Annali, 18," *Guerra e pace*, edited by W. Berberis. Turin: Einaudi, 2002, pp. 839-918; cit., on p. 870.

[75] M. Puccini, *Il soldato Cola. Uno straordinario ritratto dell'italino in Guerra*. Milan: Bompiano, 1978, p. 35.

company and stove-stoker to the officers, able to build walls for injured men and to fix anything broken on any machine, famous more than anything for being able to extract with a nail out of the tops of Austrian bombs knives, bracelets, rings, letter-openers, and even a pair of perfect spurs for Lele. Two things he couldn't do: read and write; and now that an officer is teaching him, I'm afraid that he will ruin him for me."[76]

The conviction that an illiterate person is of little or no use to people or that he might even be dangerous comes from way back, from the Catholic opposition to compulsive education, it goes along with the conservative mythology (the "socialist school master," the illiterate "subversive"),[77] it bases itself on the populist vision that replaces (and recovers) in the peasant populace its own inherited quality of wisdom. They will remember the verses of Guido Gozzano in reply to his elderly illiterate servant, "the honest and robust octogenarian" who inviting him to read called him "blessed" ("Now do a little reading for me, you blessed one who knows how to read, Read!"): "Oh, me, blessed!? I would rather not know how to read, Old One, the words of others/ I would drink, heedless of cunning flavors/ a pure wine in my cup./ And the joy of song which has strayed from me/ would shine as you shine in the depths of your eyes/ the good smile free from all contagion."[78]

The phenomenon of illiteracy, that we will continue to consider "sad," proves to be in decline from the census of 1911, but still relevant: Persons above the age of six years who don't know how to sign their name at the bottom of a document make up 38 percent of the population in Italy, an average that disguises, even at fifty years since Unification, an

---

76 S. D'Amico, *La vigilia di Caporetto. Diario di Guerra, 1916-1917*, edited by E. Brichetto. Florence: Giunti, 1996, p. 37.

77 Cfr. T. De Mauro, *Storia linguistica dell'Italia unita*, Laterza, Roma-Bari 1976, II, pp. 342-345. No less than Giosue Carducci, writes De Mauro, inveighed against "forced labor at learning to read," and against the alphabet considered "the most hypocritical instrument of corruption." Ibid., p. 343.

78 This deals with the poem "L'anafabeta," included in the collection *La via del rifugio* (1907), that we cite by G. Gozzano, *Le Poesie*, introductory essay by E. Montale. Milan: Garzanti, 1964, p. 28.

imbalance that is difficult to correct; it goes from the "light" figure of 11 percent in Piedmont to the heaviest one, 70 percent, in Calabria. The difference between males (33 percent) and females (42 percent) suggests to us the percentage of illiterates that probably comes to interest the army.[79] But the percentage is maybe lower, if it's true (as Marco Mondini writes) that the deployment here and there of Italians affects (for a host of reasons tied to emigration, to draft avoidance, and to dismissals) above all the northern—and therefore the more educated—regions compared to the central and southern ones.[80]

However that may be, the dislocations brought about along the way (the behind-lines areas with their soldiers' houses, the inland hospitals, the moments of rest in the less-exposed lines) can engender original moments of encounter from which some may teach a person to write who wants to learn.

"Guess what I am doing!" writes Lieutenant Guido Boscagli in a letter while he is recovering in the hospital. "I'm being a teacher. In the evening, since we can't go outside, I teach them to read and write, but not like they do in school, the long way, but off the cuff. They've already made progress and feel good because they can write home themselves."[81]

Sometimes the encounter can be less brusque and can have some educative ends, like in the little school of Lieutenant Piero Pegna: "I am continuing to teach the illiterates, which I consider to be more important than any lining up on parade to the sound of music: A Cpl-Maj and my attendant are helping me in this not-easy task. The soldiers already know how

---

[79] Cfr. C. M. Cipolla, *Istruzione e sviluppo. Il decline dell'analfabetismo nel mondo occidentale*, il Mulino, Bologna 2002; E. De Fort, *Scuola e analfabetismo nell'Italia del '900*. Bologna: Il Mulino, 1995.

[80] Mondini, *La Guerra italiana* cit., pp. 71-75. "Of the 5 million men called up to the army during the Great war, roughly half (2, 452, 000) came from northern Italy, a quarter from central Italy (Toscana, Umbria, Lazio, Abruzzi), and the rest from the south and the islands." Ibid., p. 71.

[81] Monti (editor), *Lettere di combattenti italiani* cit., 1, p. 175.

to read and write vowels; they love me (I got this also from hearing them talk among themselves) and they appreciate the time I'm giving them. . . . I read the *Cuore* (*Heart*) to them, and they are moved by it."[82]

Instructing the "semi-learned" also includes less informal moments. The Soldiers' Houses, founded by Don Giovanni Minozzi, an extremely active military chaplain, which spread into a network through the mountains of Cadore into the Veneto plains, are places for "moral assistance" for the troops (religion, patriotism, encouragement, songs, books, and shows). But what really helped, in terms of practical actions, manifests itself above all "in the fulfillment of a correspondence that, for reasons of illiteracy or insecurity, many soldiers needed to be guided or at least oriented in."[83] In the Vicenza Soldiers' House, one of the most frequented (1.2 million visits in four years, a movement of about 800,000 letters), the "writing halls" were constantly filled ("they're even writing in the entryway, the need and the crowd are so great"): Priests, clerics, Catholic school students teach, guide, and do the writing themselves. "We would need to build a building," writes Don Minozzi, "just to get these enchanting children to write of the history in which the healthy simplicity of the race speaks with virginal honesty of duty, of hope, of faith."[84] (Here is the "people as children" idea again!)

Also the mutual instruction, one person with the other, can transform itself into an educational moment, "a becoming conscious" discovery of truth and of new values. This is what happens, for example, to Francesco Chironna, from Matera province, who leaves for the front convinced, actually "enthusiastic to defend the sacrosanct Italian rights." At the front, a student from Benevento has the patience to teach him to read

---

82 Ibid.
83 E. Franzina, *Il tempo libero dalla Guerra. Case del soldato e postriboli militari*, in *La Grande Guerra. Esperienza, memoria, immagini* cit., pp. 161-230; cit. on p. 177. Of the figure of Don Giovanni Menozzi and on "Catholic substitution" see M. Isnenghi, *Giornali di trincea, 1915-1918*. Turin: Einaudi, 1977, pp. 12-25.
84 Cit. Da Franzina, *Il tempo libero dalla Guerra* cit., p. 177.

and write, but later Chironna learns from him to mistrust the words from the officers and those of the military chaplain, with the result that he, Francesco Chironna, becomes a rebel "against the injustice of God."[85]

The war zone, therefore, is transformed into an enormous writing laboratory, where not only what one learned in school (until 1904 mandatory schooling had been reduced to three years, from age six to age nine)[86] comes out in letters and diaries, but also one learns to write or else perfects his knowledge of writing.

HUMBLE ITALY

The soldiers who write are therefore the great majority — it may be that at the end of the war (during which time many, as we have said, learned to write) they exceeded by a great margin that 70 percent figure given initially. The figure of the solitary soldier going off, intent on reading and writing, becomes familiar also to military officials, who rarely are curious enough to find out if what their subalterns were writing was important or significant at all.

It's a question that Adolfo Omodeo asked himself in his most cited volume, *Momenti della vita di Guerra* (*Moments of War Life*), where he gathers in appendices some fragments taken from letters by common soldiers, almost all of them

---

[85] Vita di Chironno Evangelico, in R. Scotellaro, *L'uva puttanella. Contadini del Sud*, with technical critique from F. Vitelli. Rome-Bari: Laterza, 1986, pp. 231-258; cit. on pp. 241-243.

[86] Coppino's Law from 1877 that established the requirement from six to nine years was substituted in 1904 by the reform of Vittorio Emanuele Orlando that raised the requirement, at least on paper, to the completion of twelve years. Cfr. N. D'Amico, *Storia e storie della scuola italiana. Dalle origini ai giorni nostri.* Bologna: Zanichelli, 2010. It's significant that many interview statements by Nuto Revelli declare that, in their time, there was no requirement to send kids to school and that as a result schooling dwindled to a pitiable state, a place to learn to write your name and little else, because there was work that needed to be done. Interesting, for our purposes, the short statement of Francesco Abbona (class of 1892): "I finished the third year of primary school; the school was in upper Monchiero. But I learned more as a soldier than I did at school." Revelli, *Il mondo dei vinti* cit., II, p. 140.

detained in Austrian prison camps.[87] The title of the appendix "Gli umili" (The Humble Ones) reaffirms the distance that separates the officers (who, seeing the war through the "historico-political lens" understand also the intimate necessity of it) and the common soldiers, excluded from such a broad vision and who end up by "some mysterious intuition" putting themselves in the hands (rightly, according to Omodeo) of their commanders.[88] Nonetheless, adds the author, this "humble" Italy deserves to be studied with a "disinterested love of the truth."

The popular texts with which it occupies itself all come from the volume Leo Spitzer published in 1921, *Italienische Kriegsgefangenenbriefe*, the fruits of his role as an agent of the censor, serving as the director of one of the Viennese censor offices.[89] In this work Spitzer transcribes a notable corpus of tales taken from letters by Italians in Austria (soldiers living in Trentino, Trieste, Venezia; Giulians enlisted in the Austro-Hungarian army; prisoners, for the most part in Russia; Austrian subjects interned for political motives in the Katzenau Camp) and from those letters sent home by Italian subjects imprisoned in Mauthausen and Theriesenstadt. This "Italian populace" brought together into a writing community that explains itself and communicates beyond confines and from contrasting perspectives — it is typical that it becomes noticed and attributed to presumed pacifists and internationalists.

---

87 Omodeo, *Momenti della vita di Guerra* cit., pp. 263-273.

88 Ibid., p. 263. The title and appendix indicate Antonio Gramsci's correctness when we writes: "In the Italian intellectual the expression humble indicates a rapport of paternal protection and also of protection of God the Father, the sufficient feeling of a superiority that goes undiscussed, the rapport as between two races, one considered superior and the other inferior, the rapport like that between an adult and a child in older pedagogy." A. Gramsci, *Quaderni del carcere*, III, Quaderni 12 (xxix)-29 (xxi), V. Gerratana, editor. Turin: Einaudi, 1975, p. 2112.

89 The subtitle, *Materialen zu einer Charakteristik der volkstumlichen italienischen Korrespondenz*, clarified the finality of the work, translated into Italian by Renato Solmi almost a half century later: *Lettere di prigionieri di guerra italiani, 1915-1918*, published by L. Renzi. Turin: Boringhieri, 1976. On the view of Spitzer "language-censor enthusiast," see the excellent synthesis by A. Ghibelli, *La letteratura degli illetterati*, in *Atlante della letteratura italiana*, III, *Dal Romanticismo a oggi*, edited by D. Scarpa. Turin: Einaudi, 2012, pp. 472-476.

The few extracts offered by Omodeo in an appendix to his *Moments of War Life* inscribe themselves perfectly in the ideological framework of the common Italian man: They express resignation and patience ("the war of the common man is experience like a fact of nature, not unlike the passage of the seasons"), faith in God and in prayer, preoccupation with one's immediate needs, the nagging reality of hunger. Clearly beyond his comprehension (beyond his philosophy of history) are the letters from deserters "dominated by cynical cowardice" to which he devotes in his first pages a passage of indisputable disdain—"they are insignificant letters," he writes— "they attest only to the most base instincts of self-preservation and have nothing to say of historical import. And if we possessed all the diaries of the draft-dodgers, they wouldn't tell us anything because they didn't create anything historical." Deserters put themselves on the margins of historical protagonism, they avoid "diligent forces," are part of a "feeble resistance," "without will," and "completely uncultured."[90]

In Leo Spitzer's collection, on the other hand, the choice of entries isn't beholden to an ideological perspective and doesn't intend to transmit any particular message: The objective is solely that of describing the "psychology" of the Italian people. Any objective is now comfortably obsolete that might stand in the way of alternate uses and readings.

Of incredible value are the notes and the linguistic and stylistic reflections (we will take them up again later) that provide the first outlines of a common Italian ("the populist letter doesn't give so much a picture of dialects as it does the struggle of dialect with the written language")[91] and the formal composition of letters from prisoners and their families—the forms of salutation (greeting and closing), the apologies, the repetitions, the lists, the rhetorical questions, the metaphors, the requests.

---

90 Omodeo, *Momenti della vita di guerra* cit., p. 7 and note 1.
91 Spitzer, *Lettere di prigionieri di guerra italiani* cit., p. 14.

The wide epistolary corpus represents the condition of the imprisoned man more than that of the soldier, with all that it brings with it in terms of victimization, of laments, imprecations, nostalgia, pettiness, egoism. We find in it superstitions, religious practices, dreams, voices of peace.

The attitude of Leo Spitzer, we repeat, is one of open sympathy and of human understanding in the face of these imprisoned people, and yet there's something about the treatment of these texts we find unconvincing; in them we see a stretching, a constriction, the application one might almost say of a "Procrustean bed." It seems, in other words, that his systems of excerpting (Spitzer uses almost exclusively fragments, pieces, sometimes even a single line) deprives the letters of individuality, tends to make them more repetitive than they actually are, it underlines their similarities ("an incredible uniformity") more than their differences, to such a degree that it's even possible, in the end, to extract from them a model letter, an "ideal type."[92]

These are of course conclusions that support this mode of collection and the characteristics of epistolary material: Spitzer, in other words, copies and analyzes an enormous number of individual letters, one per writer, but he doesn't have the chance to read an entire exchange of letters between two people (to take just an example), he doesn't have before him the variety of writings produced by prisoners (letters, yes, but also day-books, diaries, songs collections, notes, memories); he can't bring into clear view the individuality of single writers with the uniqueness (relative, naturally) of their writing.

Our researches in the field of populist writing have led us, on the other hand, in an opposite direction, to uncover voluminous numbers of pieces of correspondence, letters, and journals that shine light each on the other, writers with the characteristics of authors, individualities strong or less so but all singular and none interchangeable; a wide range of

---

92 Ibid., pp. 274-275.

competencies and linguistic abilities, variety rather than uniformity around the same social area.

Spitzer, however, insists on the materialistic culture of prisoners' correspondence (the requests for clothing, for money, for food) even though he never misses a chance to underline, where they appear, "spiritual matters." He almost makes of these their own category among the writings, without asking himself out of what frightening conditions those letters might have come. Of the 600,000 Italian prisoners being held in Austrian, Hungarian, and German camps, 100,000 died of illness, "and the most recurring illness was, along with tuberculosis, edema from starvation. Hunger, cold, these privations were therefore the base of the mass sacrifice of Italian prisoners."[93] Also the state of the Austrian Italians, disseminated throughout the camps and villages of Siberia, was extremely hard because of climatic conditions, general poverty, and subsequently the political upheavals and the civil war that followed. How "materialistic" therefore must the letters and conversations of prisoners (both cultured and less so) be in a context so dramatic and so understandable?[94]

The "power" of the populist letters is recalled also in the Introduction of Lorenzo Renzi, where he affirms that in war correspondence there is no (nor can there be any) "explicit self-analysis" on the part of the common writer vis-à-vis his own imprisonment. "If in the soldiers' letters" writes Renzi, "we don't find passages of introspection comparable to those of someone like Gadda it is not because their psyche is simpler

---

[93] G. Procacci, *Soldati e prigionieri italiani nella Grande guerra. Con una raccolta di lettere inedite*. Turin: Bollati Boringhieri, 2000, p. 171.

[94] Bonaventua Tecchi, confined in the "poets barracks" in the Celle prison camp, close to Hanover, writes forty years later: "At first, during the hunger, no one spoke of art, of literature, nor of mathematics, nor of women, those of us who were little more than twenty years old and who, inside the barbed wire, hadn't so much as seen a woman in months. Gloomy, heavily the dark of the evening would fall on our wooden kennels, filled with spruce needles, lined up like coffins; and the silence was the only comments on the day or a careful muttering, that brought back long ago luncheons and dinners." B. Tecchi, *Baracca 15c*. Milan: Bompiani, 1962, pp. 13-14.

but merely because only an expression that is very literary and complex will allow a similar freedom. And in effect that kind of self-analysis is rare even in the letters and testimonial writings of educated persons."[95]

The reference is to pages of the prison diary of Carlo Emilio Gadda, lieutenant in the Fifth Alpine Regiment of the Italian army, captured by the Austro-Germans in November 1917 and sent to the Celle camp. Gadda, who at the time was just an engineering student and not yet the great writer he would become, goes over in the diary all his "horrendous suffering," his "terrible rage" brought on by the humiliating conditions of being a prisoner ("prison destroys in me every source of pride, either as a man or as a soldier"), by the immobility and inaction, from the forced idleness that makes him miss "the divine moments of danger, the sublime actions of battle."[96]

If Gadda keeps a vibrant and angry diary, is it true that soldiers have correspondence that is necessarily more primitive (hunger, thirst, need for rest)? More uniform, more simplified, as Spitzer makes sure to maintain? The many pages we have read, and also the numerous letters published by Giovanna Procacci, would lead one to believe otherwise. Allow us to cite, as an example, the journal of Luigi Daldosso, a farmer from Trento and an Austro-Hungarian soldier held prisoner in Pinerolo. The result of a complex and ambitious process (it also incorporates the reading he was doing while in prison), the journal is nothing more than a lengthy reflection on the inactive, lifeless (a life without life) character of everyday existence in prison. He is already writing in his first nights, "What a miserable existence, so accustomed to free living, in the pure air of the camps the days seem to me to be endless. Each day constrained to eat the same food, to walk the same steps, closed up in these tiresome walls like terrible criminals, deprived of every little entertainment, it seems impossible to

---

95 L. Renzi, *Presentazione*, in Spitzer, *Lettere di prigionieri di guerra italiani* cit., p. XXVII.
96 Gadda, *Giornale di guerra e di prigionia* cit., pp. 280 and 291.

live life, feeling like an automaton, and never to see any single thing that might even for a moment relieve the tired and beat-down thinking seemed to me something I would never experience." And again later he writes, "Soon, soon in the midst of these struggles I don't seem to be able any longer to continue with these miserable lines, and I almost don't have it in me to say on the page all that troubles me in this empty situation I find myself in. My heart is overflowing with anger and bitterness, and in my blank and shriveled brain I no longer find anything that deserves description because life in this dank abode flows always the same, like the waves of water of the irrigation ditch here."

Archives of the "I"

"It was in the first years of the '80s, almost suddenly, that a surge of interest in people's writings took shape, writings about the war but not only those, made propitious by certain documentary discoveries come to light, once again in a relatively casual way, in the corners of a territory where the war passed and left a devastating legacy (Trentino), but above all fed by a cultural and historiographical climate that has been profoundly altered."[97]

The timely reference of Antonio Gibelli to Trentino gets taken up again: The "discovery" of a consistent and distinct corpus of texts, the work of peasants, artisans, and workers, almost all of which originated in military experiences, put in motion a history "from beneath" and a new historiography of war as a mental and cultural event. In the context of the conference at Rovereto in 1985 "The Great War: Experience, Memory, Symbols" at which Italian research confronted international works like those of Paul Fussell and Eric Leed who came together to revive the debate about the First World War,

---

97 Gibelli, *La Letteratura degli illetterati* cit., p. 475.

the historians from Trentino make a first reflection on the *Populist Writings From the War*.[98]

This contribution laid out, above all else, a vast territory that had been abandoned by researchers; it focuses on the characteristics of new sources and solicits a respectful and philological approach (populist writings, it has been written, recall philological and self-critical interests not inferior to those examples that demand erudite memorializing). It brings up, in any case, the irreducibility of the autobiographical texts to a single origin, and it advances, at the level of method, the demand of biographical explorations.

The Trentine (and Triestine) writings demonstrate the unequal levels of "modernity" of the war and illustrate an experience simultaneously the same as and different than that of the Italian soldiers (one difference is the context in which Austrian Italians were forced to fight; it's a different army in which they fight as an often discriminated-against minority, tragically more alone in the exposure to violence).[99]

Starting from the 1985 conference populist writing (about the war and otherwise) attracts the interest of individual historians, anthropologists, linguists, publications, and research institutions. A complex project took place: an integral work group, an archive, a newsletter, and annual seminars.[100] These last have turned out to be especially useful. In the first meeting in 1987, recognition and definitions of the field make themselves apparent via disciplinary competences, and the approach becomes even didactic. There emerge with sufficient preciseness two thematic areas: one relating to the passage from orality to writing (cultural modalities and linguistic

---

98 Cfr. G. Fait, D. Leoni, F. Rasea, C. Zadra, *La scrittura popolare della guerra. Diari di combattenti trentini*, in *La Grande Guerra, Esperienza, memoria, immagini* cit., pp. 105-135.
99 Cfr. N. Gallerano, *Dopo il convegno di Rovereto. Riflessioni sopra il recupero della Grande Guerra nell'odierna storiografia*, in "Movimento operaio e socialista," n.s. 1986, 1, pp. 121-127.
100 Ambitious and only partially realized programming is described in Q. Antonelli, *Scritture di confine. Guida all'Archivio della scrittura popolare*. Trento: Museo storico in Trento, 1999.

results, historical time periods, public and private locations); the other makes reference to the overwhelming insurgence of the need to write.[101]

If the spread of literacy, writes Antonio Gibelli, is a long-term process of uncertain parameters, "extending the use of writing among the common people results in significant elevations that place that extension in relation to historical facts, and from these they take their motivation and significance."[102] It is the traumatic nature of the events that "separate" (wars, prison sentences, exile, forced and unforced emigration for political or work reasons, both temporary and permanent) to place a dramatic need onto writing and to invest it with a particular haste.[103] In a soldier's situation, in particular, characterized by precariousness and estrangement, writing assists in bringing together elements of an identity deeply and severely threatened. Mario Isenghi writes of this in his concluding entry: "Another interesting moment, still in relation to the question of when an ordinary person writes, is when he is acting as an 'I' as identity, as a persona, precisely because he feels the necessity of writing himself and does it, a thing that he didn't have the desire, the occasion, or the need to do—therefore an endangered identity that reintegrates itself and recreates itself (but also that forms and differentiates itself) in the moment in which he writes. Endangered identity but at the same time constructing and constructed: It is not, I believe, a type of verbal gymnastics but rather an actual dialectical situation. This is a large theme that we leave laid out, confronted, but still with everything up for discussion in the following encounters: the construction of the populist 'I' (of the 'I's), the forms, the places of this populist construction, the birth via clash over change."[104]

---

101 *Per un archivio della scrittura popolare. Atti del seminario nazionale di studio, Rovereto 2-3 ottobre 1987*, in "Materiali di lavoro," 1987, 1-2.
102 A. Gibelli, *Pratica della scrittura e mutamento sociale. Orientamenti e ipotesi*, ibid., pp. 7-20; cit. on p.16.
103 E. Franzina, *L'epistolografia popolare e i suoi usi*, ibid., pp. 21-76.
104 M. Isenghi, *Intervento di discussione*, ibid., pp. 195-206; cit., on p. 199.

In subsequent seminars bases are established for rigorous use of populist texts outside of and against "the neopopulist enthusiasm for a history that's closer to the lower class." What's interesting, writes Antonio Gibelli, "seems to me not the naive illusion of finding the writings uncontaminated by the history of the subalterns as much as the rediscovery of the subjective dimension in history, antidote against its persistent reification: the rediscovery, that is, also by means of the fact that history echoes and multiplies itself in the variety of individual and collective, anthropological and mental pathways of millions of common men and that, without reckoning with this dimension, our understanding can be truncated, atrophied, and lifeless."[105]

In the meantime, to give substance to the theoretical reflections, the National Federation of the archives of populist writing are founded with the goal of "contributing to the conservation, to the safeguarding and rediscovery of all the written production of popular origin (edited or not) with the sole exception of documents of an institutional nature (chambers of commerce, workers organizations, unions, and political parties and groups, etc.)."[106] The net of the federation, what establishes it as an agile and "rizomatic" linking structure, is the linking of historical institutes of the Resistance (Turin, Alexandria, Cuneo, Novara, Bergamo), the university centers of Genoa, Rome, and Perugia, the populist-writing archives of Trento, the archive of Ligurian populist writing,[107] and lastly the national diaristic archives of Pieve Santo Stefano, one of the federation's strong links,

---

[105] A. Gibelli, *Perche la scrittura. A un anno dal seminario di Rovereto*, in "Movimento operaio e socialista," 1989, 1-2, pp. 5-8; cit. on p. 7.

[106] Documentation of the founding is published in Antonelli, *Scritture di confine* cit., pp. 30-32.

[107] Cfr. P. Conti-G. Franchini (editors), *Catalogo A.L.S.P. Universita degli studi di Genova*, Genova 1998; P. Conti, G. Franchini, A. Gibelli (editors), *Storie di gente commune nell'Archivio Ligure della Scrittura Popolare*, Editrice Impressioni Grafiche-Universita degli Studi di Genova, Genova 2002; F. Cafferana-D. Montino, *Dalle carte dell'Archivio ligure della scrittura popolare*, in "Storia e problem contemporanei," 2002, 31, pp. 167-184.

even though it may be also jealous of its own different stance regarding archive solicitation of memorial writings.[108]

In the subsequent years the lightness of the web will have the advantage finally of disappearing, but not without leaving strong traces. The editorial column "Dried Flowers: Texts and Studies of Populist Writing," under Antonio Gibelli, is perhaps the most interesting initiative, offering a national mirror of the research and of the critical response. Pursuing the aim of realizing the variety and longtime presence of writing in popular communicative practices, the first volumes are of necessity dedicated to the Great War: letters to family from a farmer from Brescia; love letters of a young couple from Trento who were separated the morning after their wedding by the sudden outbreak of the conflict; letters from an artillery sergeant, curious and attentive, to his Roman fiancée, a fervent patriot; letters from illiterate soldiers to a wartime female penpal.[109]

Closer to home, a parallel initiative is put into place by the Historical Museum of Trento (seat of the archive of populist writings) and by the Italian Historical Museum of the War with the editorial "War Writings": ten volumes from 1994 to 2002 and the publication of forty-five autobiographical texts (journals and memoirs) and four epistolary ones.

But outside of our circuits of deliberate engagement, little attention is given to texts edited in the last twenty years by private citizens, by rural scholars, and cultural associations, local military units, and small presses: a galaxy of memoirs, journals, letters, often transcribed haphazardly and without

---

108 Cfr. S. Tutino, *Il "vivaio" di Pieve Santo Stefano*, in *I luoghi della scrittura autobiografica popolare. Atti del 3° seminario nazionale*, in "Materiali di lavoro," 1990, 1-2, pp. 81-91; Id., *Scrivere di se. Storie e memorie*, in *Vite di carta*, edited by Q. Antonelli and A. Iuso. Naples: L'ancora del mediterraneo, 2000, p. 101-118.

109 F. Croci, *Scrivere per non morire. Lettere dalla Grande Guerra del soldato bresciano Francesco Ferrari*, Marietti, Genova 1992; R. Dondeynaz, *Selma e Guerrino. Un epistolario amoroso (1914-1920)*, Marierri, Genova 1992; C. Costantini, *Un contabile alla guerra. Dall'epistolario del sergente di artiglieria Ottone Costantini (1915-1918)*, Scriptorium, Torino 1996; A. Molinari, *La buona signora e i poveri soldati. Lettere a una madrina di guerra (1915-1918)*. Turin: Scriptorium, 1998.

philological criteria, and with no information about the writer or historical context. There are, however, private and family archives that are open and that, in their own way, make it possible for people to read them. One can also imagine, in the case of the best publications, even if they are strictly local, a new kind of commemorative function, a new type of "monument," given that these days they seldom erect statues, and the memory of events and of the men that accompany them is linked to different signs.

At the same time they are making visible and available epistolary sources relative to the Great War that are held in state archives, in the archives of communes, schools, mental hospitals, and churches.[110] With regard to the early 1980s, which we have to take into consideration (and that we had to confront in putting together this anthology), it's no longer a case of too few sources, but rather the opposite, too many.[111]

Epistolary Communication

And yet the thousands of letters that we can read are a small thing compared to the enormous epistolary flux that during the conflict linked the front to the people back home: "There are in effect almost four billion letters and postcards in complex movement during the war; 2,137,000,000 sent from the front line back home; 1,509,000,000 from homes to the front; 263,000,000 exchanged among members of the military

---

110 See F. Caffarena, *Lettere dalla Grande Guerra. Scrittura del quotidiano, monumenti della memoria, fonti per la storia. Il caso italiano*. Milan: Unicopli, 2005.

111 In the participation in the eighth seminar of the federation (*Archivi autobiografici in Europa. Tradizioni e prospettive a confronto*, Rovereto, January 30-31, 1998) Antonio Gibelli has delineated an outlook of this type: "Also in this field contemporary history risks suffering from one of its most noted faults: not the scarcity but the overabundance of sources. Which becomes, here, an overabundance of people telling their own histories, having their say. And the evidence of the shortage of sources overcomes its opposite." A. Gibelli, *C'era una volta la storia dal basso ...*, in *Vite di carta* cit., pp. 159-175; cit. on p. 174.

in war zones."[112] One movement of cards and letters exceeds that of the previous year by leaps and bounds: It's tantamount to saying that each of those 39,000,000 Italians populating the country (38 percent of whom, let's remember, were illiterate after age six) was the author of 102 missives.

Of the huge accumulation of mail at the post offices some of the first to become aware were the soldiers anxiously awaiting their first letters from their loved ones. "The mail service is very confused, precisely because of the large number of letters and cards clogging up the post offices," writes Efisio Melis to his father.[113] Melis, a meticulous Sardinian, reminds his relatives to write the address of the recipient and the sender in a very clear manner, to be sure to add the 10c stamp, to repeat news for him, without any fear of boring him, and in the case of lost letters to include again in later communications the information he missed. The punctiliousness of Melis, a sub-officer in a reserve corps, destined to die at Karst in November of 1915, in reality hides a common fear: "Dear Dad, I waited anxiously too for a letter or postcard from home, when they were doing mail call. I was sure that today finally I had to receive something, but instead I have nothing."[114] And when he finally does get his first letter his happiness is touching: "Dearest sisters, I received today your dear letter with the address spelled out clearly by Dad and containing much news; please believe that I am very satisfied. You can imagine the joy of soldiers when they are lucky enough to get a letter

---

112 Caffarena, *Lettere dalle Grande Guerra* cit., p. 40. In other countries at war, Caffarena informs us, the epistolary flux is even more impressive: The French postal service made brisk work every day of the war circa 4 million letters for a total of 10 billion; through every one of the numerous censor offices in Vienna pass every day little fewer than a half million letters; in Germany, the most literate of the European countries, the flow of letters reaches 30 billion pieces. On the relationship between literacy and the letter flow in Europe see D. Vincent, *Leggere e scrivere nell'Europa contemporanea*, translated into Italian by G. Arganese. Bologna: Il Mulino, 2006.

113 In I. Loi Corvetto (editor), *Dai bressaglieri alla fantaria. Lettere dei soldati sardi nella grande guerra*, in "Officina linguistica," 1998, 2, pp. 98-99. Letter from June 17, 1915.

114 Ibid., p. 107. Letter from September 8, 1915.

from home! Such a crowd at the mail distribution! So, write often. If you can't manage anything else at least a cheap picture postcard. I write almost every day."[115]

We have already spoken, and we will speak again in a later chapter, about the reassuring and reparative character of the family letter. But we will want to return to the observations of Antonio Gibelli where he notes the "primary" need to write experienced by the peasant soldiers "with an intensity very much disproportionate to the ways and attitudes of the writers themselves."[116]

This "intensity" characterizes also the research of the tools used in writing, research that can be difficult and a source of perpetual worry and anxiety: stationery, picture postcards and pre-stamped cards, pens, stylus, ink, fountain pens, pencils, and copying pencils.

Asking forgiveness for his bad handwriting, Alfonso Lucarini, a Tuscan foot soldier, concludes a letter to his mother-in-law in this way, saying, "That's all I got for now only be compassionate with my bad writing because here there's a shortage of all ink I did it with a piece of copying pencil a fountain pen attached to a little acacia branch and that's the whole writing desk setup."[117]

The need, then, to recompose the continuity of one's own existence, of one's own familial and community ties comes to everyone, even those who don't know how to write and who must therefore in most cases enlist the help of fellow military personnel in the composition of letters. Already a common figure during the conflict, the soldier-writer has found an incarnation that is almost literary in the volume of Elio

---

115 Loi Corvetto (edited by), *Dai bressaglieri alla fantaria* cit., p. 110. Letter from September 20, 1915.
116 A. Gibelli, *L'officina della guerra. La Grande Guerra e le trasformazioni del mondo mentale*. Turin: Bollati Boringhieri, 1991, pp. 55-56.
117 Alfonzo Lucarini, from Camaiore (Lucca province), class of 1890; enlisted in the 21st Regiment infantry, 7th company, diggers; letter from July 8, 1915. Correspondence in the Fondazione Museo Storico del Trentino, Archivio della scrittura popolare.

Gioanola, *The Large and the Small War*. The protagonist, Uncle Salvino, says, "Some of the other guys who always saw me writing, gave me stuff to write home for them, and I did it happily because I've always liked writing, and also they gave me things, stuff to drink, stuff to eat. Some of the guys only knew dialect, which sometimes I didn't understand, and I had to translate what they were saying into Italian—but altogether the letters were understandable, and also I wrote all of them in a certain manner, that everyone was healthy and how were you doing? How is Mamma? I am well, only a bit cold because there's not much clothing to wear, morale is good if it weren't for the fact that I keep thinking of you, I hope I can come home on a furlough, here there's shooting but we are all well covered, don't worry about me, dear Mamma, or dear sweetheart, that I remember you always dear wife sending many kisses because it's killing me not seeing them, who knows how big they've grown, and so forth. All I had to know was who I was writing to and I had all my beautiful words ready. Then I read also the letters written to the guys who couldn't read, and I saw that they were happy with the things I said to them on behalf of their relatives, so they all loved me, the Genoans right down to the Sicilians . . . Someone would burst into my barracks at night, where there was always a candle lit: I always had a pencil on me with a nice sharp point, and I'd write for him whatever he'd tell me on the pages from protocol notebooks: If they were Sicilians they gave me two or three Indian figs, the only things that got mailed to them from down home; I remembered my father telling me about being a marksman in Sicily and he told me how marvelous those figs were. But I had to peel them so I didn't get my fingers pricked. At Quota 144 there was a lieutenant of command who always came to me to sharpen his pencil. I had a knife that cut to make perfect points, just right."[118]

As is often the case with these after-the-fact reminiscences, the memory, while interesting, can be somewhat generic and

---

118 E. Gioanola, *La grande e la piccolo guerra*. Treviso: Santi Quaranta, 1994, pp. 77-79.

colorless. More productive is the analysis of the body of letters of an illiterate soldier, Mario Tirreni, born in Monteforte D'Alpone in Veronese, and died in the military hospital in Perugia in November 10, 1918. Tirreni dictated or had written, including both letters and postcards, seventy-five pieces of mail (of course, this is what remains of his corpus, which was maybe more considerable, if we are to believe what Tirreni and his scribe affirm, that he wrote as many as three times a week).[119] For all of 1917 Tirreni's compiler of letters was Giuseppe Marini, who didn't limit himself to lending his writing but also enters directly into the communication himself. He sends his own greetings to his friend's wife, he signs at the bottom of the letter, he makes digressions to explain how things are from his point of view, like in the letter from July 28, 1917, where, right in the middle of a discourse about passes that never arrive, he suddenly enters the scene, "Kindest Maria. Please allow me to add some words of my own." He does this in order to explain the bad mood of her husband who becomes upset if too many days go by without his receiving any mail. And when the friend must temporarily leave the base or, as happens, to recover from an injury in the hospital, Marini takes the initiative to write to "Kindest Maria," because it is he who keeps the paper, the cards, the pencils, and the stamps Tirreni bought. In this triangle, the wife seems to be the most confused, and it transpires that she writes directly to Marini, complaining to him about the silences of her husband. In this way he always has to justify the long gap in news after the withdrawal from Caporetto: "I am sorry hearing you say that he could still write to you. You are correct to say so, however you know about all the inconvenient things that have occurred in these two months. I had so many postcards I had at least 30 then I will have had at least

---

119 Forty-one of these letters are transcribed by Lucia Beltrame Menini, in *Ta-pum. Lettere dal fronte. Contributo morubiano nella Grande Guerra*. Padua Panda Edizione, 2001, pp. 190-215.

20 sheets and envelopes for writing and then all of the cards of your husband that he was always giving me when he distributed them anyway to get to the end of the story, one beautiful morning the Austrians came up, and if we hadn't had such strong legs for escaping, we'd still be there with them but instead luckily we are here, but we left all out clothes and things that we had we had even 3 pencils, and so much other stuff that it was necessary for me to change jackets, sweater, drawers shirt anyway we ran away without anything apart from our lives."[120]

Communication with this much interference ended up irritating Tirreni's wife, who didn't always have faith in the intermediary's word. When her husband in January went into the hospital with an infection, she sought out different correspondents (the Red Cross, the unit commander) to find out the truth. And Marini was offended. "Either you, Maria, don't trust my word or else when you read my letters you don't understand some of them."[121]

Giuseppe Marini in all likelihood interprets his role of scribe in a unique manner; there were others who were more efficient and less invasive, and yet the correspondence not only confirms the "primary" necessity of epistolary writing but it also illustrates the complexity of delegated writing.[122]

If on the one side of this enormous spectrum that represents populist writing (writing of the common people by writers who are more or less occasional) we find the letters of Tirreni-Marini, on the opposite end, after having gone through a series of intermediate writings, one finds the group of letters by those who, while not being "writers" (intellectuals, or those who write professionally) nonetheless use language with a certain ability and narrative skill.

---

120 In *Ta-pum. Lettere dal fronte* cit., p. 204. Letter from December 21, 1917.
121 Ibid., p. 206. Letter from January 15, 1918.
122 For an anthropological and contemporaneous look at the phenomenon, see A.-V. Nogard, *Dallo scrivano pubblico. La scrittura per delega*, in *Per iscritto. Antropologia delle scritture quotidiane*, edited by D. Fabre. Lecce: Argo, 1998, pp. 205-226.

One exemplary case is that of the prolific exchange of love letters between a couple from Trentino who were separated after just a couple months of marriage. Anselma Ongari and Guerrino Botteri, she a postal clerk and he a schoolteacher, exchanged in less than five years' time 1,371 letters.[123] We find in them little talk of the war, apart from its being the cause of their painful separation, and instead much introspection, passion, hidden desire, and religion. In speaking of their own love, the couple seek also to define themselves one to the other and to tell their own story to their spouse. They build a discursive space into which enter readings made and to be made, desired and censored, novels, figures of the imagination. The passion of love and that of religion (one of the main themes of the correspondence) intertwine themselves, they use the same language, they show themselves to be stages of the same journey. Anselma (Selma) is the "epistolary genius" who brings up and engages with amorous feelings. And she, writes Luisa Passerini, is always the one who gets most excited and who ventures closest to what she considers fleshly excess as well as written excess of words, creating an intimate exchange where allusions and periphrases alternate with explicit language.[124] In its complexity, the correspondence embodies a model of loving relations that is far from that of the peasant and that, with much approximation, we may define as middle-class, individualistic, modern.

Apart from the letters addressed to family, the soldiers write also to diverse recipients, to the hometown mayor,[125] to

---

[123] The correspondence is held in the Archivio della scrittura popolare di Trento, close to the Fondazione Museo storico del Trentino. A small portion of the correspondence (forty-six letters), preceded by a full study conducted on the perspective of a history of emotions, is published in Dondeynaz, *Selma e Guerrino* cit.

[124] L. Passerini, *Introduzione*, ibid., p. XII.

[125] See, for example, G. Raviele (editor), *Lettere dall'Itaglia. Lettere di soldati meridionali dai fronti della Grande Guerra*. Naples: Guida, 1977. The letters are addressed to the mayor of San Martino Valle Claudina in the province of Avellino, Luigi Pisanello, "a wealthy and shrewd pharmacist," writes the editor, "sustained by a network of economic interests, based on his real-estate holdings, his rentals, and his census and, sometimes, by usury." In the letters the interests of the shop, family

local newspapers, to the local outpost of their political parties, to famous people. They ask assistance for themselves or for their families, they request advice and information. To the sending of packages on the part of charitable organizations, be they lay or parochial, they respond with letters of thanks. But to the soldiers without families it can happen that they get a letter from a "wartime godmother," usually a rich and educated lady intent on giving comfort and moral support, even if it is necessarily of a generic and abstract type.[126] The embarrassed responses of the soldiers betray the difficulty of entering into relations with a "lady" as well as the exceptional nature of such an event. Surprised and flattered at the same time, they are at a loss for words and things to say in their correspondence, so distant and superior and unreachable (and uncontaminated by the miseries of war) does the "godmother" seem.

The letters to the home parishes, to their local priests, in this context take on their own importance and character. The parish priest is a reference point and a spiritual confidant, but up until the beginning of the conflict he is also a representative and a passage upward, with civilian administrative officials, hospital staff, chaplains and the military organs, and downward with the soldiers' families, whom he has the religious responsibility to commune with in mourning. Often at the center of initiatives geared toward solidarity and charity, he is the first to activate the epistolary rapport with parishioners in the armed forces system, generally speaking in concert with the complete integration of religious values with military-patriotic ones. The soldiers, for their part, experience anew the common devotions that tie them to their hometowns, to their churches, and their patron saints, to whom they promise

---

feuds, and local disputes that the war didn't interrupt predominate.
[126] On the phenomenon of the "godmothers" see Molinari, *La buona signora e i poveri soldati* cit. and, more recently, also by Molinari, *Una patria per le donne. La mobilitazione feminile nella Grande Guerra*, il Mulino, Bologna 2014, pp. 211-218. Local initiatives of "godmothering" were those by the family association of volunteer work of Trentino, that addressed Trentino volunteers in the Italian army.

donations via ex voto on their safe return; they describe the religious functions they take part in; they ask to be remembered in prayers and during the Mass; sometimes they ask that their letter be read aloud in public ("Oh, Rev. Priest, my wife said she would publish it in the church during the great Mass, so that the public should know that I am very happy and that the bearer of the letter speaks truly for the writer").[127]

But with the declarations of devotion and Christian patience, these letters carry with them almost always some less conventional images of war so as to incur the censure of the civil authorities, via a signal of less patriotic faiths. In one such contradictory situation we find, for example, Don Angelo Celadon, priest of Rosa (Bassano) who ends up going on trial for having read from the pulpit, "with the aim of encouraging the parishioners about the collection of funds and woolen articles for the troops," a letter from a townsman, Vittorio Meneghetti, a soldier in service close to a military hospital in Verona.[128] In truth Meneghetti was considering with human and Christian compassion the pain of the wounded, the tragedy of those mutilated, and he confesses to a certain irony, in concluding the letter, that in the hospital one could scarcely say what was the advantage of the war: "In these eighteen men, I had every sort of injury, some of whom caused me the most pity were four who were without a leg and some others who had lost an arm; I'm telling you they were really pitiable. And to think that there are thousands of these poor men, destroyed for their entire lives, in the flower of their youth, and so many of them who have three or four children at home, poor things; it breaks your heart. And in another sense it pains you to think that these won't be the last and among them we have all of us some brother or relation who will be

---

127 Letter from Carlo Spagnolini from December 11, 1915, in C. Stiaccini, *Trincee di carta. Lettere di soldati della prima guerra mondiale al parocco di Fara Novarese*. Novara: Interlinea, 2005, p. 69.
128 The episode in E. Franzina, *Lettere contadine e diari di paroci di fronte alla prima guerra mondiale*, in *Operai e contadini nella Grande Guerra*, edited by M. Isnenghi. Bologna: Capelli, 1982, pp. 104-154; cit. on p.128.

touched by the same misery or even worse. In this hospital, there are also wounded with frozen legs and many ill with typhus. Here it's hard to see the advantages of the war."[129]

The Form of the Diary

Antonio Graziani, class of 1895, 114th regiment infantry housed in Peri in Val d'Adige, on May 22, 1915, goes up to Belluno Veronese, on Mt. Baldo, not far from the Austrian border. And here, seeing the cannon already pointing northward, he realizes finally that the war is inevitable and imminent, desired (it is language of invective that he will repeat often) by heartless butchers ("buchers"). It is in this precise instant that he decides to keep a diary: "I want to begin to describe the life I may live, which I already imagine will be a barbarous one, I understand that Ican'twriteit as ugly as it is, because even writing it ugly, Won't be like living it, All of it point by point I can't do because when there will be weeks of battle I can't write in it, but when quiet comes later. But the principal points will all be here. And so when there will be months of quiet I will try putting various days together, to abbreviate the description."[130]

Graziani, a laborer in peacetime, keeps his appointment with his diary bearing with him a truncated education and certain political and unionistic attitudes that led to his having heard the public reading of "Avanti!"[131] — but also, we think, some knowledge of various political party writings, booklets, tracts, fliers, propaganda conversations, social poetry, and hymns. In the first place we read in his decision to keep a

---

129 Ibid., pp. 128-129.
130 A. Graziani, *Diario (1915-1917)*, transcription and notes by L. Mascanzoni. Ravenna: Longo ("I Quaderni del 'Cardello,'" series of studies on Romagna from the Ente Casa di Oriani, VIII), 1998, pp. 23-55; cit. on p. 23.
131 I conclude this information from the introductory notes by L. Mascanzoni, *"Cera Cadorna ..." Diario (1915-1917) della Grande Guerra del soldato Antonio Graziani,* ibid., pp. 9-16.

diary that urge, common to all wartime diarists, to make a testimony of an event that he knows will be memorable and also to recount an experience sure to be of a violent, ferocious, and barbarous ("a barbarous life") character.

In second place, he understands the manner, not simple, in which experiences express themselves in writing. Writing also realistically ("writing it ugly") he knows how difficult it will be to fully flesh out the actualities of war, of life lived,[132] but he is confident of getting down the essential elements and events.

He foresees, in any case, that the length of the diary will be inevitably influenced by how the war progresses: If the periods of combat will be followed by days and months of quiet he will take advantage of them to put together things that took place when he couldn't write about them, delineating perfectly the typology of the populist war diary, always in the middle of the road between plan, diarist notes, and memory.

If for Graziani the decision to write is completely spontaneous, in other cases it is requested or at least foreseen. Trentinos and Triestinos in the Austro-Hungarian division, for example, at the moment of departure are given a "kit," where they find, along with postcards and cigarettes, also a little preprinted agenda (the kriegsnotizen or the kriegstaschenkalender), including a copying pencil: Besides the calendar of monthly pages, the little notebooks provided geographical and political information about the lands at war, formation of the Austro-Hungarian armed forces, an abridged history of the royal house, and some other texts that wrapped up the packet in a patriotic way (a poem, a song, and a prayer).[133]

---

[132] "The man who writes condenses things a bit, and he knows it," writes Luigi Meneghello, who adds, "Experience is a flowing, it runs all around us, we're immersed in a river, there's the flow of time, the flow of biological life and that of social life, society changes around us, with rhythms that sometimes appear even more rapid than biological rhythms. ... Writing takes something away from this flow, it is like drawing some water from a river in a bowl, and it seems to have preserved at least something of the sense of our experiences." L. Meneghello, *Jura. Richerche sulla natura delle forme scritte*. Milan: Garzanti, 1987, pp. 53, 65.

[133] Cfr. Q. Antonelli, *I dimenticati della Grande Guerra. La memoria dei combattenti*

The space allotted for the soldier to write in is small, constraining them to brief notes, just the essentials: the bare recording of facts, merely a chronological list of events (when they happen), and lists of names, places. The notebook presents itself as an *aide memoire*, "an external series of references, broken down into days and weeks that correspond to dates remembered, of which only traces come to be set down on paper, divorced, for the most part, from their emotional content, which was after all the element that determined and guided their registration."[134]

Two pages a month, one line per day. The brief notes cover the weather, work, night watch, food, gift packages, expenses, marking letters received and sent, conditions of life and health, religious and secular holidays. The intensity, constancy, the diligence with which the notebooks came to be maintained speak to the value of measuring time, to the sense of security that the continuation of days brings with it, to the desire to put into order an existence in which one has trouble recognizing himself.

Of course for us now not everything is clear, but to share what Elias Canetti affirms about the notebooks: "I know people who mock others about their calendars because there's so little in them. But only those who fill in the calendar can really know what it contains. The scarcity of notations creates their value."[135]

We follow along the little notebook of Celeste Paoli with his unit of Landesschutzen on the Dolomite front of Marmolada: He notes the alternation of guard duty and sleep, the August snowfalls, the wind, the cold, the times he attends Mass. Here is the week from August 20-26, 1916:

"20) Rest. In the morning went to Mass celebrated in the barracks, during the day more sleep the night to come the . . .

---

trentini (1914-1920). Trento: Il Margine, 2008, pp. 263-268.

134 G. Baldassarri, *Fra ypomnemata e soliloquium. Usi e ri-uso del diario individuale*, in "Quaderni di Retorica e Poetica," 1985, 2, *Le forme del diario*, pp. 29-34; cit. on p. 31.

135 E. Canetti, *Potere e sopravvivenza. Saggi*. Milan: Adelphi, 1974, p. 60.

21) At my post two hours was very cold, during the day another 2 also cold but not as bad as the night from the . . .

22) Depressed. Slept during the day also at night to come the . . .

23) Did two hours at my post and it was very cold, during daytime another two hours, very cold but not so much. The night to come.

24) Sleep during day also the night to come.

25) Did two hours at post, cold, as far as the rest, not bad. In the day another two the night to . . .

26) Rest all night. In the day the same."[136]

To his mother, whom he invites to keep a diary ("I hope you will have a notebook I want you to write on it all your happy and sad adventures whatever they are so that if you should have to die by some terrible accident, I can know how you passed your days so far from home in the fields exposed to so many dangers and difficulties."), Celesto responds in a mode that Canetti would like: "About what you asked as far as me writing my adventures, I write everything, but in a certain way so that I'll need to explain it to you, what it is, and if fate decrees that I die and I can't explain it to you, then I'd be happier if you didn't understand it."[137] Every sign, Canetti would say, conceals a life experience.[138]

Not all the notebooks are the same; some of them might contain the seeds of a diary. "No sooner is there something else to add," writes Canetti, "than has he begun a reflection on things, the notebooks leave the realm of calendar notes and fall instead into that of diaries."

But again, it is the war that determines the quality, the caliber, the intensity of the writing: a change of posting location, a hugely dramatic occurrence, a deeper involvement.[139]

---

136 C. Paoli, *La vita al campo 1915-1916*, in *Angelo Paoli, Celeste Paoli, Giuseppina Paoli, Luigia Paoli, Maria Paoli et alii*, edited by M. Paoli. Trento-Rovereto: Museo storico in Trento - Museo storico italiano della guerra ("Scritture di guerra," IX), 2001, p. 102.

137 Ibid., pp. 212-213. Celeste Paoli dies at Asiago on December 5, 1917.

138 Canetti, *Potere e sopravvivenza* cit., p. 62.

139 Citing Franco Fortini we may say that with the war conditions are determined

Domenico Zeni, another Trentino soldier in the Austro-Hungarian forces, already the author of a small notebook, buys himself a more substantial one that he calls "book." In his countrified Italian, he writes of having acquired the bigger book in order to write down what was happening, attesting that it is impossible to keep in one's memory everything that befalls him.

"I bought this book just to make a memoir of a bit of what I do during the time I am a prisoner seeing that it is impossible to keep in memory [what] happens in this time until peace comes. Up to now I made some notes in a little notebook now I've come to the point of buying one seeing that easily things happen that no one would believe who wasn't there, if God one day sends the peace we desire these cases will help our memory."[140]

The passages are clear; Domenico Zeni wants to write a journal that can present itself as a real and proper memory book, capable of conserving and transmitting a different time, the extraordinary time of war in which things happen that are difficult for those left at home to imagine. An assignment that can't be completed by mental memory's activity because only the permanence of writing is capable — when it is transformed into story — of bringing to mind in peacetime the circumstances of war and of prison, not the disconnected jottings found in a notebook even when they are supported by memories.[141]

But what are the characteristics of a war diary? The day-by-day diary mirrors more or less unconsciously the casualness of existence. It goes along from fragment to fragment,

---

for "restoring to the diary its dramatic and absolute value: In other words, when there is no interlocutor, when life has no future but only a horrid present." F. Fortini, *Ventiquattro voci per un dizionario di lettere*. Milan: Il Saggiatore, 1968, p. 199.

140 Domenico Zeni, diary-memoir (1915-1918), in Fondazione Museo storico del Trentino, Archivio della scrittura popolare.

141 A reflection on these themes that is parsed in a particularly stimulating way can be found in E. Lledo, *Il solco del tempo. Il mito platonico della scrittura e della memoria*, translated into Italian by M. Carmignani. Rome-Bari: Laterza, 1994.

without a plan or a goal, without a vision of the future. Every notation is complete in itself.

"The fragmentary nature of the diary," writes Camillo Zadra, "adapts itself particularly to reflecting life in the trenches or on the field of battle, around which movement happens according to the rhythms of stabilized direction, beyond the scope of the soldier." Space contains him, advancing, retreating, remaining in one place for days and nights, walking interminably, eating and fasting, drinking, sleep result from the descriptions that we have completely unchained from day and night, from some usual kind of regularity, in a condition of continual exposure to death; this doesn't mean that the soldier doesn't have moments of "normalcy"; it means rather that he lives, when he is at the front, entirely situated in a state of perennial instability and mutability that surrounds him, preventing him from gaining perspective or distance sufficient to gather the wholeness of his own experience.[142]

In this fragmentation of perspective only the basic entry of date and place, the temporal measuring into days, weeks, months, years offers a kind of recomposition. The diary is "based on a date and place," writes Jean Norton Cru, titles and subdivisions make a blueprint; these basic entries "constitute a scene."[143]

This reduction of perspective, this limitation of the field, this tie to the present, to the here and now, discourages and oppresses the more cultivated diarists, the officer-writers. Silvio D'Amico writes about this, after having found the pages of his own journal to be insignificant. "Basically this system of noting down things evening by evening is a silly illusion. The only thing that one remarks on are some particulars, the closest ones, not the most important ones, also because the importance emerges later. The essence of a fact almost never makes

---

[142] C. Zadra, *Quaderni di guerra*, in "Materiali di lavoro," n.s., 1985, 1-3, pp. 209-236; cit. on p. 223.
[143] J. N. Cru, *Sulla testimonianza. Processo alla Grande guerra*, translated into Italian by C. Casalini. Milan: Medusa, 2012, p. 59.

itself known right away. Only at a distance in the memory—which veils, idealizes, deforms, but sees the whole—are the characteristic lines grasped."[144]

And yet a large part of the power of and the interest awakened by wartime diaries (including Silvio D'Amico's) is found precisely in their "direct grasp," in the gaze of the soldier/diarist who goes from the trench to a forest and becomes lost in unknown territory.

Naturally we mustn't ask diaries, and even less the populist ones, for circumstances and details about facts as they are understood by military history: the tactical maneuvering of attacks, defense, advances, the capture of men and destruction of materiel.[145] One turns to diaries to understand how these assaults and retreats, these destructions come to be seen and experienced, and what repercussions they have on the body, the personality, and the mind of the soldier who goes through them. On closer reading, the diary entries, even the most condensed ones, tell us something about either the mind and thinking of the soldier going into the war zone or else about his alteration after coming into contact with the violent, military, and coercive world. Glenn Gray, an American philosopher who fought in the Second World War, rereading the entries in his diary observes that, with regular exposure to homicidal violence "men can retain the memory of civilian life and obstinately resist, as I forced myself to do, the pressures of violence and irrationality. They can write home or

---

144 D'Amico, *La vigilia di Caporetto* cit., p. 145. A reflection rather similar paves the way also to Gadda's text, titled not coincidentally *Impossibilita di un diario di guerra*, in Id., *Il castello di Udine* (1934). Turin: Einaudi, 1975, pp. 29-43.

145 Cru, in the pamphlet of 1930, warns of the "superstition of military facts":"Life on the front has taught us different," he affirms in his typically sanguine manner. "Some may object that these memories contain too few so-called military facts; the author relates, abuses, believes in psychological facts and details of his own material life: eating, drinking, letters, packages, lice, mice, the rain, the mud, nocturnal maneuvers, permissions, etc. Where can one find in here a history worthy of Thiers? It's almost fact-free. It's true, and this is the pertinent point. We need to be careful of memoirs that have too many facts and that assume a historical style; here is a testament that wants to be communicated and that tells above all things I haven't seen." Cru, *Sulla testimonianza* cit., pp. 30-31.

to their lovers convincing themselves that they are still the same. But to the soldier who has abandoned himself to the life of war, who has weighed the experience of killing while avoiding the act itself, or who has traveled far enough down the chaotic passageway of battle, it's not permitted for him to remain unchanged. At least the majority of men, whether they want to or not, end up acquiring the status of combatant. The states of his soul and his interior disposition are shown by the presence of others and by the surrounding atmosphere of threat and fear. He has, in part, to surrender to others' will and to more powerful forces. He becomes in a real sense a fighter, a *Homo furens*, which is always what it has meant to be soldiers."[146]

Writing and Time

Most often soldiers write their memoirs after the events they personally witnessed, either at the end of the war or many years later. Instead of the "here and now" of diaries, memories get projected onto the past; soldiers try to reorganize their recollections and put them in a certain order. Populist or more cultivated, they all divide up, speaking generally, the characteristics of the autobiography in this way, as expressed in one of the more classic descriptions: "Autobiography is a giving of form to the past. It imposes a plan on a life and, as a foundation for it, creates a coherent history. It determines certain stages in an individual life, it builds ties among them and defines, implicitly or explicitly, a certain coherence in the relationship between me and the outside world."[147]

---

[146] J. G. Gray, *Guerrieri. Considerazioni sull'uomo in battaglia*, translated into Italian and critically annotated by E.M. Massucci. Trento: Fondazione Museo storico del Trentino, 2013, pp. 46-47.
[147] R. Pascal, *Design and Truth*, in A. Pizzorusso, *Ai margini dell'autobiografia*, il Mulino, Bologna 1986, p. 190. Cfr. also by Pascal, *Cos'e un autobiografia?*, in *Teorie moderne dell'autobiografia*, edited by B. Anglani. Bari: Edizioni Graphis, 1996, pp. 19-32.

And yet the times, the modes, the results of memoir writing differ from person to person. It is striking, for example, that many memoirs are written during the war but by people who consider themselves "outside the fray" because they are prisoners or injured or demobilized or else displaced to internal service, definitively outside the theater of operations. "From the place where he writes his memoir, the soldier looks at his own past through a crack from which, individually or in a group, voluntarily or less so, he has left the war."[148]

The point of view is, in other words, that of one who considers that his experience of fighting the real war is over. The relative nearness of the writing to the lived events gives the memory a particular freshness, a greater precision in geographic details and chronologies, a richer adherence to how things happened, all characteristics that later writings tend to lose. As far as different ways to give form to recollections of war we can cite some interesting cases from among the authors in our anthology.

Alfonzo Cazzolli, from Trentino, enlisted in August 1915 to the Austro-Hungarian army, begins his memoir the 31st of January 1918, in Manchuria, as an Italian citizen, while he waits, far from the front, a transport back to Italy. This incipit is surprising: Instead of following the usual chronological criteria, Cazzolli reveals in advance the crucial event of his history—his desertion, which left him, in June 1916, in the hands of the Russians. "On the day of June 8, 1916, around 5:00 in the evening, tired and depressed, after long suffering and anguish, I turned myself in to a battalion of Cossacks; within two hours I found myself together with two Italians, G. Mazzalai from Trento and G. Boldass from Monfalcone, Friuli. We surrendered to the Cossacks, as I said above, in the small village of Potosloki. On August 23, 1915, about 6:00 in the evening, I left . . ."[149]

---

148 Zadra, *Quaderni di guerra* cit., p. 228.
149 A. Cazzoli, *Ricordi e Memorie*, edited by C. Zadra, in "Materiali di lavoro," n.s., 1986, 1-2, pp. 185-206; cit. on p.185-186.

The evidence given to the act of desertion signals immediately to the reader the distinctive mark under which the writer intends to file his war experience. And in fact the rest of the memoir runs from the date of his departure for the front and is nothing but a long description of his progress leading up to and putting into action his exit from the ranks of combatants.

A large part of the memoir writing of Trentinos has these characteristics: It forms itself in the context of the war, limits itself to describing one segment of the experience, and demonstrates with more or less expressive power the unifying design that links the different moments of life at the front.[150]

Let's take the case of Alessio Menapace, who emigrated at a young age to the United States, where he worked as a miner, and was called up to fight at thirty-seven years of age. He writes his memoir in the spring of 1917 in a rest home in Innsbruck, after a serious injury partially invalided him. He himself added to his retrospective tale the sign of an unnameable condemnation of the coercive meaning of "homeland." Because of his family's poverty, he writes, he was constrained to emigrate and had worked very hard; he was able to give relief to his parents' "prickliest thorns." But here the war breaks out and he is recalled and forced to fight for Austria. The reader will easily understand, he writes again, that this homeland, "for which I was forced to sacrifice, which threw me by the throat into this enormous snare—it's not mine. But my real and true land, up until this period the one in which, with my willingness for tireless work, I earned my living and

---

[150] A good example of a "project" based on feelings and passions rather than on events and chronologies is offered by the incipit of Cesare Dusini: "how to spend time so as not to remain in idleness, how to do it so this prison seems not so boring and long? It's really painful to see oneself here locked in a room, stretched out on a shelf, without ever being able to go outside unless you're accompanied by one of our officers. To cheat time, I will prepare myself to write my whole story, beginning with the first of August 1914, in other words from the outbreak of the war in Europe. Pain, agitation, fear, hate, cowardice, disillusion, hope, hunger, thirst, lethargy, all must get filtered into these few lines, even the love that some ray of sun on a cloudy day comes to brighten little by little the bitter heart of the prisoner. Kirsanov April 1, 1916." Cesare Dusini, memoirs (August 1, 1914 to November 25, 1915), in Fondazione Museo storico del Trentino, Archivio della scrittura popolare.

supported my family with honor and spent the larger part of my life, is that blessed land that I will call for all my life and for all time, the mother of the poor, of good will: America."[151]

Very different is the memoir of Albino Soratroi, who was born in the then-Austrian Ladino enclave of Livinallongo and for that reason was drafted into the army of the emperor. He began to write in 1970 at the age of seventy-two, and he is the last of the valley's veterans to survive the conflict.[152] And likely this is the strongest motivation for him to pen the text that became something like a last will and testament. Luciano Palla, who was the curator of Soratroi's memoirs, hypothesizes another reason for his writing: "Maybe it was reading books about the war in the Tofane [area of the Dolomites], which he himself actually lived through, that made him understand the importance of his experience."[153] The memoirist cites two volumes directly in his own work, "this [the heroic character of two Austro-Hungarian officials] one may encounter also reading the volumes by Burtscher, *War in the Tofane*, and Piero Pieri's *Our War Among the Tofane*."[154]

---

151 A. Menapace, *Mia vita in guera*, edited by Q. Antonelli. Cles: Pro Cultura Centro Studi Nonesi, 2012. This deliberate and unusual choice of an elected homeland contrasts with the simplifications that Trentinos and Triestine people would want deployed for Austria or for Italy. And it goes to add itself to all the definitions of "homeland" that we find in the autobiographical texts by Trentinos, where in large part they define themselves according to location, but where we also find affirmations given for the purpose of negating borders and nationalities. Cfr. F. Rasera-C. Zadra, *Patrie lontane. La coscienza nazionale negli scritti dei soldati trentini, 1914-1918*, in "Passato e Presente," 1987, 14-15, pp. 37-73.

152 He writes in the conclusion of his memoirs: "Of all of us who were in Val Travenanzes together with the Fodom [the speakers of Livinallongo's dialect], mentioned already as there being five, I am the only survivor. All the Fodomi mentioned as being with me in prison have disappeared, I was younger than all of them, and now it's some years later and I am seventy-two (in just a couple months!). Cosa di Salesi, March 1970." A. Soratroi, *I miei ricordi di guerra e di prigionia (Maggio 1915-Febbraio 1919)*, in *Simone Chiocchetti, Vigilio Iellico, Giacomo Sommavilla, Albino Soratroi*, edited by L. Palla. Trento-Rovereto: Museo storico in Trento-Museo storico italiano della guerra ("Scritture di guerra," VI), 1997, pp. 175-262; cit. on p. 262.

153 Introductory note by L. Palla, ibid., p. 173.

154 Soratroi, *I miei ricordi di guerra* cit., pp. 198-199. Quoting exactly the titles of the two works, Soratroi means to bolster the veracity of his account. Piero Pieri,

The result is a "chilled" text, of low emotional temperature, given that Soratroi wants to confront himself with military history, from which he tends to take vocabulary, point of view, and the pretext of objectivity. More than half a century after the conflict, in a radically different place (Livinallongo just after the war became part of Belluno), Soratroi, like so many other memoirists, relates not only what he remembers but also what he knows, the information he has gained over time, reconstructions made by others that had become part of his culture and his identity. The account of this Ladino former soldier presents us with one of the fundamental problems of memory, which is that "one doesn't remember in isolation, but with the help of the memories of others," that we often (more than we sometimes are willing to believe) borrow tales heard from others but even more, that "our memories are filed in collective stories, themselves reinforced by commemorations and public celebrations of related events."[155] Apart from reading the different historical reconstructions, how many public commemorations will Soratroi have taken part in in his lifetime? And how many conversations, tales, anecdotes will he have heard and exchanged with his co-militarists from those times?

Still other modalities. The memoir of Duilio Faustinelli, a shepherd from Valcamonica, class of 1893 and corporal in the infantry at Karst and in the mountains of Asiago, brings up a complex relationship to oral storytelling. Faustinelli writes at the end of his text, "I wrote this diary some years after the

---

one of the more noted military historians, was also a combatant/official at Tofane. His work, *La nostra guerra tra le Tofane*, was published in magazines in the 1920s and then reissued and supplemented in book form in 1930 by l'Editrice Perrella di Napoli. But later on many other editions came out (the editor indicated one in 1973).

155 P. Ricoeur, *Ricordare, dimenticare, perdonare. L'enigma del passato*, translated into Italian by N. Salomon. Bologna: Il Mulino, 2004, p. 54. Ricoeur takes up the notion of "collective memory" of Maurice Halbwachs: see his *La memoria collettiva*, Italian edition edited by P. Jedlowski. Milan: Unicopli, 1987; *I quadri sociali della memoria*, translated into Italian by G. Brevetto, L. Carnevale, G. Pecchinenda. Naples: Ipermedium, 1997.

war it deals with, then after 1953 I wrote everything together in a single volume . . . in 1954. Now I am tired of describing so many military facts. I am stopping my hand for anyone who wants to read it."[156] It seems he understands that in expanding the "journal" (in common parlance and not merely among the common people, every autobiographical text is a "diary") it passed through various phases (not counting typewritten manuscript in 1975 and published book in 1982). In 1980, before the book came out, he put out a long oral account transcribed by Giorgio Sbaraini.[157] So it is that we have from Faustinelli two texts that, when compared, are unsurprisingly like copies of each other. We find first of all the same number of events (the two texts are set out in a succession of facts exactly like a popular fable that proceeds from one trope to the next).[158] The order can change slightly, but sooner or later they all come back: the Italian artillery firing on grenadiers, praying to be saved from the assault, the temptation to shoot oneself in the hand, the finding of a precious little box, the captain who kills two soldiers in cold blood, what seems like a bout of fever, the thirst suffered at Asiago, etc.

The medium—the saying aloud of the story in the presence of the interviewer, the writing down of that story with long years of having adapted it and making it longer with digressions, reflections, etc.—seems inconsequential.

Actually, the rote repetition of events (like in the oral fable, an extremely cruel fable, in this case) harks back to an original oral tale, replicated within the context of the social milieu of the country as if to "ossify" itself, and this is what one finds subsequently in dialectical expressions and typical stock phrases. But also the modalities most typical of the

---

156 D. Faustinelli, *La "Cattastrofe,"* edited by Circolo culturale G. Ghislandi. Esine: Tip. Valgrigna, 1982, p. 92. On the spine the book carries a different title: *Diario di guerra di un pastore canuno*.

157 Fontana-Pieretti (editors), *La Grande Guerra. Operai e contadini Lombardi* cit., pp. 268-318.

158 The reference is to V.J. Propp, *Morfologia della fiaba* (1928), Italian edition edited by G.L. Bravo. Turin: Eunaudi, 1982.

writing impress themselves on successive accounts as they are re-told. We can't otherwise explain the end of Sbaraini's interview when Faustinelli not only repeats word for word the last section of the written text but also goes so far as to relate the text of the signature: "After so much effort, having arrived back home on June 12, 1919—enough with khaki life! [*basta naia*] Finally free from purgatory, if not outright hell, I bid you farewell, Destiny and Miracle. Here signed Diulio Faustinelli, martyr escaped through the eye of a needle that I barely made it through..."[159] But from another point of view this conclusion is supremely expressive of his entire life experience as it played out under the sign of Destiny and above all of "Miracle" (Faustinelli placed in the pages his "blessed clothes," or his scapulars with the holy images that he wore on his chest for the entire war), a miracle moment by moment invoked and always received.

In sum, with his memory exercises, Faustinelli confirms that writing, paradoxically but inevitably, erodes oral memory. Alberto Asor Rosa comments on this with tremendous clarity, "The greatest producer of memory energy comes by writing: Writing for those who do it consumes and eats up more than any force in the world because words, once written down, suck life from their roots, and when there is nothing left to suck, they consume them until they disappear.... When one has written down his own memory on the page, he loses the memory, and what he later recalls is what he's recorded, no longer the thing that, up until a moment before, he thought had happened."[160]

Diary is also the title of one of the most interesting, with some elements of exception, of the populist memoirs, which we have been able to read in its entirety only in recent years: We refer to the war notebooks of the shepherd from Abruzzo

---

159 Fontana-Pieretti (editors), *La Grande Guerra. Operai e contadini Lombardi* cit., p. 318.
160 A. Asor Rosa, *L'alba di un mondo nuovo*. Turin: Einaudi, 2002, p. 19-20.

named Francesco Giuliani.[161] A largely self-taught shepherd, an impassioned reader of the *Divina Commedia* and of chivalric poetry, himself the author of poems, and a skilled woodcarver, he writes during the 1950s, alternating prose and verse, a memorable war story (765 manuscript pages), based largely on detailed letters written to his wife. The diaristic element to the letters (which is also a kind of writing of the present) upholds the entire literary and poetical re-working and is determinative in the creation of a very original text that avoids easy classification. Although writing in the 1950s, Giuliani doesn't use the kind of words one would expect from his era,[162] but he reuses, re-founds them, turning them into poetry (there are ninety-three compositions in total), texts written forty years earlier. Therefore, from the diary we find chronology, the precision of references, the instants of great clarity, reflections born at that moment; of the memoir we find an ordered design, a unitary structure, elaborated writing. And above all, what characterizes the project is a radical opposition to the war, a reinforced dissent, an unhesitating pacifism.

Assigned to the 13th Regiment infantry, Giuliani in 1915 is at Karst, in 1916 on the plains of Asiago, in 1917 at Ortigara, and in 1918 at Montello; he is wounded three times, and the Spanish flu almost finishes him off. And yet his point of view

---

161 F. Giuliani, *Diario della guerra 1915-18 e Lettere dal fronte*, edited by P. Muzi. L'Aquila-Roma: Japadre Editore, 2001. An extract from the notebooks was published by anthropologist Annabella Rossi under the title *Diario della Grande Guerra scritto da un pastore*, in "Il Contemporaneo," September 1961, 40, pp. 58-95. Other pages appear in the anthology *Se ascoltar vi piace. Dai quaderni di Francesco Giuliani*, edited by M. Gentile. Turin: Lindau, 1992.

162 It is an expression that we pick up from Annette Wieviorka, where she writes that "the testimonial, above all when it finds itself inserted into a mass movement, expresses, beyond the individual's experience, the discourse or discourses preferred by society, in the moment in which the one making the statement tells his own story about the events he himself lived." A. Wieviorka, *L'era del testimone*, translated into Italian by F. Sossi. Milan: Raffaello Cortina, 1999, p. 14. The agreement between this and the reflections of Paul Ricoeur and Maurice Halbwachs is evident.

is that of a civilian, or even better, according to Gray's definition[163] we have cited elsewhere, he is a man who does not want to transform himself into a "combatant" (*Homo furens*) but, on the contrary, he aims to oppose violence and irrationality ("I don't want to teach myself how one assaults a trench, neither to point a rifle, when the target is a man").[164] In the case of Giuliani one isn't dealing with just attitudes reducible to populist "non-involvement," to resignation, to an absence of patriotic enthusiasm, to negative dullness, but rather with a reflection of the value of peace and of the irrationality of war.

THE POPULIST ITALIAN

The texts of popular origin, including those collected in this book, are never easy to read; they demand of readers an unequivocal cooperation, an affectionate (if not loving) attachment of substitution; to add punctuation where there isn't any, to interrupt the flow of words, to introduce some simple fixes to the writing.

To put it another way, the soldiers express themselves in a (written) language defined as "common Italian" that departs in a more or less noticeable way from the norms of standard Italian and presents traces of the regional spoken and dialect languages to the written, vocabulary (lexical), and syntactical level (it is "the type of Italian imperfectly acquired by those for whom dialect is their mother tongue," wrote Manilio Cortelazzo more than forty years ago.)[165]

---

163 Gray, *Guerrieri* cit., pp. 46-47.
164 Giuliani, *Diario della guerra* cit., p. 357.
165 M. Cortelazzo, *Avviamento critico allo studio della dialettologia italiana, III, Lineamenti di italiano popolare*. Pisa: Pacini, 1976 (1st edition 1968), p. 11. Tullio De Mauro also proposes a similar definition for identifying that which seems to him like a "language over a dialect" cfr. T. De Mauro, *Per lo studio dell'italiano popolare unitario*, in A. Rossi, *Lettere da una tarantata*. Bari: De Donato, 1970, pp. 43-75. A discussion starting from the definitions by Cortelazzo and De Mauro in G.C. Lepschy, *L'italiano popolare*, in Id. *Nuovi saggi di linguistica italiana*. Bologna: Il Mulino, 1989, pp. 37-50.

But before beginning in earnest allow us to dwell for a moment on the situations in which soldiers found themselves writing and on the material conditions that give it context.

The typical expressions of regret about bad handwriting that accompany the sign-offs of the letters are surely a "kneejerk politeness," but that doesn't mean that they don't have anything to say about the real difficulties that soldiers at the front had in moments in which they are transformed into writers.[166] Of the scarcity of paper, of stamps, and of pens we've already spoken, but the act of writing presupposes a space, a posture, some flat surface to lean on, a source of light. To write is a "risk": One writes on a plank balanced on one's knees, inside a shelter (a cave or a shed) where one is constantly hemmed in by movement, pushed, where it is impossible to have a moment to oneself and enjoy a minute of intimacy. A good account of this is given by Giuseppe Capacci: "I, who for five days haven't received letters from parents and from Maria, sat right down to write to my fiancée; it is almost evening, I establish myself on my burlap close to the entrance writing on my knee, while outside it's snowing. A soldier was standing upright by the door, and I asked him if he could move because I couldn't write; he said, "Go outside!" I was angry and told him what to do with himself, and he came at me with his hands at my face as though he had been angry at me for a million reasons. So, I leapt to my feet to begin to fight; I couldn't see anything anymore, kicking and punching as though he were a German! The paper and ink fell to the floor, I broke the pen on him: The fight didn't last long; I felt someone grab me by the hands, two soldiers pulled us apart, and it was over; for that night I had to stop writing."[167]

---

166 On the apologies for "bad writing" and the uncomfortable situations in which the soldiers find themselves when writing also A. Bartoli Langeli insists, *La scrittura dell'italiano*. Bologna: Il Mulino, 2000, pp. 160-161.

167 G. Capacci, *Diario di un contadino alla "Grande Guerra,"* edited by D. Priore. Florence: Aska Edizioni, 2014, p. 48. Cfr. also G. Bellosi, La voce "in un pezo di carta," in *Verificato per censura. Lettere e cartoline di soldati romagnoli nella prima guerra mondiale*, edited by G. Bellosi and M. Savini. Cesena: Il Ponte Vecchio, 2002, pp. 41-90.

In this typically difficult situation the fact that writers who by their social standing or their level of education should produce rather uniform texts, instead, give life, as we have said, to their letters and to their diaries that are all different in their linguistic portrayals. In the tension with the written norm, the populist writers use every mode of writing to which in some period of their lives they have come across. Relatively few of these modes were scholarly, more were from business language, from newspaper writing, and from popular literature.

Lorenzo Coveri affirms this, "With the definition of popular writing it's necessary to abandon the oral dimension that excludes writing, the cultivation that excludes the popular: It deals with defining an intermediate area, heteroclite, of meeting between different cultural and linguistic models, in the middle between document and invention."[168]

In this autobiographical space we find therefore a huge gamut of manifestations: texts that avoid showy adherence to written norms and literary mediation or influence, in which the interference with dialectical speech is strongly revealed (they are almost pure transcriptions of speech) and by means of different intermediate solutions—writing, on the other hand, via "narrative joy" and outside the necessity and the coercion of models that are too restricting (as is plain to see from the piece of the Capacci memoir cited above).

Also in the corpus of the texts we have chosen the reader will find a wide range. But we should give a closer (and analytic) look to those entries that were more difficult to understand. The sense of confusion they communicate comes from, in the first place, the tendency to reproduce in written form speech as spoken (eliding words together, and vice versa, breaking words up into parts, the incapacity to correctly distinguish the phonic continuum). In addition to these phenomena comes the uncertain distinction between capital and

---

168 L. Coveri, *Italiano popolare, scrittura popolare. Una prospettiva linguistica*, in *Per un archivio della scrittura popolare* cit., pp. 87-102; cit. on p. 94.

lower-case letters,[169] the absence or casual attention to punctuation, spelling, the interchangeable use of phonemes (T and D, B and V, C and G, S and Z, O and U), the lack of double letters when they should be used and, in order to seem hypercorrect, incongruous doubling of them elsewhere.

The syntactical construction is almost always arduous and awkward: logical concordances, redundant pronouns, accumulated prepositions, polyvalence of "that." The legacy of dialects, found also on other levels, is most evident in vocabulary, although not with the frequency we would expect.[170]

In the texts from Italians in Austria we see emerge the so-called austriacano (Austrian + Italian), an Italian-German jargon that reproduces German-sounding words following a path of formal resemblance and phonetic use with a definitive grammatical integration (la canistra: military rucksack; il gerghero: the soldier, and so on).[171]

But rather than dwelling on the weaknesses, it serves us better to underline again how the populist writings are a product of a tension, of an effort (which has something grandiose about it) to abandon one's dialect and the oral world to come closer to Italian writing and to its models and types. It has an obviously "amphibious" quality. But this enormous striving to give form to one's experience in the "new world" in which the soldiers find themselves flung can only arouse admiration and compassion.

---

169 It is a very timely observation by Glauco Sanga, in *Lettere dei soldati e formazione dell'italiano popolare unitario*, in *La Grande Guerra. Operai e contadini Lombardi* cit., pp. 43-65, cit. a p. 57.

170 For a more detailed analysis see Glauco Sanga, cited above and, among the many that take up the topic of popular Italy, see Gaetano Berruto who in *Sociolinguistica dell'italiano contemporaneo, La Nuova Italia Scientificia*, Roma 1987, seeks to describe the most typical among them: cfr. pp. 105-138.

171 Cfr. M. Bonfanti, *L'austriacano nei diari, nelle memorie e nei canzonieri di soldati trentini*, in *Pagine di scuola, di famiglia, di memorie. Per un'indagine sul multilinguismo nel Trentino austriaco*, edited by E. Banfi and P. Cordin. Trento: Museo storico in Trento, 1996, pp. 101-122. For a complex analysis of the Trentino corpus, see Q. Antonelli, "*Io o' comperato questo libro ...*" *Lingua e stile nei testi autobiografici popolari*, in *Pagine di scuola, di famiglia, di memorie* cit., pp. 209-263.

In conclusion we would do well to point out Stefano Catucci's method of reading and understanding the language of these texts: "The various forms of populist literature reveal not only an esthetic charm but also the truth and intensity of a language that is fragmented, rhapsodic, incorrect from syntactical and grammatical points of view but exactly for those reason are more ardent and effective at getting across the potential shock drawn from the experience of war, or more simply its fragments. Of course, we are still dealing with texts whose representative violence and immediateness cross over frequently into aphasia, almost as if the need and the impossibility of telling were not two opposing principles that reciprocally canceled each other out, but instead two faces of a single process."[172]

---

172 S. Catucci, *Per una filosofia povera. La Grande Guerra, l'esperienza, il senso: a partire da Lukacs*. Turin: Bollati Boringhieri, 2003, pp. 218-219.

Chapter 1.
Italians on the Russian Front

The Italians who were sent in 1914 to the eastern front, in Galizia and Bucovina, to oppose the Russian units, are the Italians of Austria: roughly 55,000 Trentinos, 30,000 from Friuli, and 32,500 men from Trieste and its territory. On August 5 Emperor Franz Joseph declares war on Russia, and the easternmost areas of the empire become immediately contested terrain.[1]

At the departure of the "Italian" soldiers, subjected to the mass draft of all capable men between the ages of twenty-one and forty-two, there were no manifestations of collective enthusiasm, no exultant patriotism, no expression of that communal sense that takes the name *Augusterlebnis* whereas elsewhere, in Austria as in Germany, the first days of the conflict were characterized this way. Profound consternation, bitterness, an oppressive sense of uncertainty, hope for a quick conclusion, presentiment of death: These were rather the thoughts and feelings of the soldiers and their families reflected in many of the war diaries.

Unloaded quickly at the small stations in the center of Galizia (Sambor, Rudki) after seven days of journeying in livestock cars, Italian Austrians looked with sleepy eyes on the countryside in its worst possible light: the bad roads, the mud that attached itself to the marching feet ("All mud, mud, mud! Mud in the water, in the air, in the streets, in the meadows, in the fields, everywhere. It seems like the people too are made of mud"),[2] the swampy terrain, the suffocating heat, the

---

[1] Essential work edited by Gianluigi Fait, *Sui campi di Galizia (1914-1917). Gli Italiani d'Austria e il front orientale: uomini, popoli, culture nella guerra europea*, Materiali di lavoro-Museo storico italiano della guerra, Rovereto 1997. A history "from below" in Q. Antonelli, *I dimenticati della Grande Guerra. La memoria dei combattenti trentini (1914-1920)*. Trento: Il Margine, 2008.

[2] Botteri Guerrino, p. 16.

ugly gray skies. And also passing through the small villages in the country they are struck by the dismay of confronting the Polish peasant populations and their way of living: They are struck by their poverty, by the decrepitude of their homes, by the lack of cleanliness, by the abundance of parasites, by the promiscuity of people and of animals. The presence of Jews in particular, so numerous and so striking, leaves an indelible mark on the journey through Galizia, such as to feed among the soldiers anti-Semitic prejudice, already widely diffused in the nation by the Catholic Church's publicity.

"A singular race, these Jews!" writes Guerrino Boteri. "Unctuous with the strong, hypocritically weeping to those in command, they become like griffons with whoever honestly wants to pay; they are hyenas with those who become their debtors! And they get money out of everyone and everything. They sell hot water for tea and coffee, pieces of black bread at 5 Korone per kilo; they sell honor, reputation and . . . even their daughters, just to get money! They are the strangling lasso of the Poles that let them drink and murder."[3]

Sent quickly to the front, the "Italian" soldiers, dispersed into a multiplicity of corps and troops, are immediately engaged in the bloody battles of Rawa-Ruska and of Grodek where the armed Austrians organize a line of defense with the object of stopping the crushing advance of the Russians and retake the city of Lemberg. The battle that begins on September 7 (one of the bloodiest ever to be fought on the eastern front) will last four days and will conclude with the clash of Austrian forces that will leave thousands of dead on the fields.

"Two-hundred thousand dead," according to Arnaldo Fraccaroli, war correspondent for the *Corriere della Sera*, "the torn-apart earth lines itself with cadavers like a vast cemetery. The hospitals are filled with wounded. They are improvising hospitals in houses, in the schools. And they sign them with a red cross on the roof. On the roof: It's a signal that constitutes

---

3 Botteri Guerrino, pp. 19-20.

a novelty in modern warfare, made necessary by airplanes."[4] After the failure of the battle of Rawa-Ruska, the Austrian forces make a retreat toward the river San, rightward tributary of the Vistola; here the army of Dankl attempts to mount, without success, a second line of defense.

Among the Austrian soldiers posted to the left bank of the San, low and swampy, there is Gabriele Zambelli, who two years later (in prison) remembers the "horrendous spectacle" in which he had to take part.

"When I was at the garrison," he writes, "I didn't know what it was, the thing called war. I saw the wounded, but the truth is I still didn't know. Oh! What a horrendous spectacle on the banks of the river I was slated to see, to hear. [. . .] In the dusk began the scene, really moving, how could any man resist such a scene who has been educated in the school of Christ? A wave of screams lifted from the muck: those who screamed for help, those who screamed for their mother, those who screamed 'friends, help,' who screamed 'God help me save me,' 'Italians, help me I am hurt and I can't move and the water is reaching my throat, help me my friends, the water will soon drown me.' These voices I heard distinctly from amid the confusion of other shouting and the yelling in different languages. Such a scene went on for more than half a day, and then there was complete quiet."[5] A spectacle made more horrid by the powerful reflectors that cut through the darkness of the night and made it possible to continue the battle, with the Russians on the higher shore mowing down the army that uselessly tried to cross the river.

The retreat transformed itself into a haphazard getaway that halted only at the entrenched fields of Krakow.

In these first months the Austrian Italians encounter, often with desperation, a modern war that to the thunderous bombardments, the explosion of shrapnel, and to the machine-gun

---

4 A. Fraccaroli, *La presa di Leopoli (Lemberg) e l a guerra austro-russa in Galizia*. Milan: Treves, 1914, p. 125.
5 Zambelli Gabriele, p. 180.

strikes added also bayonet assaults, hand-to-hand combat, the frightening charges of the Cossacks, and then the destruction of villages and the harvests and the systematic work of the military hangmen, who wage their own war of cleansing, judging presumed spies and Galician saboteurs.

Joseph Roth writes in one of the last pages of the *The March of Radetzky*: "The Austrian army's war was begun with military trials. For days and days the traitors, real and presumed, stayed hanging from the sacred trees, a warning to the living. But no matter where the eye looked, the living were fleeing. All around the corpses that hung from the trees there were fires, and already the foliage was beginning to crackle, and the fire was stronger than the eternal, murmuring drizzle that announced the bloody autumn."[6]

The savagery of the clashes is reflected in the number of those fallen: At the end of 1914, after five months of war, the Austro-Hungarian army had lost 994,000 men, the Russians more than a million.

Among the writings from this time one can find more than one mention of Trentino, Friulian, and Triestian soldiers made objects of scorn and infamous insults. In effect the "Italians" were objectively victims of discriminatory measures in recruitment, in the assignments to corps and in furlough allowances. Add to this, once Italy joined the war, the diffidence of the commanders, which gave rise often to punishment and mistreatment, almost seeming to want to avenge themselves on their "ally-traitor." Thus it is that the ill humor, if not outright hatred, is directed at the body of officers, who were majority German and Hungarian, who among the Italian soldiers rose to power as a kind of omnipresent "ideological enemy."[7]

This chapter dedicated to the "Italians" on the Russian front concludes with the dramatic departure of the spring of 1915, when mass conscription comes to be extended to young

---

6 J. Roth, *La Marcia di Radetzky*, translated into Italian by L. Terreni and L. Foa. Florence: Tea, 1990, p. 406.

7 Cfr. O. Uberegger, *L'altra guerra. La giurisdizione militare in Tirolo durante la prima guerra mondiale*. Trento: Società di studi trentini di scienze storiche, 2004, p. 318.

men of eighteen up to men of fifty. Gone the illusion of a brief war; it became all too clear that its character was total and its duration lengthy.

Giuseppe Lunelli, tradesman, was born in Villamontagna (Trento). Enlisted in the 4th Regiment Hunters (Kaiserjaeger), he was sent to Galizia with the first units. In his diary he described his departure, then he stopped; he didn't write again.

At about 7 in the morning Antonio Pedrotti came into town, coming from the Cognola Town Hall with the announcement "The general mobilization of mass conscription."

So, all those up for military service had to report to their command center within twenty-four hours. Everyone read the announcement and were despondent, I also was very unhappy. I went right home to get my things together and to console my family with cheerful words. Just about the same time, Valentino Pedrotti and Gioacchino Decarli showed up to see us; they had to report to Trento to go look after the military cavalry. And that was the first time I cried: to see my friends leave and not to know if we would ever be able to see one another again. Two handshakes, a kiss on the cheek, and then "Good lucks" together with some tears and a good goodbye.

Afterward, I went to Luigi Fracchetti, who gave me one last shave. My heart was beating stronger and stronger the closer it got to be time to go. I went back home to get my stuff, on the breast of my shirt I hung the medal of the Blessed Virgin and a little oval piece of cloth with a little picture of the Sacred Heart and the word, "STOP."[8] I took with me some cutlery, shirts, handkerchiefs, and socks: When the packing was done, the

---

8 These are images of the Sacred Heart, printed on cloth, that get sewn onto the inside of the jacket at the height of the heart or else on the inside of the hat. The injunction to "Stop!" is directed to the enemy bullet.

only thing left to do was the hardest, most emotional thing, giving my dear parents and brothers a final goodbye. They were all around me and I didn't know what to say. I had to ask their forgiveness for everything I had done and to give them all one last kiss. What bitterness in my heart! Such pain! In that moment I didn't know how to begin.

My father prepared for me a wallet with 200 K and put it in my hands and I began to say my goodbyes. My poor mother was the first, who, with tears in her eyes, pressed her warm lips to my cheek and gave me a last kiss—I did the same and in a suffocating voice asked everyone's forgiveness. During that emotional scene my brothers came out with pained cries and wept. So, then I began to kiss them one by one and to ask for their forgiveness. It seemed as though my heart would burst through my chest with the tremendous pain. I fled to the kitchen because I didn't know where to hide from the pain. I found there Giuseppe Ciurletti and Beniamino Bampi, who gave me courage. After I was in the kitchen a few minutes my father called me to him again. Seeing my father with the holy water and my siblings and mother all on their knees to give me their blessing, the final blessing—it was something I had never seen and couldn't believe was happening so soon, and I froze and couldn't say a word. "Giuseppe," my father said, "I am giving you the last and holy benediction." Once again I felt pain in my chest, tears fell from my eyes and with trembling legs I knelt and with my hands cupped I received the last benediction from my loved ones. I rose, kissed my mother again, and she said, "Go to war, my son, take care of yourself, and trust in the Blessed Virgin and you will return. Yes, I am sure of it, you must return, goodbye my dear son, goodbye!" And my brothers did the same, "Goodbye, Giuseppe, goodbye!" And so it was that I was constrained to leave, with a shattered heart, my beloved family, without knowing if I would ever see them again.

Umberto Artel was born in Riva, on Lake Garda, in 1887; a stationer, typographer, and reader of books, he was among the founders, in 1911, of the local Socialist group. At the outset of the war, he was brought into the army and in August was sent with the first transports to Galizia.

August 12 [1914]

Goodbye, my beauty, goodbye!

At 1 in the morning my battalion left. Nobody knew the destination, but everyone was imagining a place of arrival, but the most common opinion was that we were going to Alsace-Lorraine by France, and this thought makes people feel a bit better, even though one has the sense that in that locality the fighting is awful. The specter of Russia frightens us and is general over all of us. On the road.

A real crowd of people, not cheering but greeting us warmly, has come with us up to now, well into the night to this station in Bressanone.

When the train begins to move the women cry, while those of us who can't bear to show everything that we're feeling wave our berets at them.

Along the whole railway through the countryside, wherever the train stops they make these warm demonstrations of support for those on their way to war. I arrive in Innsbruck.

A huge mixed crowd was waiting for us at the station. Aristocratic ladies and rich burghers, country women with eyes swollen from crying offer us every kind of food and drink, cigarettes and sweets and medals of the Madonna. The demonstration of support and encouragement lasted the whole time we were in the station.

A line of little teeny kids accompanied by teachers and nuns surround us shaking our hands and trying to jump up and hug us, and because they couldn't quite make it we had to take more than one of them and raise them up to the level of our faces to receive their kisses, which were returned effusively.

Oh, those sweet innocent kisses; you don't know, little ones, how much you pull at our poor hearts. Your kiss is a good luck charm, but we too have left our own children down there in our houses, sweet little angels, and old folks bent over with age, our moms who close their already abandoned rooms, who cry for the departure of their boys, in the cruel doubt that they will see them again.

May your innocent and dear kiss be a good luck charm and that one day our mammas will embrace again those sons for whom they cry now as though they were already dead.

Set back down on the ground, these little ones moved away in a big flock and with all their might yelled their, "Viva the Imperial Tirolese Hunters!" while the elegant young ladies and daughters of the commoners continued to hand out gifts.

The sharp whistle of the train and the horn sounding simultaneously let us know that it is time to go. We all take up our places in the train wagons and, after a few minutes, the huffing machine pulled us away while the enormous gathered crowd at the station and along the tracks waved frantically with loud cries and fluttered their handkerchiefs and their flags.

We are far away by now, but we seem to be able to still hear a "Viva!" sent to us from the tiny Innsbruckers, and a tear falls impertinently down the cheek before we can wipe it away.

St. Giovanni of the Tirol. It is the last town in the Tirol that separates us, possibly forever, from our own land. And here in this town, a sigh of sorrow rises imperiously in our heart and we ask ourselves: Will we see these places again? Mama and our friends, the pleasant hills, the silver rivers, the dear purple-colored lake, will I see them ever again?

Even clearer to me was the sensation of what loomed above me and how many were the threats we faced and a terrible knot closed my throat and while my companions silently admire the picturesque countryside, I let my tears fall at the thought that maybe I will be sacrificed to an abstract idea, for an unknown cause, for a country not my own!

August 13

In the morning we get up early. Now we are in mountainous Salzburg. The entire way we have been seeing Landsturm[9] guards posted; they are guarding the train tracks, bridges, and coasts.

All these old soldiers greet us sadly and while the train keeps going and going past them it seems to us as though the old soldiers are saying to us: Farewell, poor boys. You're going to the war, but there will come a day when this land, bathed in your blood, will also be trodden by us and we will catch up to you and join you. Now you leave your houses weeping, but tomorrow it will be us, even if we are older than you. This Motherland also wants our arms that are weakened by work and by age. And we will come to give her our help. We will come sadly, but we will come.

And the train rolls on and on and on. In a small village it pauses.

---

9 Tiroler Landsturm, the territorial militia.

We see a woman in poor clothes anxiously coming up, followed by two little kids, one of about ten and the other around eight. The woman looks worriedly, lost, through all the train cars and the two children are pulling at her skirts. Her eyes are huge, her face emaciated. Poor woman.

But a corporal is hanging out of my train car and peering at the road and while the train is still moving he jumps to the ground. He runs up to the woman who, in tears, takes him into a maternal embrace.

The train stopped. Absolutely forbidden to get off ... In a corner of the small station a group of girls blow kisses to soldiers and wave their handkerchiefs. And the women weep. They weep for their sons who have already left for the war, they weep for us who are going under the Galician knife without realizing it.

The Salzburg territory is behind us; we have come into Northern Austria.

At Linz we see a solemn display. There is an enormous crowd and a military band. But, weird thing, this exquisitely Austrian war, so desired by Austria, instead of raising enthusiasm, is endured with evident emotion. Everywhere there is a sense of shock and terror, and everyone is upset. All the parties that they throw for us express distress. Also in Linz, the women, and also many men, who come to greet us soldiers and to give us their gifts, weep, and we, the real victims, have to act brave and laugh at all the commotion.

    August 14

Toward 7 in the morning we get to Vienna. They brought us in through a commercial station so that, if someone had gone there wanting to buy something, it would have been pretty hard for them.

But Vienna also supplied us with the generosity of the citizens, as they have done everywhere else we've gone, because to remove from us every embarrassment gracious and kind young women run to provide us with whatever we want, declining every attempt at compensation.

I am adding, in these hurried notes written on the way to who knows where, the name of a gracious young Viennese woman, with bright and kind eyes and hair like bejeweled gold, beautiful as her good and generous soul: Mizzi Vompatc-Vienna X Neus Eilgut in order to send her my memories of the camp.

She gave with immense self-effacement. She leaves in my soul an infinite memory of radiant sweetness, in the strange moment in which one enters the immense host of Austria's death-bound.

August 16

After two days and two nights of extremely boring travel we had crossed Hungary and entered into Galizia. All the way to Buda-Pest, one hopes, but now no one has any doubt but that we are going to be fighting the Russians. All of us are resigned to it now. Farewell to dreams of deserting.

Russia is not France. Come what may, at this point the only hope that encourages us is that the whole thing will be over soon.

Toward evening they made us get off the train; we are at Starzava. Galizia. We march a couple of hours, and so we camp in a field to spend the night under the ceiling of stars.
I don't feel the need to make poetic references, but nevertheless it occurs to me that the sky is adorned with an infinite myriad of stars that seem to me more luminous than those one sees over Lake Garda. Here camp life begins.

I am writing by the light of an acetylene torch for cooking. They set guards, and the entire battalion is going to sleep on the cold and damp grass.

Angelo Paoli was born in Denno (Val di Non, in Trentino) on August 4, 1890. He followed in the footsteps of his father and learned the trade of a cobbler. At the outset of the war he was drafted and enlisted into the 1st Regiment of Landesschutzen and sent to Galizia. He took part in the bloody battle of Rawa-Ruska on September 7.

It was just dawn when we got the order to advance. It was September 7, 1914: the terrible day that will always be remembered by all the Tirolean Imperial Hunters.

As soon as we were spotted by the enemy it seemed like the end of the world broke out: cannon fire, gunshots, machine-guns' rapid-fire shooting, the bullets whistling everywhere; the dead and wounded were heaped around: some with no legs, some no arms, those with heads split open, those wounded in the belly who were losing their intestines. The situation was impossible to describe.

Little by little we reached a trench filled with our guys: There we stayed for maybe an hour, there in the trench it was all blood and corpses, you didn't even know where to step. The order came to advance further. I made it maybe 300 steps and found a hole dug in the earth, I threw myself in it like a dead man; I couldn't advance any further.

I stayed like that around two hours, I fired some more shots with my rifle, but I couldn't even raise my head. After a bit, I heard a voice at my left side, I raised my eyes and saw there a German from my company and he told me that all our guys were getting out. He had no sooner gotten those words out than a bullet cut through his throat. He fell back, screaming.

I lifted my eyes a bit and saw the Russians, distant from me by about 250 feet and firing with full force. I was desperate; I didn't know what to do. "If I stay here," I told myself, "they'll kill me, if I flee I'm as good as dead." I couldn't even look at that poor guy they'd shot; I gathered what courage I could, lifted myself a bit and wriggled like a snake across the ground, then I got up and ran and I got into another of our trenches: There the dead and the wounded were piling up on one another; you couldn't even take a step without stepping on them.

The wounded yelled, "For pity's sake, don't walk on me!" The unwounded and the wounded who could stand, all of them fled. When I was in the trench, the bullets were coming from everywhere, I got hit slightly in my left hand and in my thigh. But once I got out of the trench, from among the half-dead and the wounded, I set off running like a desperate man. I had my gun in my hand and my pack on my shoulders and running made it hit me over and over in the back. It was like an animal running. Amid the enemy's gunfire that was coming from every direction I kept running an hour and a half without stopping. When I was a little bit away from the danger, I slowed down and from the fatigue I felt after running that course, I said to myself, "If I don't die this time, I won't die at all." I got to the medical unit, they bandaged my hand and then I went in search of my company: There were almost none of them there, and the companies were a mess, disorganized because of so many killed and wounded that were left there on the battlefield.

That day was immense: My life was hanging by a thread; it was a miracle that I stayed alive. For a month and a half or two, when I remembered that day, September 7, I got again the chills of fear and horror I felt that day.

Giacomo Sommavilla, bookkeeper, was born in Moena (Trento) in 1878. Enlisted into the 3rd Regiment Landesschutzen, 2nd Battalion, he arrived in Galizia on August 24, 1914. Assigned to transport duty, he reached the battlefield on September 8.

Galizia

On September 8, 1914 we are marching from 7 in the morning, taking the road through a wood, when two shrapnel exploding very close to us — one soldier of the Red Cross unit got hurt — made us run every which way. On that day I saw many Russian prisoners, there were around 150, all in a group, they were in good spirits, because they were saying that now there was nothing to fear. A while later I saw more Russians, wounded ones, who were coming to us, all together and in good shape; the enemy retreated, and the rest of the day passed without interesting incident. Night came and finally I could sleep.

The next day, since one of the drivers of the company's food transport was sick, I was picked by the captain to be lent into that service. I went willingly because that way I could travel more comfortably and was almost out of harm's way. The terrain we were marching over was all covered with cadavers, with their faces all distorted, splashed with blood and mud, with the eyes open from the pain and probably also from terror.

Those cadavers were in a state that made you scared just to look at them. You could see there were crosses stuck in the ground meaning clearly that there was someone buried there, maybe some official. You could see along the road many guns and other war implements, all of it presented a most horrific spectacle and meant that a fierce battle had taken place there.

The battalion penetrated a narrow valley crossed by a poor road. A dense forest covered both sides, making it more gloomy; those of us with horses came up last. When at around

8 we heard ahead of us that the battle had begun, the guns and machine gun made their awful voices heard and possibly also claimed some victims; with the horses about halfway through the valley, we stopped and awaited new orders.

Before midday we could see the wounded pass by, pale and dripping blood, who stared at us with bewildered expressions, asking us, almost all of them, for something to drink. Some were still trembling with fear, some swearing at their fate in a thousand ways. The battle went on until nighttime, with heavy losses on both sides, but no one meant to give up, those of us with the horses moved away. Early next day we tried to go back in to carry the food rations to our combatants, seeing that the day before they hadn't gotten any.

We got to the place where the battle had taken place the day before, and it was a gruesome sight everywhere you looked, many soldiers from both sides had fallen, one next to the other they were lying there unburied, all of them filthy with their own blood, with their eyes staring and glassy, awaiting the pious hand of the sapper destined to bury the dead. We were waiting for the best moment when we could get close to our ranks, but unfortunately the challenge persisted, and it was very difficult to advance; we waited until evening, and then we decided to go back to a safe place; we had to throw away the food, as it had begun to rot.

Fioravanti Gottardi, a farmer, was born in Brentonico (Trento) in 1887. Enlisted in the Landesschutzen, he arrived in Galizia on August 12, 1914. He too took part in the battle of Rawa-Ruska.

On the 7th [September 1914] we fold up the tents and go on an exhausting march across the steppe. The thirst was unbearable and we can't find even a spring, not even a pool in which we can bathe our arid throats. The next morning, going over a hill I see many corpses covering the ground from the day before. Going through a thick woods I see even here bodies of Russians fallen under trees they were hiding behind. When we reach the edge of the woods, the horrific spectacle of the battle presents itself before our eyes! The thunder of the cannon, the explosions of the bombs, the agonizing cries of the wounded blend together with the last rolling groans of the dying! My mind is like a mill; it's impossible to think or form a clear idea.

In a moment my family springs to my mind, but the commandant's yell makes me forget everything: Forward to the assault! Coming out of the woods, we advance, mixing with the other lines, and at the sound of the drum and the horn we attack the Russians. The yelling was tremendous, so much so that the enemy turns tail and runs. What a massacre! When night comes, they order retrieval, but only then can one be sure how many of the company are missing. So many wretched families!

While we are advancing for the plains on the 9th, the enemy artillery targets us and begins the extermination. My poor battalion! The projectiles fall like rain and we don't have any defense. Death was circling all around me. The commander of my company, seeing the dangerous situation raises his voice and shouts: "Save yourself if you can!" Poor guy! It may have been his last shout, inasmuch as I never saw him again that day. When it occurs to me that he fell, I am unhappy, because with us Italians he was very good, being himself Italian. With luck I saved myself, or maybe it wasn't my time, given that a grenade burst two steps from me and threw me another ten steps away. I got up feeling a bit beaten down, but fortunately unharmed. That evening under the command of other officials I fought all night long.

The 10th they gave us a bit of time off behind a little mound.

The 11th of September we spend the whole day in front of the Russians who are retreating while also slowly fighting. Also on that day we renew the companies and cover the corpses with earth. When the night comes everything becomes calm again, disturbed only by the glare and crackling of the villages in flames that burn all night. I look around me and see just two of my buddies, and the rest were from different regiments. We talk a bit and find ourselves amazed to be alive. With that, we decide to go in search of our regiment, since it had been twenty-four hours since we had any food.

Arriving at a nearby village, we see a barbarous sight! Strung up on the beam of a cabin fourteen civilians of all ages hang dead. I knew that they had fired at the backs of our soldiers, and for that they had been condemned to death.

We ate a few potatoes we found in the cabins, and we sleep on a pile of straw.

The following day, 12th, we find an artillery official on request who tells us that our regiment is marching in retreat. He shows us the direction and, after having walked all day, toward midday we find them gathered behind the hill. Wretched regiment! Where are all the men? Out of my regiment there remain fifty and some companies were destroyed completely! Poor Trentino, how many of your sons has this war taken from you. But thinking too much about that only makes me angrier! Two hours later we leave in the opposite direction for the battle field and the march goes till nighttime.

Guerrino Botteri, teacher, was born in Trieste to Trentino parents in 1882. He got to Galizia on October 2, 1914, when the Austro-Hungarian army was retreating under the power of the Russians' attack.

October 9, 1914

Infamous day! Never in my life have I been so close to that state of the soul they call "desperation" as I am today: never have I heard so many comrades and comilitarists call for death to free them from such atrocious torture. But let me begin from the beginning. We leave early in the morning, we go through a village: we see women enlisted in the army who, with their characteristic short-handled Galizian spades, shaped like a T, clear the layer of mud, half a meter thick, that's covered the road. It looks as though they are shearing the road. And we keep walking.

It's evening. We see a village in the distance. The little cottages each with a barn seem to be beckoning us to rest there; the water that is falling faintly and cold and light seems to help us to call a halt. We see soldiers turning from one house to the next; we're kidding ourselves looking for shelter here. But the village ends; we stop, and then we go; we stop again and then continue. A horrible march, with marching songs that lengthen and shorten the regiment with mournful runnings and stoppings, and it makes it like an enormous gray caterpillar that stiffens and extends itself to move forward, making its moving rings crack. And yet it keeps going. Maybe it makes only a km an hour, with a march that brings blood to the shoulders and oppresses the breath. But it goes on.

The soldiers, that to us seemed to be in charge of quartering, were starving like us; with eager eyes and ready hands, they rummaged through the houses to find something to quiet their eager lips. And it goes on. Forward, at night in the cold, in the mud, with a screaming hunger, up a hill that wouldn't challenge us were it not for six hours of exhausting and horrible marching.

As of midnight, the cold wind is blowing, frozen, on the sweat-damp foreheads cold with fatigue and with hunger, and up there, on the summit, where the even more cruel wind seeks flesh and the water lashes against the face, up there we stop for an hour to get the squads in formation. Whoever isn't where he's supposed to be is a "pig" a "shit-dog" a "villain" "damned." Poor It[alian] youth, poor fathers of families whose sweet affections you've abandoned, so many nests of sweet caring for the nation: You hear the recognition of your huge sacrifice! You are "vile shitty dogs"! the cold burns, and the water lashes! One of my friends begs that someone kill him; he doesn't want to, he can't go any further: He is worn out in body and soul. Through my teeth I seek to comfort him, but it dies halfway in my throat. He rises, keeps going. Forward: forward again like mute machines, resigned, rendered stupid by pain, by tiredness, by the cold, by the water that slices us alive: forward to stumble on roads with a half meter of mud that slips, slides out, trips, and betrays. Shoes, stockings, overcoat all drip with mud and water; hands that seek the foreheads soaked in sweat coat the face with omnipresent mud, the legs bend and . . . onward. It's 4 in the morning when we arrive at some abandoned houses where finally we take a break in front of a fire, so many people dragged through this Calvary! No one sleeps; no one eats; no one drinks. We are just silent, still. Stunned, in front of the fire that dries the mud that we see up close! Beware if you don't have thoughts and prayers to God on days like this. The world is too black! In Him I found the strength to maintain silence. Thanks to Him! [...]

The morning of the 17th of October I found myself sleepless, beaten, unable to stretch out at my post!

A day of crazed fear, was the 17th. A fear like that that takes one by night, and that torments one who can't rebel.

All day we were closed up in the bell tower that had become a target for grenades and enemy shrapnel, without our being able to move, nor see, nor fire back. The grenades thundered, exploding around the boards as they trembled. With a dry and broken shout the split boards from the roof fell on our heads; beyond a meter over our heads they told us that bullets avid for our blood passed by: And we stayed still! Still, waiting idly for death, like Christian gladiators in the Coliseum, waiting for the sharp fangs of the hungry beasts.

Modern war has something frighteningly sad about it: The individual disappears, he becomes a drop in a river of lava that slowly, with a fatal urge jumps ahead, stops, goes backward. The drops don't count for anything: If one of them stops, it freezes, it is lost, no one pays it any mind, if that drop squeaks, chirps, before extinguishing itself, its cry is overpowered by the enormous spongy creaking of the river.[10]

So it was that we, closed in the bell tower, where from moment to moment a grenade could have made us a terrifying carnage, under the constant threat of death, which screamed around us, with two women ripped up by a grenade, dragged and abandoned in a hurry in front of the bell tower — we, I say, lived in that day all the anguish of someone tied up, defenseless, who finds himself circled by the wild beasts that seem to devour him, from minute to minute . . .

Toward midday the storm is worse: The entire belfry is creaking, it's crashing boards up above; not far away houses burn; to the left and right in before the crackling gunfire continues. A lost soldier enters the bell tower. He is from Bocenago (Eusebio Boroni). He lost his company on the morning of the 14th. He's been staying until recently in the ditch that we crossed on the morning of the 14th. He sees dead, injured, blood, fear. He is starving, among many more starving than he.

---

10 Guerrino Botteri seems to pick up on, more and better than other soldiers, the nature of modern war as "machine," as "robot." Eric Leed reports in his book *Terra di nessuno*, a description of war (attributed to Rudolf Binding) as a glacier curiously similar to Botteri's: "What else is humanity if not a moraine under the weight of a monstrous glacier? This glacier crawls slowly toward the valley, and nothing seems capable of lightening the weight. When at last it melts, when the pressure on the moraine lets up, all that remains is a vast and desolate expanse of rocks, that know nothing of the glacier. Such is this war. Whoever compares it to an old campaign in which the two adversaries wills' face off frankly is wrong: in this war both adversaries are frozen on the ground and only the war has its own will."
E.J. Leed, *Terra di nessuno. Esperienza bellica e identita personale nella prima guerra mondiale*. Bologna: Il Mulino, 1985, p. 49

With stumps of candles, from the church, I warm a tin of jam. Both he and I are tormented by hunger. Then on a cross, that I would like to erect on the grave of the dead of the 15th, I write the names of two of the fallen: I can't put it up as long as it's daytime. I await the evening.

It slowly arrives. There comes a calm in the flurry of the ferocious ire, while the night makes the fire among the huts behind us more frightening.

We go back to the trenches. I was dreaming, a disjointed dream. My wife had died: The ties to the earth had broken. I wanted a fiercer battle, I wanted to see eternal Love, and to find again the land of my life. A cannon woke me. It was dark: I was in the war. Just as well. Sleep returns, I dream. I was consecrated a priest. A husband and a priest: a terrible position that raised a wall of prohibitions between two great and infinite loves, infinite in their difference. I was suffering! A shove from my buddy liberated me from the nightmare.

Third sleep, third dream. I am at home, among my beloveds! I breathe with full lungs: The war ended without leaving the wounded nations bloodied with hate and revenge. The world smiles with peace, but the dawn comes up greeted by the furious crackling of gunfire that rings out nervous, dry, insatiable.

October 18

And the entire day the music of the firing, the shouting, the thunder, the explosions continues.

It's just been said: a day like the others. But it's long to live it: The moments agitate, shake up: One becomes nervous.

And, when God desires it, it becomes dark. An order: *Vorwarts!*

Forward!

One takes one's gun, jumps out of the trench and . . . forward, mute, with eyes that see everywhere, except for where one puts his feet.

We go ahead like this, three or four-thousand steps, among thin trees, when we get to a naked field, which, after two-hundred meters rises and becomes a hill from which the Russians fire.

Our advance is not disturbed: We halt before coming out into the open. Hands to shovels, in a quarter of an hour each one of us has a little hole and a little bank: into the holes, with the head against the bank: It's night. Does one sleep?

An infernal shriek of grenades that explode a dozen paces behind us says no. The bullets that whistle around us confirm it. The fire on two houses at the end of our line of occupation makes us understand that the Russians know where we are, and they won't let us sleep.

Chapter 2.
The Blessing

In the spring of 1915 the party in favor of the war filled the plazas. The interventionists came from the petit bourgeoisie and the bourgeoisie: Among them professionals, intellectuals, and students stood out. The country folk are absent; the people are, for now, a distant and unknown reality, even if they are present in the lines of the army that control the demonstrations.

"In the month of April [1915] the strikes began: The city seemed filled with students—they were studying how to make war. Not a single day passed without a picket line; free egress was abolished; different days there were general strikes; it was all indifferent; neither the trams nor cars were working.

"We had circled the entire center of the city; on every route that went to the Cathedral there were cavalry and infantry—no one was getting by there! It was frequently necessary to fix the bayonets, seeing the bad situation. Looking down those long streets filled with youth on strike, you can't see even a stone of pavement, just straw hats. What a racket! Phenomenal yelling, long whistles, as if they wanted to turn everything upside down. 'But you have to get out of here, scoundrels,' we soldiers keep saying, 'you'll get a taste of the war soon!' But once they see the glint of the bayonets, they let us through.

"There was an old Garibaldian guy, with his red shirt, and with a bunch of medals on his chest; he was leading the others and they were yelling, 'We want the war! Long live Salandra, death to Giolitti!' Horrible things it rattles my nerves to describe. When they brought our rations into the middle of the piazza we four were eating while the young ladies on the terraces watched us, smiling, the way one looks at enemies.

"Reading the news one can see that the war is being concluded, listening to the discussions of the ministers. Giolitti was saying, 'Even if the war ends victoriously, it will be for us a terrible loss.' That certainly is no lie."[1]

The author of this page is a Tuscan peasant, Giuseppe Capacci, drafted into service in Milan in the period of the great protests for intervention. Overwhelmingly occupying the scene there are the students with their straw hats, middle-class folks, and aggressive and radical words spoken.

They came from school bringing with them heroic dreams and aspirations obtained from an epic burst of energy related to reunification. "It's war we have dreamed of since childhood" — confesses one of them — "when in the first books we read it was borne upon us to hate the Austrian army."[2]

So it was that the declaration of war was greeted with such expressions of collective enthusiasm (the "holy enthusiasm of '15") in which seemed to be reborn the Garibaldian spirit of the reunification.[3]

"One leaves the barracks yelling 'Viva!' and promising with great screams to the crowd that they are about to see a piece of the body of Franz Joseph," writes Antonio Baldini.[4] Hurrahs, yelling ("the storm of yelling"), screams, songs, drinks, flowers, musical bands accompany his voyage to the front. Upon reaching Sacile, in Friuli, camped in an unconsecrated church, overcome and encouraged by the "affectionate and obliging face of the Fatherland" he falls asleep "thinking vaguely about the war, unable to imagine for myself anything concrete."[5]

To go to war without a clear cognizance of the nature of the conflict, without knowing which frightening events

---

1 Capacci Giuseppe, p. 24.
2 A. Omodeo, *Momenti della vita di guerra. Dai diarie e dalle lettere dei caduti 1915-1918*. Turin: Einaudi, 1968, pp. 16-17.
3 P. Melograni, *Storia politica della grande guerra*. Rome-Bari: Laterza, 1977, I, p.11.
4 A. Baldini, *Nostro Purgatorio, which I read in Il libro dei buoni incontri di guerra e di pace*. Florence: Sansoni, 1953, p. 8.
5 Ibid., p. 15.

came about from 1914 and after on the other fronts, seems baffling. And yet, as Melograni writes, almost all the soldiers (not only officials and students) "imagined war in the way it had been represented to them in history books and in popular lithographs, thinking that they would be going to the attack accompanied by marching bands and fanfare. [...] That there would be two or three great decisive battles and then, before winter, that victorious ending that everyone hoped for."[6]

The war as interpreted by Lieutenant Scarpocchi, as is seen in one of his letters, is also characterized by a faithful optimism and a fervent patriotism. The strange (and possibly a bit sacrilegious) baptism by water in the Iudrio stream, to which participating officers and perplexed soldiers submitted, can be interpreted as a rite of passage that brings them toward a world that for only a brief time longer would be unknown.

Bruno Scarpocchi was born in Tuoro (Perugia). A lieutenant in the 74th infantry regiment, he died July 5, 1915 during the first battle of Isonzo.

Kosana, March 26, 1915 4 p.m.

My dearest ones:

[...] On the evening of the 23rd from the report of the 18th we knew that mobilization had been announced, from the extraordinary report of the 22nd we knew that we were to cross the border at 4 the next morning. That night I barely slept. I got everything in order on the assumption that everything will have been completed during the night and in the briefest possible time, and on the other hand without letting any of the soldiers suspect that we weren't supposed to know anything. Awake at 1, depart at 2:30, ready to cross the border at 3:30. My battalion and the 2nd on the first line, the 3rd

---
6 Melograni, *Storia politica* cit., p. 12.

in the second, to the right and the left we had brigade after brigade. At exactly 4 a cannon fired giving the order for the general advance. Everyone was a bit emotional. The border where we were was along the Iudrio River.[7] I crossed the river and dunked my head: I felt inside me an infinite joy. It was a baptism, and also I had the proud thought of redeeming the blessed soil of the fatherland; who knows — I was just happy. Then I took the water in my clasped hands in a bowl and climbed up the little bank to bathe the heads of the company. Everyone understood the sweetness of the blessing that was in my thoughts. Everyone took off their caps and offered themselves. Even the soldiers, poor simple animals, who seem closed off from every delicate feeling, offered themselves too. I took a branch of a hawthorn tree, I dipped it in the river's waters, and I shook it over a thousand bared heads of the soldiers. It was the baptism of children by a child. After fording the river we had passed the river and in order of battalion we continued on. The small country houses were either empty or else occupied by women. The last of the men had been called up to service the previous Thursday. Speaking of which we found on the door of one of the little houses the announcement calling for the roundup of men aged 18-50. According to the announcement, only exempt were imbeciles, men who had lost both arms or both legs, or an arm and a leg and those who were blind in both eyes! Just as well we weren't fighting the idiots!

The population, women and a few elderly and babies, received us with a cold joy. They were happy enough, but they also were afraid because the Austrians told them that we were going to burn everything down.

Of enemy soldiers, not so much as a shadow, not even the Financial Guard because everyone fled when we appeared.

---

[7] Tributary of the Isonzo.

Around 7 p.m. we reach an area close to S. Martino Quisca, a town inhabited not by Italians but by Slovenes, who had the customs of Friuli, and almost all of them know how to speak the Venetian dialect and almost none of them German. At 10:30 finally we stopped in a street: We slept on the ground. We were too exhausted not to drop off immediately. During the whole day all we ate were some eggs, but the fatigue was stronger than any other desire.

Yesterday afternoon my battalion came up to the advance guard here in Kosana, 2km from S. Martino. Up to now, no Austrians.

Chapter 3.
Beyond the Border of Irredentist Lands

Beyond the old border the Italian army must measure itself against a population with little enthusiasm for the war and for Italy. General Cantore, struck by the lukewarm reception from the inhabitants of Avio, in Trento, supposedly said to his companion, "You Trentini are all Austrianized."[1] And "Austrianized" was also how the peasants and priests of Friuli seemed to the General Staff. The spying psychosis that quickly spread in the conquered areas sees a proliferation of spies who could signal the movements of the Italian troops to the Austrians using complex means.

We find again the climate of those first days of war in the diary of Francesco Giuliani, an Abruzzese infantryman whose personal experience of war is among the most acute and moving accounts ever written.

"The morning of the 26th, while we were halted on the side of a road ready to move out, two carabinieri passed by on horseback, they were pulling behind them an old man who was barely able to follow them, he was fastened at the wrists by a chain, shoeless, his clothes were hanging off him in shreds, and reduced to that state he made a pitiable figure. Word was going around that he had been caught cutting telephone lines, but I never did find out if he was responsible.

"We went through Cervignano; it was all decked out in flags but deserted. There was just one man up on a balcony with his wife and a young woman. The young woman made a menacing gesture toward the soldiers passing by and that maybe meant that the thrashings we had coming to us were just ahead of us now.

---

1 M. Peghini, *Avio 1914-1918. Un paese tra due frontier. Da periferia dell'Impero austro-ungarico a "terra redenta"*. Avio: Biblioteca comunale Arnaldo Segarizzi, 2009, p. 107.

"That evening we stayed in Campolongo, which was almost deserted; those few inhabitants who hadn't fled kept themselves hidden out of fear of us. In the streets were some barricades that served no purpose. We couldn't see lights on in any houses, everything was dark, and the sight of the empty town left an ugly impression on me."[2]

Also in the pages of Giuseppe Garzoni, reproduced here, we find again the voices of draft dodgers, betrayals, spying, executions of civilians. After true and false news—the voices, the rumors around the tragic events that took place in Villesse began circulating immediately in an atmosphere of suspicion and fear, brought back to life decades later in the memoir pages of Duilio Faustinelli—are here in the anthology. In short, after some exchange of fire with the territorial Austrians and the local police forces, the Italian officer in command, Major Citarella, found himself surrounded by hostile civilians, who blamed him even for the flooding of the River Torre, the tributary of the Isonzo. So much so that on May 29 he decides to transform Villesse into a fortified camp, barricading the streets of access to the town. He therefore takes hostage all the male citizens between the ages of fourteen and fifty-five, for a total of some hundred men whom he uses at the barricades like "human shields." Therefore one needed only a burst of gunfire to take out five men, to which one adds one man who was killed at the gates of the cemetery on May 30. After which Villesse, which had been considered a lair of traitors, was evacuated and all its inhabitants interned.[3]

---

2 Giuliani Francesco, p. 11.
3 Cfr. L. Fabi, *Villesse 1914-1918. Piccole storie di una Grande Guerra*. Cremona: Persico, 2003, pp. 15-18; M. Pluviano-I. Guerrini, *Le fucilazioni sommarie nella prima guerra mondiale*. Udine: Gaspari, 2004, pp. 203-205. In an inquest conducted after the war by the army is was recognized that there was no hostile act on the part of the inhabitants, mostly Italian sympathizers, but that there were no nighttime attacks either. Lucio Fabi writes: "At night, without knowing it due to an error, the soldiers were shooting among themselves, which results in a report executed by the military authorities on the ordnance manufactured in Bologna." Fabi, *Villesse* cit., p. 50.

Francesco Giuliani, who witnessed the terrors brought about by militarism, dedicated to those executed at Villesse these lines of poetry:

> The regiment of the third battalion
> passed by Villesse, a nearby town.
> Here, without reason, and against all reason
> Were executed more than one citizen.
> A deed of a greater man, like Nero
> Pitiless, blasphemous, ferocious and murderous.
> And to the terrified population
> Remained their cruel destiny.
> That furious soul was not placated
> By prayer, by laments or cries
> And whoever wanted to acted to cut down life.
> Surely, my reader, you don't feel
> The fear that was felt there
> When those few extinguished are seen.[4]

"The prevailing attitude of the Italian army with regard to the occupied populations," Lucio Fabi has written, "is revealed to have a colonial nature, as if it came from the stockpile of the previous experiences in Libya."[5]

Yet the most common "acts of war" committed against civilians were different: destruction of houses that were temporarily abandoned, raiding of livestock, theft of clothes and goods. Among the many that we have read, the descriptions by Giuliani, Giulio Mazzera, and Garzoni appear the most vivid and so go along with the "painful observations" that Giani Stuparich included in his diary:

"Today is a day of painful observations. In the tent we met up with two of the cycling officials, who came to talk to our captain and with the colonel of artillery. So some of these cyclists pop by, all dressed up and looking like they just accomplished a glorious mission. Having leaned the bikes

---
[4] Giuliani Francesco, pp. 11-12.
[5] L. Fabi, *Gente di trincea. La Grande Guerra sul Carso e sull'Isonzo*. Milan: Mursia, 1994, pp. 300-301.

against the wall, they were surrounded and one of the officers they had come to see came out too. They tell us that they searched the houses, and one opens a handkerchief and shows us the 'precious loot': golden things, rings, chains, earrings. I was expecting the officer, angry, would grab the hand of the shameful idiot of a thief and punish him. Instead he smiles, shrugs, and goes back in the tent. The guys from the regiment went back to telling us of their exploits. I can't listen any longer, and Carlo and I move away from them. I am thinking of the poor women who were robbed and of our country that has come to be treated as an enemy."[6]

Duilio Faustinelli was born in Pezzo in Valcamonica in 1893. He was enlisted into the infantry in the 13th Fusilleers Pinerolo Brigade. He wrote his memoirs in 1953. From thirty-eight years of distance he brought back the voices and rumors that led to the execution of six civilians in Villesse, demonstrating that he was still convinced of their guilt.

The night of May 23, 1915, a couple minutes past midnight, we heard the horn that sounded the alarm: It meant the beginning of the war. Senior and junior officials were roused to fury (they really seemed like butchers), and they soon gave the order in a loud voice to put up the tents and come together ready for war and to affix our bayonets to our guns. And this was the morning of May 24. War declared against Austria-Hungary. And that night there was a great confusion: who

---

[6] G. Stuparich, *Guerra del '15. (Dal taccuino d'un volontario)*. Milan: Garzanti, 1940, pp. 63-64. Among the officials complicit in this there is also Paolo Monelli, who in occupied Calsugana looks on benevolently while his "boys" open up the casks of the refugee Trentinos in Austria and rob them of their belongings: "The 63rd goes back to Borgo to rest. . . . The soldiers line up with their demijohns, their flasks, their mess tins full of wine, roasted chestnuts in the pan, a petticoat over their arm, a top hat in their backpack. The poor spoils of war. From Borgo to Marter the way is marked by a trail of red in the snow. At the re-placement of the machine guns from Feltre to Ponte del Zaccon there is a refreshment bar; those boys had taken a barrel from it, they had broken it open, all the soldiers passing by are supplied with a cup full of wine." P. Monelli, *Le scarpe al sole*. Milan: Mondadori, 1981, p. 35.

had misplaced his pack, who his food pouch, who his blanket, who his shoes, etc., etc. It seemed like the end of the world, and it was still very dark: Then we formed ourselves into lines, and then we began advancing, all prepared for battle, to go up against the enemy who unfortunately was awaiting us just across the border that was nearby. In the countryside on towers there they posted lookouts, who flew their own flags.

We proceeded toward Cervignano, Campolongo, Palmanova, toward Villa Vicentina, step by step. In those first days of the war, I felt several times the desire to clamber up trees, with my gun at the ready, always on the lookout to see if I could see some movement of the enemy who awaited us at the front.

Having reached Villesse, a little town close to the Isonzo, we found ourselves prisoners on an island; they, the enemy, realized it and diverted the course of the river to the other side, and we were stuck there for twenty-four hours.

We weren't well provisioned, also in munitions, so in that period the engineer bridge-builders made us a pontoon bridge out of boats in order to free us.

In the meantime, our officers had discovered some spies, among whom were the priest of that area: There were nine or ten of these townsmen who were discovered while they used a telephone hidden underground, and they were then shot. The situation began to look unclear. Then on June 4 we came to Villa Vicentina, and here about 2 km from the Isonzo the enemy was entrenched. Sleeping was out of the question.

At sunset of the 4th of June they had added me to the 2nd Regiment Grenadiers. That same evening they distributed rations of bread called "pagnotta," almost all of it rotted because it had sat in the sacks for a number of days, but we had to consider it as valuable because one didn't know when the next bread might come, seeing as the war had already commenced.

Francesco Giuliani, shepherd and day laborer, was born in Castel del Monte, in Aquila province, in 1890. He attended the first years of elementary school, but then he continued on his own, teaching himself. Recalled to arms May 15, 1915, he was assigned to the 13th Regiment of infantry. On May 24 he was already in the war zone. In May of 1916 he was transferred to the upland plateau of Asiago. Giuliani is the author of a complete memoir, made up of diaries, poetry, reflections and further considerations on the war.

Aris di Monfalcone, June 10, 1915

Behind the lodge where we are staying, just a few steps away, there was a nice house belonging to some rich family, the soldiers would sneak over there and mess everything up, there was a commotion, and they all stole some things.

I went myself, out of curiosity, and I was amazed at the extraordinary luxury I saw there: all the rooms were furnished beautifully. Upholstery, soft carpets, mirrors, doorjambs and more doorjambs made of ebony and mahogany, chandeliers, porcelain cups, statues, little figurines, chairs, silk curtains, and velvet; and who knows how many other things that I couldn't even describe. I went into a bedroom with a very comfortable bed; the walls were adorned with nice paintings and other objects; on a nightstand a shelf of books, a bundle of letters; on all sides objects of luxury the likes of which I had never seen before. A lady's hat with ostrich feathers on it, silk dresses, linens that filled the cupboards. I had the courage to take just one book. In that room some beautiful lady had lived, it was like a nest for a lovesick dove. Surely the inhabitants of that village lived an enviable life.

The next day I went back but the stuff was all out of place. I went to the room I've mentioned and I saw the hat thrown down on the floor and someone had the insolence to satisfy a bodily need there. With that action he left a commentary on

Italian civilization. All the closets were opened and the linens pulled out and thrown about haphazardly, the mattresses and cushions pulled out of the bedding, the mirrors and paintings destroyed, the towels pulled apart to be used in like socks in shoes. They threw out the green-gray waistcoats and took the ones they liked. Some of them had changed shirts in there, and they did well: the one they left had become populated with lice. Some idiots had tried to put on ladies embroidered shirts and stockings. There were those who had put on the fancy shoes and jettisoned the ones they had had. They cut up bedspreads to make ankle stockings, which we weren't permitted to wear. There must have been some among them who were crazed with destruction: they broke plates, bottles, cups: anything that was fragile. That imbecile Brandani took a black silk dress; maybe he hoped to bring it to his fiancée when he returned, if that was his fate: he had cut it carefully so it would fit inside a towel, and he carried it in his pack for two or three months; finally he decided to throw it away.

Mongardi installed himself inside the house, and one day, who knows why, he lit it on fire; suddenly on the roof rose a column of smoke that attracted the attention of the enemy, and a few minutes later the cannonades began. The first went a bit high, the shrapnel fragments hit the shingles of a house a few steps in front. A grenade landed at the base of a mulberry tree and completely crushed it. Next door was a woodworking shop, and the windows went totally to pieces. And all of this was just what we saw around us. The fire quickly went out, the smoke disappeared, and the enemy stopped firing. The lieutenant colonel in charge of the battalion came and yelled at Mongardi for being so imprudent. That stupid mistake came close to being a disaster and that's why I am right to always say that no one understands war. While the enemy was firing we huddled behind the wall inside the lodge, and our fear was great.

The village was uninhabited, there remaining just a boy with a sick mother and no means of carrying her away. A sergeant had grabbed this poor boy and demanded to know how many Austrian forces were at Monfalcone. This poor terrified and uncomfortable guy didn't know what to say, or maybe he didn't understand, and that cretin of a sergeant insisted, and after a little bit he was no threat.

Every day we went to dig trenches, and from the houses we took all the wood necessary; we were authorized to take apart the doors and windows that would work for covering the trenches.

Not far from the village there was the Zoratti mill and pasta factory, a very imposing factory building, we got the order to strip it of all its wood. In no time flat, everything was turned over inside. Doors, windows, tables, benches all the wood that was there was carried away. Some set themselves to picking the locks on the drawers, the cabinets, rummaging around among the letters and registrations, hoping to find something that wasn't there. There were sacks of bran, and some guys amused themselves by emptying them, and scattering it everywhere, others enjoyed smashing up all the machinery. They were all vandals out of mania for destroying whatever there was.

One day while we were digging trenches, we were discovered by the enemy, who quickly greeted us with a violent volley of gunfire; the bullets whizzed by. Suddenly whoever crouched down, from behind a cry, but all he got was a wound. The storm passed, and we regrouped behind a house, but a few minutes after, cannon fire and shells began to arrive, broken shingles fell around us and we were in danger of getting hit on the head by them. The captain, seeing that the danger wasn't letting up, lined us up one behind the other and like that we went to take cover in our quarters.

After a week, we went by the trenches that we had dug almost to the slope of the hill and at the top we found our little headquarters.

All the stuff that was in the houses, not only what was useful but also not useful, was brought into the trenches that were decorated with mirrors, paintings, gramophones, bedspreads, sheets, mattresses, couches, and, as it had rained almost every day, the trenches were full of water and mud, and not being able to dry anything off, all that stuff ended up ruined.

Giuseppe Garzoni was born in Buia, Udine province, in 1888, where he finished just the first two years of elementary school. He emigrated then to Germany to work in the brick-making furnaces. Called up in May of 1915, he was assigned to the 6th Rifle Regiment. The story of Garzoni isn't very clear – the timelines seem to cross – and yet the violence against civilians is very vivid, as is the atmosphere of hostility surrounding them.

The morning of July 27, 1915, arrives; they gave us the duty change off the first line after ten days. So the morning of the 27th we turned back into the second line. We made up the tents and then washed. The next day they would order us to be line guards along the line of one wing. It was raining hard. The street that we were supposed to go down was a slope, ravines, few guards. So many times we slipped and fell, like Jesus Christ when he went up Calvary: He had the cross and we our backpacks with gun and 15 kilos of munitions. So we arrive at the place. There was a house; we got ourselves settled in. The soldiers there were mad because it was good there.

We changed our clothes, lit a fire in the hearth, and then dried the clothes. No more sleeping on stones. We had a nice mattress of wool that had been abandoned by the inhabitants of the town called [illegible]. We slept well all night.

Then in the morning they inspected the telephone lines. We were five men with the corporal major. During the day I went to the abandoned houses to see how the owners had left them. I felt a great displeasure seeing these furnishings all destroyed by our soldiers after the civilians had fled. They got out of there the 5th of June, because some of them were spies; and that night they killed, hidden in the forest, all those wounded who passed by and they killed also some officials. The day we chased them out was Saturday. From 11 a.m. till midday they were to supposed to have left everything indiscriminately. In the houses one could see that they had been making butter and they had to leave everything and go. In the cellars one found everything, the hidden wardrobe was all trampled by those who had come to see. The grain had been carried off by our soldiers. I saw broken sewing machines, clocks, writing tables, armoires. In those houses there was a pitiable mass of ruin.

I took for myself a pair of wool socks, a waistcoat, and other useful things. I was thinking to myself: "If this disaster happened in our land besides suffering for the war itself, I would also suffer for this." Then I go back after visiting all the houses. There we made our own meals; one went every evening to get provisions from command, a Ravana, a half-hour further south. During the day, we went to Terranova[7] to buy wine and other things. And there one could eat and drink. There one could forget about the war if it weren't for the wounded who were brought down from miles away every day, because in that area also there were some little camp hospitals.

One day we took a crate of bees, we killed them all and took out the honey, four liters of honey; there was always enough fruit.

---

7 Possibly this is Ternova d'Isonzo.

In that town there remained just a woman and a man. The woman was old and sick. The man had been judged insane by doctors. Both were left there in the town. The man was in fact mute. But one day our officials discovered that instead he was a spy for the Austrians, and they shot him immediately. So then there was left just the one woman, to whom we gave some of our rations.[8] She wanted only coffee and sugar and we gave her all the sugar that we had received from command and she thanked us very much. She was still in her house, and we brought her food.

In that town I washed all my linens; I hadn't been able to do it since leaving for war.

In that time I wrote home a letter registered mail. I sent my greetings and they wound up published in the newspaper. Those ten days I lived like a prince.

Giulio Mazzera was born in Busseto (Parma) in 1889. Enlisted into the Rifle Corps he was sent to the Trentino front in Valle del Chiese. In the first days of June he went up the valley to Condino, where he witnessed, scandalized, the devastation of the homes abandoned by civilians who had fled some days before. He too reported hearing talk of spies, telephone lines, and firing squads.

We make our way along covered paths, and after an hour or so we get to Condino, our advance town where we find a corps of riflemen on guard. It's a nice town but totally deserted. They let us into a house that was still part occupied and, when we head up to the second floor, we find the bedrooms all wrecked, mattresses on the floor, the armoires open and filled with linens all messed up and, not being officials, the soldiers got into the chests and raided them, some found

---

8 Possibly a mix-up of letters: It is the soldiers who bring their rations to the single woman.

watches, some pins, others tried on stockings or linens; there were some other valuable things, but they were heavy and bulky and no one wanted to bother. I watched and didn't dare take anything; it seems profane to me to see people consuming these things that others had taken so much care to preserve, and I don't dare touch anything, on the contrary I move away and then in the cellar we find wine and cheese in these little shapes, but 10 kilos the biggest and so everyone took some of those and they offered it to me and I accept some also. After a half hour I don't know why instead of working in town or going ahead, we go back a half a km and pass by a church with a catwalk suspended from it by means of steel cords and we go to work in the trenches already begun in line with the others in the valley where we were the last few days (today I got my first letter from home, dated May 28 ...)

June 8

Today's a rest day all day, cleaning, papers, and lottery playing. Today we learn more details about Condino. We know that the rifle corps and the second platoon of our company who went into the town yesterday afternoon worked at making barricades on all the streets and every hundred meters with overturned carts, barrels, window timbers, and furniture of different kinds.

And so the soldiers — left to themselves and free to go in the houses still with the idea of finding something to eat and drink since they had been without for so long and also to find something of value — abandoned themselves to an orgy of destruction, they invaded stores, cafés, and hotels and also private houses. And when they were high on wine and liquors one can imagine what point they arrived at. All this was told to me by those of them who returned and had some bottles, cheese, postcards, pendants; maybe they were exaggerating a bit but unfortunately it's mostly true. I don't have the words to condemn the conduct of those in command during these shameful episodes from the exalted Italian civilization that so condemns Germany where it's done the same.

Yesterday in Condino a spy was executed, one Giacometti, owner of a sawmill who was in contact with the Germany and Italian military command for the supply of some lumber, who also after the exit of the population stayed in the town and it is discovered that he had a telephone in his house by which he communicated with the fort, telling them from hour to hour where the majority of the concentration of Italian troops were so they could shoot into the middle and so came the deaths of some riflemen . . .

September 3

In Condino with the 7th. I was forgetting that from the first of September the 9th Company of the 62nd Infantry is arrived and will be here until the Saint's day; they've come here to get Condino into shape! Oh, dear, at this point they are too late. This morning I went out to check on a telephone line that had broken in town when a cart drove over it, and I saw some soldiers from the 62 who were putting more or less in order whatever they could and cleaning up; they removed the barricades of furniture and made them again out of rocks and stones. Now there is a great strictness about anyone who carries off any object, so much so that they sent someone to go with me when I went across town to go to my work zone. What's bad about this town is that in the first days after war broke out this town was abandoned to itself and no surveillance over it and the soldiers seized the first moment of indecision to begin by looking for wine cheese butter liquor; then from there they started taking linens, still just as much as they needed, and in the meantime to look for money and valuables to the point where they got so used to it they didn't feel like they were committing a crime. After five or six days four policemen came, but in a town this sparse there was little they could do; after a month or more with the police a command guard of twenty-five came and they began to arrest people, so that today apart from someone who will go for fruit, the rest the town is starting to be treated with respect (after having been devastated!). In this company of guys I have found only one known to me, a certain Medici from S. Secondo, and he actually lives in Carzeto.

Chapter 4.
The Deadly Rumbling

The close encounter with war is, first of all, as Gibelli writes, a real and proper "sensory bombardment (be it of a visual or, above all, auditory type) that hits the combatant, subjecting him to stimulus of an unprecedented variety and intensity."[1]

The rumbling of modern artillery forces itself on officers and on soldiers entering the war zone with a "sonorous imperialism" that would be hard to underestimate.[2]

"The closer we get to the real war," writes the young Lieutenant Filippo Guerrieri, "the more one enters into a mysterious kingdom; you can't understand anything on account of a loss of coordination, you get every variety of news, but all of it is contradictory. The wounded speak, but in their discourse there's too much subjectivity, a confusion of ideas. The only news source that's secure this close to the front is still the newsletter of Cadorna, which comes with the newspapers when they arrive.

"Meanwhile there's a continual rumble of intense shelling that seems to come directly from hell; we follow with the naked eye the blast of the enormous artillery shells, ours and the enemy's, that meet in the sky, whistling, yelling like screams, screams like those of a wild beast. At night, in the mountains there's a strange lightning in the sky like that of a stormy night; in the dense darkness great blinding columns rise; these are enemy signals that throw off waves and flashes of light into the trenches where our soldiers wait vigilantly, ready for defense, ready for offense."[3]

---

[1] A. Gibelli, *L'officina della guerra. La Grande Guerra e le trasformazioni del mondo mentale*. Turin: Bollati Boringhieri, 1991, p. 164.

[2] The expression comes from R.M. Schafer, *Il paesaggio sonoro*, translated into Italian by N. Ala. Milan: Ricordi-Unicopli, 1985, pp. 113-114.

[3] Letter addressed to family from August 14, 1915, in F. Guerrieri, *Lettere dalla*

There is no writer, cultivated or less so, who doesn't try to describe, with ordinary and sometimes familiar images, the new soundscape that one little by little discovers — optimistically for some; for the vast majority of others, with real terror.

"The atmospheric vault above us," writes Giani Stuparich with a neat metaphor, "is a fabric of whistles, a net of steel strings, rumbling, thrown from one invisible extremity to the other."[4] And later, "The shelling has resumed, even stronger. Some grenades leave angrily: *Nyow!* Spinning, the biggest ones, in the air. The sound lends sense to the sight, because we seem to be able to see them spinning in a spiral. Those ones that land, go forward tired and slow. But there's an Austrian battalion very nearby: *boht-nyow, boht-nyow, boht-nyow*, with a regular rhythm, one after the other."[5]

Ottone Costantini, some of whose letters to his fiancée we present, pays special attention to the sounds of war: large-caliber shells coming so close "with a characteristic tired-seeming crawl that makes you think of a train on a long track or of a thin fabric tearing";[6] the rifle shots "seem to break apart" in the moist earth: They are "fiery jolts and crashes";[7] the bombings produce "doubled and terrible bursts of tonality like a bass drum";[8] the machine-gun sound is "death's motorcycle."[9]

---

trincea (Libia-Carso-Trentino-Macedonia), edited by E. Guerrieri. Calliano: Manfrini, 1969, p. 79.

4 Stuparich, *Guerra del '15* cit., p. 44. Silvio D'Amico, another intellectual who will become famous, notes: "At night, a huge din; one understands that for every enemy blow that arrives, something less than thirty of our own go out. The howling of our Artillery Campaign is irritating; they are dry blows, the echoes extending in the mountains in a hoarse growl. It makes you think of enormous dogs, or also of the roaring of wild animals in an enclosure when they sharpen their teeth against the wooden partitions of their cages." Note from December 3, 1916, in S. D'Amico, *La vigilia di Caporetto. Diario di guerra, 1916-1917*, edited by E. Bricchetto. Florence: Giunti, 1996, p. 38.

5 Stuparich, *Guerra del '15* cit., pp. 58-59.

6 Costantini Ottone, p. 70.

7 Ibid., p. 82.

8 Ibid., p. 104.

9 Ibid., p. 79.

The thundering of artillery, dominator of the battlefields, is followed by the devastating bursts of shells that destroy trenches and underground refuges and hit behind the front lines. The physical experience of bombing is highly traumatic for everyone, as the texts of our anthology attest. To these we must add a portion from a very dramatic letter from Ottorino Davoli, a painter from Reggio Emilia, who describes his first experience in the trenches: "As for me, I breathed through a nighttime attack under terrible fire from every weapon known to man, I endured a slow (and for that reason more terrifying) bombardment, clinging onto boulders . . . together with my men. It's terrible . . . to have to hold still . . . immobilized with the ears straining, listening to the far-off firing of the cannon (this comes from practice too) to hear the noise and the iron-gray approach of the shell . . . it announces the arrival blow that tears the air and then the immediate explosion! . . . Then to look . . . there and amid a dense and high column of dirty smoke . . . to see trees leap into the air, fragments of human bodies (if they are recognizable) clumps of earth, boulders . . . the rain that follows, covering everything! Ah, it's really something. And then immediately afterward the question: Is anyone there? And awaiting the next hit! This time it's moved toward us . . . how close will the explosion be? This is modern war! Greater than any attempt at human defense, greater than the grander possibilities! Enough; I don't want to go on."[10]

The heavy cannon are utterly dreadful: The Austrian 305, for example, with a sound like a train when launching at maximum velocity, provokes real terror. "It takes your breath away," confesses Luigi Gasperotto in his diary: "The fog returns, when suddenly an immense, anguished, terrifying scream arrives, and stays, extends itself and comes nearer, growing louder, angrier, more cruel and ferocious. And while the air all around trembles, and your heart stops beating and

---

10 Letter from September 30, 1916, in E. Paterlini Brianti, *La Grande Guerra nella memoria reggiana. La guerra del 1915-1918 rivistata attraverso lettere e documenti tratti da archive pubblici e private*. Reggio Emilia: La Buova Tipolito, 2006, p. 210.

your breathing gets shorter and your eyes widen like in a dream transfixed by the terrible awe, the scream ends in a crash and in a storm cloud, and out of the crash and the cloud comes a whirlwind of dust, of rocks, of iron, from which the air stays long darkened and a hail of splinters arcs and descends almost sweetly in wide rays all around you. It's the 305.

"Monte Coston has given the alarm. Everyone is running to take shelter in the observatory but not before another hit, better aimed, waving overhead, hurls men to the ground like twigs. . . . In the meantime Lt. Cabib of the 1st Artillery explains to me that every 305 hit costs 3,000 lire and weighs 420 kilos. . . . The eighth hit lands, the last, one prays. Enough for today. Austria has just spent 24,000 lire, or kroners, with nothing to show for it. But I confess that the 305, heard for the first time and without having prepared my soul for it, takes your breath away."[11]

---

[11] L. Gasparotto, Rapsodie (*Diario di un fante*). Milan: Treves, 1924 (4th edition revised and expanded), pp. 32-33. It seems that in the cemetery of Cervignano an unexploded 305 shell was transformed into a headstone. Alfredo Valenti notes in his diary: "October 1 [1916]. Up at 3:00 the carts are attached and we go to Cervignano with thirty carts and we take on 3000 blows, at the Cervignano station we see a giant warehouse filled with chests each one of which contained one of those monstrous projectiles that are 305 caliber. At about 11:00 we are in the barracks, and they give us food. When we are permitted to move about, I go to visit the town cemetery, on entering one finds a monument in the form of a 305 which had fallen at the beginning of the war, fired by the enemy on the encampments of our soldiers close to Sagrado, but it did not explode, and so it formed the monument to all those many who fell who were buried in that cemetery, and where one notes a large number of infantry officers fallen at Karst." Valenti Alfredo, pp. 30-31. And here is Giovanni Comisso who sees in 1916 his first 305: "One day a notice goes around that a 305 cannon has arrived at the station at Cormons, and it brought us all a great relief — we too then would have a piece of 305 with which to respond to the daily firing of the Austrian 305s placed in the dense public gardens of Gorizia. It passed by solemn and huge, although covered by cloths so as not to be glimpsed by airplanes and it went among the acacia trees on the hills of Subida. I was curious to see it, and one afternoon I went down the muddy paths to the adjacent observation post from where one could see down in a hollow the 305 crouched down like a giant toad." G. Comisso, *Giorni di guerra*. Milano: Mondadori, 1980, pp. 65-66.

Mimo Genga was born in Colbordolo (Pesaro) on August 18, 1894. A bricklayer like his father, he emigrated to the United States at a very young age. He went back to Italy in April of 1914. He was recalled to arms on December 13, 1914, and enlisted in the 37th Regiment infantry.

Plava, June 6-7, 1915

We passed the days of June 2, 3, 4, 5 with few instructions. Then on the 6th, accompanied by Maj. Franchi we went down along the hill a ways, on the other side where the enemy were; though nobody knew that. Calm, tranquil, we were building a trench when suddenly we heard in the distance the rumbling of shelling; I at first didn't know what it was, all of us stood up and looked around, "What's that?"

"Nothing, nothing; it's a fly buzzing around!" responded Maj. Franchi.

All of us silently went back to work on the trench, but it wasn't over yet. Another four or five minutes later we heard another mortar firing, much closer than the first one. We all laughed; it went so far that none of us heard the explosion. Another few minutes went by, and the third rocket was frightening: You could hear the cannonball approaching. It's impossible to describe the fear. We all fled, running one way and another. Trembling, we went back to the camp. But it still wasn't over. After half an hour a similar shell blast of 152mm exploded two or three meters above my head. Fortunately it was a short shot; if it had been even 5 meters closer it would have taken out the whole camp. I didn't know where to go; I was shaking like a leaf, but that too passed.

The next day, June 7, we were supposed to make a false advance even further down from where we were the day before, June 6.

We were to leave at 3 in the morning, before the first meal; everyone was getting ready; at 1 we went down as a crowd into a ravine where there was a stream, in a big mass we were under this cliff to refill our water flasks that we'd need in the false advance. All of a sudden it seemed like the world was ending; it was a 305 mm missile that exploded on the left side of the stream, in the middle of all of us who were waiting to refill our water bottles. My God, what screaming! Stones, dirt, splinters covered our innocent bodies. I saw two of my friends rolling by the side of the river, covered in blood. I had no idea where to run to. A third friend of mine was hit in the leg by a rock and was unable to walk. None of us had our hats on anymore, me, who was so afraid of blood, was yelling like a crazy person, calling for my mom: "Mom! Help me, help!"

I put my dear friend on my shoulders, and I got out of there at top speed. While I was climbing, I don't think I had even gotten twenty steps along, here terrifyingly came another 305. Oh, lord; this is it. I lay down on the ground without even breathing; I felt the heat of the missile that went by swiftly so close by and wound up exploding in the ravine, 200 meters below me. This one went by too; I took to my path again, I arrived at the tent with my buddy on my shoulders, and we were more dead than alive. At 2 an infernal rain of bombing began; and the advance was suspended.

Ottone Costantini, account clerk, was born in Osimo on February 18, 1889. He was called up on May 23, 1915 to the 3rd Regiment fortress artillery. He wrote to Sandra, his fiancée in Rome.

July 24 or 25, 1915

Under a beautiful sun, in the most lush of the greenery, in front of a pub, beyond Civildale toward the front. Lots of car traffic, howitzer cannon munitions, courier trains . . . a party, a show of orders and of incomparable, incredible activity; the cannon grumbles from afar. Just now the king passed by in his car, going toward the front; we cheered him. Our calm and confident enthusiasm doesn't allow for even a shadow of fear. Many prisoners go by, enemy battalions defeated. The strength of Italy.

Ottone

>July 24 and 25, 1915

My dearest lady,

We've almost reached the goal. From the village . . . where I am we heard extremely close by the angry rumbling of the cannon at long intervals. Mount Nero ahead of us is frightening and it seems that by the dream of some crazy person it is occupied; and yet the alpinists and the rifle corps are there.

It's 8:30 in the afternoon. Among the first shadows of the evening, beneath the fog and the rain, we can hear far away firings and suddenly the blast of a sinister enemy grenade. There are short intervals, and then the fury is reignited in the semi-darkness. Just then we hear a tremendous racket closer by followed by that characteristic whistling of the big shells that splits the air. It's one of our pieces a few meters from us that is joining in. It's a tremendously beautiful spectacle, one feels gigantic! All of this right under my very eyes and tomorrow or after I too will be among the combatants . . .

>August 8, 1915

Dearest Miss Sandra

By my break in writing these last days you will have understood that something new has happened and this is a change in our position. Now we are within view of the enemy on the same line of campaign artillery. In fact, other batteries are behind us. We haven't yet started firing but it's clear that when we do our battery will be terribly ridiculous. Just yesterday four shells of large caliber fell close to us.

Soon I will be off to the gun battery, the order to fire came. Till we meet again? . . .

I am back. The firing was a few hours and will be only as a test for the target practice and to adjust the shots. I was saying, then, that two of the four shells passed over me very close with their characteristic slow crawling that makes you think of a train on a long track or of a thin fabric tearing: interminable. For fear . . . believe me that it's completely not done, but I threw myself face down on the ground under a tree and just then it exploded again right next to me on an exposed piece of ground. The emotion that comes with the danger of gunfire is complex, because it varies depending on the conditions of the area and one's state of mind. The night before we got to Cividale the sound of the distant cannon gave me a gloomy feeling, and the trains of injured men that passed us coming out as we were going in made me feel like a man who reluctantly leads his ox to the slaughterhouse. But this sad moment was brief, surely the result of two sleepless nights on the way and of malnourishment. At Cividale I encountered an enormous quantity of trucks and a huge column of towing vehicles. An enormous movement! The spirits on that day already were on the rise, and I heard the lively gunfire and cannonfire in the distance with enthusiasm. Once we reached the first front I spent many hours of rest admiring the unfolding of the artillery battles and the high columns of smoke from the shelling of the enemy against the massive walls of the mountains. In other hours, artillery fire but not even a shadow of the enemy shells. But finally the order to advance came. We got up at

2 a.m. dismantling the pieces and then away in the night to stand guard by the side of an impressive ravine.

I was in command of a wagon with the mortar. I was outfitted with twelve troops and four pairs of oxen. The night was extremely dark, on the heights that were our destination that selfsame night began a furious enemy grenade attack. I don't need to tell you what an awesome effect those red metallic flames with flashes of liquid silver had; it was a shower of stars, like something from a fairytale, something unreal.

Then came the water, and we went and went on in perpetual silence passing little shadowed woods, finding the way invisible. At least three times I had to stop because of accidents; it would have taken very little for the whole thing to have collapsed into the ravine, animals and men with their heavy loads. But the Virgin whom you pray to was maybe watching over us and we made it happily all the way to Isonzo.

August 14, 1915

Very kind Miss Sandra

I'm writing to you in a moment in which history will count among the glories of Italy. The cannon which for thirteen hours hasn't stopped its deathly rumbling today reached an intensity of fire that was catastrophic. After two nights with no sleep I found myself this morning able to rest until 1, when around 4:00 a formidable cannon fire woke me again. It was the beginning of action so long awaited with bated breath.

For anyone who hasn't been part of the unfolding of a modern war, it's impossible to conceive of the grandiosity of the spectacle. More an auditory spectacle than a visual one, but a marvelous spectacle nonetheless.

All the tones of the rude and powerful metallic voice were in that volcanic orchestra. The air, continually assaulted by rumblings, by thunder and by echoes of the nonstop explosions, resounded with an immense complaint, mixing all the tones. It seemed like it was a nightmare, and yet the sun was still shining in a cobalt-blue sky. In this sound-laden setting the scope of our work was among the most interesting. The assault over, brief and energetic commands moved men and heavy instruments. Intercrossing plumes of rocket fire and shoot, shoot, always in the most perfect calm.

Antonio Graziani, bricklayer, was born in 1895 in Belricetto (Lugo di Romagna, Ravenna province). Enlisting in the 114th Regiment Infantry, he was sent first to Trentino: In May 1916 he would be working in Val Lagarina, between Mount Baldo and Mount Zugna. In October of 1916 he would be transferred to the front near Karst. He died on June 7, 1918, in circumstances that are unclear.

September 1915, Serravalle-Val Lagarina, Trentino

On the 10th we have to mount guard in the trenches in Serravalle. We spend the entire time on guard duty, from the 10th to the 18th. On the night of the 18th we go back to the Serravalle area, and there we rest all night. On the 19th everything was calm in the town, some of us were writing, some others thinking about their families. Suddenly at 4 p.m. the adversary began a strong bombing attack. Everyone just froze, hearing a blast that no one believed was possible. We all asked ourselves what it could be. We hear the sound of the second shell that little by little was coming closer: It sounded like a train in the air, it exploded in the area where we were. In the strike it flattened three houses. From all the smoke there was, nobody knew which way to run. A little later I saw some wounded men, and I set about helping them along with a friend of mine

There were people running this way and that yelling, "Oh, God!"

My friend and I gave each other courage, and we wanted to go to the place the disaster had taken place, thinking that there might be other friends of ours buried in the wreckage... The next day it became known that there were eight dead and twenty-two wounded. For five days the bombing continued. In these days we eat at night, but nobody wants to eat because of the lingering impression left by those unheard screams. Then we discover that we are dealing with a 420 because one of the shells didn't explode.

Giuseppe Capacci, farmer, was born in Monterchi (Arezzo) in 1895. Called up to the 8th Regiment infantry at the end of September, he was sent to the front at Trentino, to the Passo del Tonale. In the spring of 1916 he would be transferred to the eastern front. In June he would be on the front line in the zone of Monfalcone.

October 19, 1915

There, on the mountain, one begins to hear the defects of the war: You can hear the rumbling thunder of the explosions from our cannon, which were hiding themselves in the hidden valleys. In the first days, curious to see what it took to fire them, we went to the place: When the cannon fired the first shots, we were just stunned and we became terrified. Later, more used to it, this agitation passed. After the shot is fired, one can hear the shell rustling in the air until it has gone beyond the mountains. When it would get to its destination, the official who was manning the observation tower would telephone with information about whether the shot had been straight; otherwise he would estimate the distance, to the left or the right, until they had fixed the shot's aim.

At those times there weren't many weapons; when both battalions entered the action the first times it seemed like Judgment Day: It was all thunderous, the valleys were ringing with it, then the noise would die off. The 19th of October was the first day I remember when with my company for the first time we found ourselves under the fire of the 35th Austro-Hungarian. That day I stayed in the camp while the others went to the fort to work. It was about 8:00 in the morning and I was reading a letter from Maria; I heard in the air a strong wind, a sharp sound, then nothing. The first time didn't hold my attention. At the second landing, I didn't know what it was, but I got up to run and ask a local worker what it was. He answered me, "They're 305 shells; it's the enemy shooting at Ponte di Legno."

Oh! What terrible listening! It didn't seem possible to me that anything could make such a racket! It seemed like a train, or a piece falling out of the sky; every six minutes another one of them arrived. Some soldier told me that on a regular basis the Austrians sent their regards. Then they stopped firing on the village and started shelling the fortifications where my company was working. The first shot was long; it wound up over the encampment. Oh, what a surprise! I threw myself to the ground; it seemed like it wanted to flatten me! After hearing the crash I raised my head looking at the spectacle: The shell had fallen beyond me more than 50 meters, where it contrived to make everything disappear. The ground and the stones that it had lifted and thrown had destroyed the trunks of the trees! No storm could have achieved a similar effect to the same degree: It plucked an enormous plant out by the roots, the same way we would cut a stalk of wheat. Others around there were torn down.

Another cannon blast reduced into fragments the iron grating of the fort. My colleagues were there working, but no one was hit; they didn't hang around even for a minute; they got out of there right away. Everyone was agitated and spilled out of the encampment among the firing in the midst of the thick forest. You didn't hear the boom when they shot, you only heard it when the shell came up from Monticello, louder and louder the closer it got.

In that town, Ponte di Legno, one hit a four-story palazzo: It made half of the whole place disappear, from the roof down to the ground. The newer soldiers were much more afraid of the bombing itself than the damage it brought about. From early morning until 2:00 in the afternoon the Austrian 305mm cannon continued to fire: It made me so upset that I couldn't sleep all night. It seemed I could always feel it coming.

"Everyone has to get used to it" it's said among us soldiers. "This was so as to get the effect: When we will find ourselves in the trenches, where the shells come more frequently upon us, and with no possibility of fleeing your assigned post, and you will hear the screams of your companions who have been crushed, that's where pride and excitement vanish and one begins to think a bit about the Creator!"

Chapter 5.
Machines Against Diggers

As had already happened on the French front, so it was that the Austro-Hungarian theater of war seems to have been quickly dominated in an exclusive manner by the digging corps.

"In the narrow spaces of the trench," writes Eric Leed, "war reveals itself to be work, and not in the ethical sense, but rather in the ancient meaning of the word."[1] Work as struggle, suffering, hardship, continual effort. An effort frequently rendered vain by the devastating bombings from the enemy, so much so that in the trenches, writes Leed, war seems to assume a character of a conflict "between implacable machinery and diggers. The war machine could grind up the results of months of excavation work, but spades and hoes end up restoring balance, and everything starts all over again."[2]

Of the methodical process of endless and pointless work Antonio Gibelli too insists that after having brought back some testimonials from soldier-workers, even those who were accustomed to hard manual labor, he was forced to conclude that "the logic and the motive for the shifts are fleeting, inasmuch as they depend on an unknown and superior design. In the same way one can never grasp the overall logic of war, which presents itself as a casual sequence of assaults and repositionings, waiting and retreats, digging work and building work quickly rendered useless. The work is perhaps normal, but in a context that makes more fleeting the meaning and logic, and therefore more clear the dispossessed nature."[3]

---

[1] E. J. Leed, *Terra di nessuno. Esperienza bellica e identita personale nella prima guerra mondiale*, translated into Italian by R. Falcioni. Bologna: il Mulino, 1985, p. 130.
[2] Ibid., p. 135.
[3] Gibelli, *L'officina della guerra* cit., p. 108.

The sense of waste and uselessness of the completed work pervades also one of the more polemical pages of Silvio D'Amico, an intellectual and officer who actually believed in the war. He writes on January 2, 1917: "And all this work, work, work, all these thousands and thousands of men who climbed up to the heights of the Vallone, all this effort of will, intelligence, and tenacity, all these roads and lanes made step by step carrying on shoulders each and every rock, all these caves . . . all these caverns blasted out one after another, all these artillery pieces disassembled from other positions and dragged and reassembled here, hundreds and hundreds of them, really thousands: all these enormous batteries put together, the gun emplacements, the recoveries, the ammunition storage shelters, the armories, one after another, these telephone lines laid, guarded, repaired day after day, all these thousands of tons of shells, carried in the trucks a few at a time, unloaded one at a time by night, hidden and covered with branches, the entire plan determined down to the last detail, studying the maps, the range of placement, the figures of adjustment, the infinite care, the regulations, the back and forth, the shifts, the refueling, the daily provisioning, the means of transport, the tractors, the horses, the mules, the oxen; and the water taken on, the humidity absorbed, the incurable illnesses contracted; and the hopes, above all the enormous hopes that also the skeptics didn't confess to themselves [...] all this is useless, was useless, went rotten under a sun that didn't want to face it; better to pretend it never began; even better to send away the munitions, abandon the gun emplacements, the caves, the recoveries, the storage shelters, the repairs, the roads, leave here the remarkable feats of engineering construction that were built, with all the innumerable materials collected, tables, beams, iron girders, metal plates, sandbags (the bags alone cost thousands, and they will remain here to decay) and turn back in order to do the spring over, and to begin *everything* again."[4]

---

4 D'Amico, *La vigilia di Caporetto* cit., pp. 70-71.

This extract from D'Amico, even though it conveys things very well, is still a partial description and, ultimately, optimistic. Other officials denounce the senselessness of their orders, the absurd pretext of making soldiers work beyond their capacity, the lack of adequate materials and instruments. A Piedmontese lieutenant writes to his father on May 26, 1916, "If I don't vent this to you immediately, I might explode! . . . I am taking part in a jumble of solemn nonsense, so much that it becomes unbearable. . . . We are working for fifteen days without a break, under the almost constant rain, with 120 exhausted wretches who've been on the campaign a year: We are supposed to make fencing but we have little wire, no nails to attach it with, and no hatchets to chop the stakes (the brilliant infantrymen make stakes with their bayonets fixing the wire with thorns taken from the bark of trees). We are supposed to dig trenches, but the rocks are hard, and the picks can't pierce them. We need gelatin to ignite the mines, but they didn't give it to us because a platoon of miners was supposed to arrive but there's been no sign of them. We need to raise the parapets with beams, but the beams can't be cut with bayonets, and in the entire company there is but one saw. Sandbags would help, but they gave us 150 for a line that's a kilometer long!"[5]

But such rationality and general positivity that the vision of the officials maintained, given that they believed in the war, is nowhere to be found in the texts of the ordinary writers we've chosen. The letters and pages of diaries by soldiers demand, to the contrary, that we enter into the dark and anguished universe of the trenches, in order to know the chaotic and topsy-turvey world where traditional and natural times of the cycle of the seasons are gone, such as day and night, waking and sleeping, working and playing.[6] Those trenches, those caves,

---

5 Giuseppe D., author of the letter intercepted by the censors, for having expressed critiques that we have read will be condemned to six months in prison. In B. Bianchi, *La follia e la fuga. Nevrosi di guerra, diserzione e disobbedienza nell'esercito italiano (1915-1918)*. Rome: Bulzoni, 2001, p. 465.

6 Leed traces a convincing parallel between the work of mining and wartime in

those recoveries, so well described by Silvio D'Amico, are inhabited in reality by a populace that finds itself degraded by filthiness, a "populace of troglodytes" amassed in small burrows, more like worms, mice, moles, rabbits.

Angelo Venturi, day laborer, was born in Borgo San Lorenzo (Florence province) March 9, 1891. He was sent to the 6th Regiment rifle corps. He died on November 21, 1915 at Mount Podgora, near Gorizia.

Combat zone, July 9, 1915

My dear father,

If this reaches its destination, it will surely make you happy to hear where we are. We are in burrows like wolves: During the day it's absolutely forbidden to leave them lest we be discovered; if you do, watch out! We're in the line of fire of four mountains all supplied with massive artillery, and so when it's getting to be evening everyone goes out to do our business and to eat a little bit of rations. In other words, everything is upside down, from morning to night. This however shouldn't make you worry too much; being hidden like this we are not in grave danger; we're in the middle of a forest and so it would be very hard to spot us.

You will have read many times in the newspapers the names of Gorizia, of Mount Pogdora, Sabotino, Monte Santo, and we are right underneath these mountains, further on from Isonzo, and we are awaiting the moment to enter Gorizia. But it's a very impatient waiting, with the enemy so strong, entrenched in these positions. In other words, it's the point where the

---

the trenches: "In the trenches the hardest jobs were performed at night; during the day one sleeps or else mounts guard, and many soldiers complain about being constrained to live in the darkness. The apparatus of war often is nothing more than a variation on that of mining work." Leed, *Terra di nessuno*, cit., p. 190.

bone is strongest. You can imagine that for two months our artillery has directed its fire over Mount Pogdora and they plucked it all like a chicken. There's not a tree left standing, not a morsel of land where they haven't thrown a high-caliber grenade, but their trenches are still there and they don't surrender; they are armored as much as if they were making the assault. But we have had to retreat without result. The enemy is not leaving these trenches, and when they hear the shells of our artillery that raise huge clouds of thick smoke, they flee to their underground shelters. They're covered and so can't see anything. Only at night do they begin frequent attacks that our excellent artillery knows how to silence. And so it is that so much of the night and the day over our heads pass furiously whistling the large and small caliber shells, friends and enemies interchange with perfect order. Now we are accustomed to this and don't pay it much heed, we're all very impassive in the face of this sweet sound that doesn't let a moment pass by without splitting the air. I've written this to you just so you know something about what's happening, but I beg you not to give it too much thought and get frightened because I am fine. Don't read this letter to Mamma so that she understands what's going on. With the hope of being able to write you when we've crossed the River Isonzo. Warm hugs and kisses from your son Angelo.

Greetings to my friends; let me know Tugnaz's address.

Farewell: Let me know if you receive this letter.

Battista Belli was born in Soresina (Cremona). He was drafted into the 65th Regiment infantry.

August 9, 1915

With my letter I come again to tell you that I am in good health at present and so let's hope always to be. My dear ones, although I find myself in danger, still I hope always to see you again. If things go well and I have the grace of God to remain unharmed I think that at the end of this month I will descend from these mountains where I am now. It is since the beginning of the war I and my comrades are here passing over, up and down, night and day like so many nocturnal birds.

Here almost everything is done at night; we work making trenches all night long. We need to make three or four kilometers of mountain in order to go get food, and even that at night because the food caravan doesn't leave its place so as to escape notice. In other words, if I am able to return to Italy I will want to say that it is because of Grace. However, as much as I'm doing hard work, thank God I have not really suffered, and let's hope it continues always like this.

Although here almost every day it rains and one sees also snow and fog, it always passes. One day or another let's hope always that God wants to make peace, that all this will be finished for everyone, for those of us who are here to labor and also for you who are there always, night and day, thinking of your sons. But what do you want to do, my dear parents?! How much you have thought of your sons and you are so worried about them, so that everything stays the same. Only God can put a hand on the head of each one of us to bless us. Every day I recite prayers especially now that I know that you at home are praying to S. Luigi, and I every morning say always the "Gloria Pater" in order to have the grace to return again to embrace everyone in the family.

I will finish writing by greeting you all, the whole family, Papa, Mamma, sisters, brothers, Luigi and his sons, all the relatives, friends, all those who ask after me.

Alfonzo Lucarini was born in Camaiore (Lucca province) in 1890. He was sent to the 21st Regiment infantry, Company 7, trench diggers. Letter addressed to Mrs. Anna Cannizzaro of Camaiore.

September 21, 1915

Most Esteemed Madam:

Yesterday with the utmost relief I received your letter containing so many pieces of information. Thank you for your thoughtfulness. Here everything is going marvelously well for now; it's important to stay ready, however, for the enemy has his ear tuned to our movements, assisted by spies who remain in the area. All the entrenchment operations and other jobs must be undertaken at night because in the day we can be taken in the line of fire, which would result in a massacre. During the day one sleeps holed up like badgers in their burrows, and at night we work; even our rations we need to take in the tents because in the daytime there isn't a road with sufficient coverage to transport them to us. But as I have said before, we are not lacking anything: coffee, wine, lemons, sugar, anise, everything, however, outside normal hours; but we enjoy them just as much in our nocturnal life. There are no lights; I can't remember the last time I saw a lit lamp; we have to smoke during the day because at night we can be seen.

It's here that all of us regret the loss of young Benedetti, who was struck down with an illness, so suddenly that the doctors immediately made us all get inoculations against that devastating disease. I would have so many things to tell you about, but it will be better to tell you about them at greater length on my return. I share the most cordial greetings with Gildo and Firma, a kiss to Adelina from me. Signing myself your humble Alfonso.

Luigi Teoli was born in Brescia in 1886.

In the trenches, October 9, 1915

Beloved wife,

I am proud to have received your postcard informing me essentially of the optimal state of your health and also that of our dear children, Mamma, and my sister, and in so in return I can tell you that I too feel fine, but I am burdened with lice that I am obliged to carry with me via my skin by doing so much biting of me, and I can't change clothes or bathe because I am here in a trench underground and nearby the enemy: His trench is only about five meters from mine, and for this reason we can't move except to piss, but always on our knees.

Once a day a soldier comes to give me meat and bread and water like they do to prisoners, at night on the other hand I have to fire constantly to avoid the enemy coming to take me where I am and make me prisoner. And this goes on for six days, and so I came here on the fourth and they will give me the duty change on the 10th, and so for another six days we are here resting, except when there's some fighting, in a small town a bit further back where I will try, if I can to hunt down the lice, but I am sure that after a day I will have them again because the trenches that we just made a few days ago are filled with these animals who even try to get in my mouth. Eh! My dear wife, if you knew the life I was constrained to live! And all in order to see if I will be able to bring my skin back home to you, and to my kids . . .

Antonino Cella was enlisted on April 20, 1915, into the Tolmezzo Battalion, 6th Company, 8th Alpines with the rank of corporal trumpeter. After having been sent to Karst in the spring of 1916 he would reach Mt. Adamello.

After this period of my convalescence was finished, I returned to Gemona where I remained until October 20, 1915, when I left for the front to rejoin the 4th Alpine Regiment, Val Batea Battalion, on the Isonzo, specifically at Volaria. On the 28th of the same month, we ascended Mt. Mertzl, a difficult position and unassailable, with us halfway up the mountain while the enemy is at the summit and could hit us not only by firing on us but also using rocks and by blocking every one of our movements. After nine days in the trench, in the mud, suffering the cold, we went down to Volaria, a town that had been taken over and evacuated, from which two days later we left to go down to Vodil to the left of Tolmino, another difficult and dangerous position being hit by large-caliber artillery. Here in the large trench where one mounts a lookout for platoons every 24 hours, there are enemy cadavers only a few meters away from our embrasures, already rotting and dismembered by our artillery shells. This circumstance nauseates us and takes away our desire to eat our rations, which consist of tins of meat, all the more so the bread is frozen in the cold given that we can't move unless it's nighttime. In that post we changed the watch twice, then on November 24, 1915, from Camno we went up again onto Mt. Mertzl but via a different route, where we resisted seventeen days of action, among the cold, the rain, and the mud without any relief.

In such a position we had to work entire nights in which the darkness allowed us to be unseen and unbothered by the enemy and for that reason none of us knows any rest, suffering also from thirst because we are out of water on this mountain.

Francesco Giuliani, shepherd and laborer, was born in Castel del Monte (L'Aquila) in 1890. He attended the first years of elementary school but later went on to become an autodidact, reading and teaching himself. Called to arms on May 15, 1915, he was assigned to the 13th Regiment infantry. On May 24, he was already in the war zone. In May of 1916 he would be transferred to the upland of Asiago. Giuliani authored a complete memoir, made up of diaries, poetry, reflections, and later meditations on the war. We are publishing two letters addressed to his wife.

Ronchi, October 20, 1915

Five months of this unhappy way of living have already passed, and who knows when I will be able to see you if the Reaper isn't cruel and wants to spare me. I never lose the hope of getting through this, and it helps that others too are hoping, but for many hope is in vain. This place where the war is being fought is frightening and could justly be called the kingdom of death, of woes and pain; in the trenches one could write what's written on the doors of hell: Abandon all hope, ye who enter here. Nights and days are always sad; it's not possible to have even a moment's peace, happiness is gone, in every face you see torment and hardship.

If some days the sun shines and the bombings quiet, only then does one find a little comfort. When there is nothing to do, everyone's only occupation is writing letters and cards; maybe the fear generates more love for parents, wives, and kids. There's so much letter-writing that each company sends a bag of mail daily; the one that arrives at the same time as that one departs is just a teeny thing. With what anxiety do we await news, who receives a letter is for a time happy and content, as though the letter brought him salvation.

Food also is bad; it has to come from far away, it gets distributed at night and besides is cold, and many times the only meat ration is not clean. Twice we have had tuna rations, and this was so good that it brought back one's appetite. I have one thing going for me, and that is that nothing turns my stomach, nothing takes away my appetite; I eat everything happily and probably even too much and I always feel fine. For me, who am not used to an easy life, all the discomforts of the trenches don't bother me so much, but there are other things that no one feels they can withstand. I can say, as did rightly a monk of the times of the siege of Florence, "You see in what sad times I have to live." If everything that here one suffers through were at least for a just cause, one could just about get through it with some resignation; but I am certain that no such just cause exists.

Ronchi, October 26, 1915

I always want to be sure you don't miss my news, and however they may be you won't miss them, you don't need to worry; as long as there's life, there's everything. Seeing as how in the front line things are too bad, in a few days we're moving to the second line; in trenches around certain houses, and there is next to us the Ronchi cemetery, which one day I was curious to see. Here the dead aren't neglected as they are at home, one can see that they take care to keep everything up; but the war won't let anyone rest in peace. One sees many tombs whose roofs have been taken off by grenades and the beautiful marble pieces reduced to fragments. Also few Italians sleep their last sleep there.

The trenches where we are sheltering are a little less than a meter deep, covered with branches and with a little earth, and many times someone falls through who is too heavy for the branches to hold. The trenches are so narrow that we can't stretch out our legs; the muddy walls drip constantly with water since it rains almost every day, for a bed a bit of hay reeking with stench, and the fleas swarm over our clothes like worms on a carcass. You might be thinking we would do better to live in the houses, but they are riddled with danger. In order to be a bit more comfortable a couple of us took up lodging in a carriage, which was almost totally buried underground and was placed like that for the purposes of the trench; it's disappointing that the entrance is uncomfortable, but once inside one's nice and dry, and there I'm as happy as Diogenes.

Here one may enjoy the freedom that I am always desiring; one can be a little bit calm; during the day you don't work and at night no one watches over you. I hope that for a while, my darling, I can give you good news.

Roberto Gandini, farmer, was born in Villa Poma (Mantova) on August 10, 1890. He was called up in May 1915 to the 9th Regiment of artillery. He was the author of a very detailed diary.

November 23, 1915

Last night about fifteen of us left and went to Redipuglia, where we found some beams that we needed to transport to the trenches in order to make a lookout shelter. Redipuglia is a town that seems should have been very beautiful, but now you can't find a house that hasn't been broken up and the greater part of it has been reduced to ruins. There's a church that's completely sunken in, all you can find is a poor Christ figure hanging from a wall that looks like he is thinking about his predicament.

We each take one of the beams and head back up. The road is tiring and filled with rocks. We head up and soon we hear the whistling all around us of the bullets from enemy rifles. Two of them land so close behind me that they really start me thinking. And yet on we go! And after a bit of a pause close to a shelter we recommence the climb and arrive at a place where we need to be totally silent so as not to tip off the enemy.

Here I would like to write to you everything I was thinking in that moment, but it would be too long. I will say only that in that moment I looked at the moon, so beautiful, and I thought that also from my home one could see that moon and maybe my dear ones were looking at it at the exact same moment and turning their thoughts to me.

We made four trips and the last one was the most dangerous. We were walking one next to the other me and my friend Fornaciari and after hearing several whistlings here and there one came in our midst. We passed a terrible moment. Finally we get back and little by little go to sleep, chatting about the evening that was anything but tranquil. The day of rest here passes calmly cooking the liver that we took from the butcher. In the evening we go to the gun battery.

Carlo Spagnolini was born in Fara Novarese on March 16, 1884. Sent to the Italian Army, he wrote to Father Gaudenzio Manuelli, the parish priest of Fara Novarese, demonstrating his devotion to San Damiano.

From the front, December 11, 1915

Rev. Archbishop I would like now to write you one or two lines: The other day we went to work carrying lath up into these mountains in order to make shacks and there were some Austrians there who shot to the right and the left, there were bullets that were whistling by us, but I appealed to San Damiano and I got back unharmed.

The memory of San Damiano is always with me; every minute our Saint comes to my mind; if I am able to return I want to make a beautiful painting and place it before our protector San Damiano. Now we don't go out to work because the Austrians will see us; we go instead at night; the hardships are huge up in these mountains at night, with the snow a meter high; our feet are always wet. Now we are encamped in the middle of a forest, in a shack made of lath. Here it's terribly cold, it will be a serious matter if this glorious peace doesn't arrive. To do this arduous work and there is the danger of dying! Oh, Rev. Archbishop, what hardships we must go through here in this place I find myself!

I have my mind turned to the Lord and to our protector San Damiano and to our Little Madonna delle Grazie. Above all I will have always in mind San Damiano, so that he protects me and I may return gloriously to my poor family.

Oh, Rev. Archbishop, please forgive me for sending this letter without a stamp, because here we are in the middle of the woods, and it's impossible to get stamps, but I believe that you will be all right with it.

Oh, Rev. Archbishop, my wife says that you might let her read my letter publicly in church during the grand Mass; I would be so happy if she could read it and say that I am in fact the author, the one who wrote it.

Many greetings and a handshake from your musician Carlo Spagnolini, brother of Pietro, Luigi, Damiano. Many greetings, Reverend; many greetings to your family, to Signor Battista and his mother. Please excuse my handwriting and if there are errors in the letter.

Every minute the figure of San Damiano comes to my mind.

Giovanni Zanni was born in Belprato (Brescia) in 1889. He was enlisted into the 77th Regiment infantry.

March 8.4.1916

My dearest family:

From the depths of a giant trench I describe for you my miserable life. I find myself in the trenches, thirty meters away from the enemy. We are here like prisoners, during the day one can't even raise a finger, at night we are careful in our holes so as to not be caught in an assault. All day and night we hear the enemy, who says, "Come, come, Italians, together with us."

When we answer, they trust us and say to us, "Come if you are able into our trenches." Looking out of the embrasures of our trenches we see the wire fencing full of dead bodies from five or six months ago and no one can go out to take them in, we smell a terrible stench that we can't withstand. These there we have before us. At night at 11 they bring us food to eat, and nothing else happens at night afterward, we eat in the trenches, behind the pathways. We are always tormented by cannon fire and gunfire, and at night they throw into our trenches grenades of every grade. My dear father and all my family members! We won't see one another again; God wants it this way. I am on Mount Sabotino; you will have read in the newspapers that it is a good position! They say that the soldiers who were here before us had sacrificed 10,000 men, and we aren't even halfway up the mountain!

It's more than twenty days since I saw Cousin Zubani, and we won't see each other again; I am very scared I won't see him again. I owe him his money. And how can I pay him back? I wrote also to the two brothers. In any case, I don't have anything else to tell you. I greet you from my heart, and I kiss everyone in the family, bye, farewell.

I am your wretched son

Giovanni Zanni

My dear ones, pray to God for me, who am in an ugly position; only you can save me.

Ettore Travostino was born in Gattinara in 1887. He enlisted in the 76th Regiment infantry. In 1917 he moved to the machine-gun unit as quartermaster. The war zone of which he was writing is the Carnia, the location is situated on the Udine-Pontebba line and "directly underneath a piece of high ground that guards this little city, now deserted, from 400 meters."

War Zone May 11, 1916

My dear ones:

My regiment has left and with them the Gattinarese company members, among whom I think is Cousin Mario, whom I have not seen again since when I left San Daniele. The only ones left here are my company, specifically trained to complete the work of the defenses, together with the engineering soldiers. And we will have them for some months, before rejoining the regiment. For this reason life isn't so bad, because we're working with a certain moderation; all one can do during the day is sleep, and at night we go to Mount Fortino where the pick and the shovel await us. We come back before dawn, and it's about an average of five hours of work. Of the day, sleeping steals some hours, particularly after rations, because of cooking and cleaning our clothing. The most important thing is that we are relatively safe. Many greetings from your Ettore.

May 19, 1916

My dear ones:

I am still here working. Now I have done everything: wood cutter, brick-layer, manual worker, and bellboy. At night with the rain and in the good weather on festival days and working days, with no distinction whatsoever. This week the Austrians bombed several houses in Pontebba with much fire and barbarically. But they didn't try any offensive. We actually ran, from fear of grenade fire, but we ran quickly to the shelter on the other side of the mountain, burrowing ourselves in little openings in the rocks. Now it seems as though calm has returned. But you write that I don't say much. What is it that you want? There really isn't much time. Working all night long, sleeping during the day, and I get mad when they wake me up to eat. As far as health goes, I am very well. I got a postcard from Cousin Basilio. Reciprocate my greetings. To all of you I hope we will see one another soon. Send me Cousin Mario's address, and write me often. Ettore.

War zone May 26, 1916

My dear ones:

I receive today your letter. Just as well you are hurrying, to the better of the farm work. Once you're done with the hay, you can more comfortably take care of the vines. I am still here working like usual. You are asking me how one can do so at night, in the dark? Of course we don't get to see the results of the finished work. It has to be of a very relative efficiency. And yet it keeps on going like this. They are defenses that should have been here already before the war began, and finished in the daytime by skilled workers. But here we always arrive late, and everything is done sloppily, with a lot of waste and few results. What should be able to be done well in a week's time takes a month and turns out badly. As far as the ins and outs of everyday life, by now I am used to them. I continue to enjoy the best health. Many best wishes to you and to all our relatives.

Ettore.

    War zone June 12, 1916

My dear ones:

Today, the day of the Pentecost, we reached the Quota 1,800. Further up there are the Alpine troops, who climb among the living rocks, where they drag themselves with cords. We are sheltered in good entrenchments, covered with pine trusses, clods of earth and tarred-over card, to keep water from getting in. There are also fireplaces so we can warm ourselves up by the fire. We take turns mounting the watch, and in the other hours of free time we work to fix paths and covered walkways or else to put in new wire fences. Last night suddenly a snow storm came up. In short time everything was white to a thickness of 20 cm. But it disappeared quickly with the first sunshine. It seems almost impossible. In aggregate the cold isn't too harsh, and one handles it just fine. It's like how it is at home in January. Now we are moving closer and closer to nice weather. The danger is very relative. I am still in good health. Many greetings, Ettore.

    July 12, 1916

My dear ones:

Don't believe that we live in a state of constantly being soiled on account of laziness regarding cleaning and changing the linens: no. I wash myself from head to feet every fifteen days at least. The dirtiness reigns instead where we are constrained to rest, and it is here that every week a little bit of everything gathers: They are burrows dug out into the earth, very wet and populated by insects of every kind, so that when we sleep they come on us to keep us company. What we need is good disinfection treatments repeated often; instead, we have none. As such, we remain dirtier and dirtier. Notwithstanding which, my health is still good. The clean air of these mountains is what keeps us well. And so I hope to remain. Many greetings to all. Ettore.

Alfredo Valenti was born in Alzano Maggiore (now Alzano Lombardo in Bergamo) on May 19, 1888. His family was relatively well-to-do. He attended the first years of middle-school attached to the lower seminary. Called up to the army on April 29, 1916, he was assigned to the 3rd Artillery Regiment mountain unit, 164th battery. He died in the camp hospital on October 24, 1918.

December 1, 1916

At 4:00 they call us because the food is being distributed and it consists of coffee, which I drink right away, and of broth, a nice ration of meat, and a single piece of bread. At 7:00 we're woken and we start working with our picks in order to build a shelter for the group commander; it's work that lasts until 6:00 in the evening with no interruption. All day long it was a cursed bombardment, and Austrian grenades of 152 caliber went off very close to us. Having eaten our second rations at 7:00, we have to go to reassemble the new gun emplacements on an exposed site, and so each one of us works in silence. Once we got the first piece mounted, grenade fire landed around us; seems certain that the moon gave us away. Then we go to bed and I fell into a deep sleep, and at 4:00 they bring us first mess, then we recommence the work with picks to make the border wall and we keep on working until 10:00 not paying any attention to the enemy, who could observe me. Around 10:00 however while moving the second piece, another round of grenade fire made me have to take shelter immediately; a rock thrown by the attack hit me in the leg hurting the limb a bit, but it was OK. When it seemed the enemy was easing up, we managed to put in place the second piece. At 1:00 they fire the first shot, mostly to make sure the aim. And so we need to fill up bags and dig in order to make shelter. In the evening the rations of food didn't come because of the intense bombing, and so we eat the reserve food and then sleep.

December 3, 1916

At 1:30 I have to take a shift guarding the piece; at 3:00 someone will come to relieve me; at 5:00 finally the food arrives; I eat and fall back asleep. At 7:00 we have to take down the pieces and move them into the valley mostly to have them cleaned, and so we transport them quickly because the enemy is in front of us raining down grenades on us, making it hellish, and so it continues all day; different grenades fall in our valley but they all remain intact, and all day we work briskly and dig again our own shelters, mostly in order to make them safer, at 5:00 (finally) exhausted I am able to rest while I wait for the food to come, at 9:00 at last we are given food, the cooking being stopped on account of the massive bombing. Around 10:00 we begin to hear the gunfire and it gets more and more intensified, it's a counterattack that lasts until 11:00 followed by a devilish bombardment, the grenades fall like a thunderstorm; finally I go back to sleep.

December 4, 1916

It's raining. At 4:00 they distribute the food, and so we go under the shelter to eat, write, smoke a cigarette, and just lie there doing nothing until 10:00. The bombing today isn't as bad; it seems one should celebrate the protectress of the artillery. Anyway there is work to do refilling the bags to use to cover the shelters, it rains, though, while were doing it; right in the middle of the valley a 240 explodes, luckily no one was hit. At 5:00 we go to find shelter and wait for the food delivery, which comes around 8:00; in addition to the food, there is the matter of attending whether there is mail. Anyway, I'm going to sleep.

Giovanni Bussi, tailor, was born in Cossano Belbo (Cuneo) on March 15, 1898. He was called up in 1917 to the 255th Regiment infantry.

May-June 1917

Today I went on fatigue duty together with some comrades from my squad. As we were passing through a place beyond the bottom of this valley I saw some soldiers making big ditches and others who were digging others in which they had put bodies wrapped in tent fabric, one on top of the other like anchovies and they spread lime over before covering them up. We had made a halt and I asked them why they were burying so many of them together. They responded that those were the remaining dead who were all mixed together because burying them one at a time was impossible, so much so that they didn't know who they were, and that now they had to make more holes because they had more dead bodies to bury and that they were victims of gassing.

It's the third day that we have been here and today we go up to check out the front. One quad at a time must go up and do work on the second line where they are building a gallery. We go up behind a Waloon via a path made like a staircase. At the top you come out to a slight slop where there are two walkways; we take the Granatieri walkway. It's a walkway made in a zigzag form, but here and there cannon have poked holes, so it's dangerous. To get to the part where they are making the gallery we go along a stretch of the second line, every once in a while we hear the hit of a cannon and we throw ourselves on the ground. The soldiers on the line laugh because we haven't figured out how to tell the difference between a hit that is outgoing and one that's incoming.

Where we're building the gallery there is a motor that works with heavy oil and it uses a drill bit with compressed air that they use to make holes in the rocks, then they insert gelatin tubes in those with a detonator and a fuse; they close the holes, compressing them well, then they collect all the fuses which are of varying lengths and they light them. You leave and you count the explosions, then armed with a short-handled pick-axe and a lantern on your belt, shovels and wagons, you go in and take out all the material that's been blown up, and then you start over again. The squad I'm part of is made up almost entirely of guys from my area or else very nearby.

Rations arrive only at night, most times it's like the gum they use to put up posters. It's seasoned with cheese such that the mess tin is always covered in oil. You can't wash them because the water here isn't even drinkable and if you try to go find some it would mean your hide, because it's not the kind of oiled-cloth bag you carry water in but rather your own skin.

Chapter 6.
The Enormous Olive Press

The title of this chapter is an expression taken from the diary of Carlo Salsa, who when seeing a landscape where corpses piled up, mixing frighteningly with garbage and excrement, thinks of the group of soldiers as "a pitiful human pulp clutched helplessly in the gear mechanism of this enormous olive press."[1]

The dimension of death, the experience of being around the dead bodies of their comrades and of enemy soldiers, seeing the decomposition, the unbearable odor that the cadavers emit are the elements that make up this everyday experience of the trenches. Because war is above all else a question of bodies.

Salsa writes, "On the lower walkway soldiers have to remain in a crouched position so as not to become targets; the uneven sides of the shelter barely reach up to your head. It's impossible to move, this grave we're in is filled with smushed bodies, with stiffened legs, with guns, of munitions boxes that crowd together, of overflowing trash: Everything is stuck in the mud, which is as strong as red mistletoe. Little by little forms become visible, things define themselves around me. A side of the trench is completely swollen with dead bodies that mix together in a confused tangle: It's only with difficulty that I can trace the individual human shapes among them. They are almost all corpses of Austrians: Many — starched by an unctuous patina — are spilling into the slurry in the same way, in the same placement as sardines. One sees some of their heads lined up along the edge, some others that sway, and others that don't register except by locks of pitch-black hair. . . . Carefully, with a stick, I lift aside a flap of the tent that covers a tangle: a fetid wave meets me. But in that instant I

---
1 C. Salsa, *Trincee. Confidenze di un fante* (1924). Milan: Murisa, 1995, p. 65.

was able to discern five or six dead bodies who stared speechless into an open hole in the middle of them. Only one of them raised his livid face, turning toward the heavens the sneer of his naked jawbone."[2]

The grime, the intimacy with animals (flies, lice, mice), "the frightening mixing of body and waste matter, contamination and contagion from biological waste (excrement, blood, brain matter), dirt and mud,"[3] are topics that appear with regularity in the letters and diaries of the soldiers. But they crop up insistently also in the literature of those officials who, closed off in the horizon of the trenches, develop an unvoiced grudge about not seeing or knowing, about being just a number. Luigi Bartolini, among others, writes, "Trenches. Disgusting tunnels, gut-wrenching, that were filthy with excrement and with mud and that stank of decay or of calcium chloride emptied by soldiers from the infirmary over the piles of cadavers. A 305 grenade hits; and the trench is reduced to mush; the earth mends itself, the living remain hidden; but meanwhile everyone was expecting to die, one nibbled at the hardtack scavenged from the pockets of the wounded; one drank putrid water that trickled from above, over the decomposing bodies."[4]

The letter from Lieutenant Marcello Pasti is less macabre, but no less dramatic if one considers that it's written while waiting for his own death and is almost completely suppressed by the censors. The young engineering student simply affirms that Karst was becoming a giant cemetery: "You have heard, Alberto, that night when I was up, after having come from Ca' Tron, what a stench the warm air of the first days of May brought from that cemetery that is Carso, and those were the recent victims. On the 23rd they gave us the order for action. Unfortunately the Austrians are all just opposite us so that

---

2 Ibid.
3 Gibelli, *L'officina della guerra* cit., p. 188.
4 L. Bartolini, *Il ritorno sul Carso*, Mondadori, Milano 1934. Here we are citing from the volume by M. Isnenghi, *I vinti di Caporetto nella letteratura di guerra*. Vicenza: Marsilio, 1967, p. 24.

hitting them is extremely difficult, and also right now, unless a miracle happens, we won't go to Trieste. The two engineering companies placed at the disposition of the infantry have been really badly hit. Command has said that the losses are enormous, the gains paltry. Brigades last just a day.

"Of two regiments that went up on Wednesday and Friday only one of them came back down. Yesterday evening we had to clear the old first line of cadavers. Terrible!

"It was nighttime, and all I saw pass by was dead bodies. What a job we found ourselves doing, and to think that I didn't want to study medicine so as never to have anything to do with cadavers! But I continue on as best I can, trying not to look, so as not to have to explain anything to myself. And so I proceed with the wounded; to the long lines of them, I have to shrug my shoulders. Not to think, is the thing. The poor infantry is beaten up by battle, it's shattered by death, it's abandoned in groups like macabre ruins after a frightful tidal wave. And infantry continue to come, even now they are coming up, they come new, fresh, and tomorrow they won't exist. . . .

"But it's better not to think. Let's hope that, for the sake of this poor infantry, the war ends soon, tomorrow, the day after tomorrow . . . if not, the poor beautiful youth of Italy!

"For me, don't give me a thought, don't worry; Mamma doesn't know any of this, and that suits me fine.

"Don't you think, you folks there, about the waves of life that go out from Italy and break themselves against these cliffs of death? Every one of these young kids deserves a monument. Let us hope that peace is near. Write to me from Ca' Tron. Keep me abreast of everything and, once the offensive is finished, let's hope we see each other then. An embrace, Marcello."[5]

---

[5] Letter from May 26, 1917 to his brother Alberto, in *Ta-Pum. Lettere dal fronte. Contributo Morubiano nella Grande Guerra*, edited by L. Beltrame Menini. Padua: Panda Edizioni, 2001, pp. 176-178. Marcello Pasti is born in San Pietro di Morubio on July 26, 1897. A student at the Univeriisty of Padova in the school of engineering, he then becomes a reserve lieutenant assigned to the 1st Regiment engineers. He dies

The camp hospitals, set up right behind the front, can become places for privileged observation: The broken bodies of the enormous and unstoppable gearworks of the war all pass by here. For this reason the diaries of doctors and nurses, when composed with humanity, are capable of correcting the "war vocabulary" of the military writers.[6] In this anthology we have included some pages taken from the diary of Giuseppe Ruberti, a seminary student stationed in a medical ward. Here we add the dramatic notes of medic Lieutenant Fulvio Minetti about the battle zone of Isonzo (November 10 to December 2, 1915).

"November 12. It's daytime and we are out in the open in front of the enemy. Grenades and bullets whistle from every direction. I find an armored shelter and occupy it, staying the entire day stretched out, eating a little bit of bread and cheese. In the evening I go back to S. Lucia Under the Waters.

"November 13. I slept in an unimpressive compound, dirty with mud and threatened by bullets. It's impossible to imagine a sadder life than this one, even being in peril of death means less than ordinary discomforts, which are unthinkable to those far away. We argue even about food, which up to now has been healthy and abundant. We've had wounded along the way, and they begin to show up here as well. Transporting the wounded is a real problem; the conditions of those wretches are horrible.

"November 14. It's raining and snowing. The wounded are coming, along with some who are dying, and they receive treatment by God's grace! There's a lot of mud and no water, no space, stupid personnel, and resources and equipment are too limited. So many ill men.

---

on June 2, 1917, in camp hospital no. 57. The sentences redacted by the censor were restored by the editor and written in cursive.

6 The reference is to the famous saying of Arthur Schnitzler: "They say: He died a hero. Why don't they ever say, He sustained a splendid, heroic mutilation? They say: He died for his country. Why don't they ever say: They cut off both his legs for his country? (The etymology of the powerful!) The vocabulary of war is invented by diplomats, by military men, by the powerful. It should be corrected by veterans, by widows, by orphans, by doctor, and by poets." A. Schnitzler, *E un tempo tornera la pace* ... edited by G. Lanza. Milan: Feltrinelli, 1982, pp. 52-53.

"November 15. Mud and cold. Stench of cadavers; rations depleting. In the dispensary it's not possible to stand upright; one sits uncomfortably. Water drips from everywhere. Medications pro forma. Our work is useless, our sacrifice is in vain, what they need here is good stretcher-bearing staff and besides that a real dispensary, with this system, we have neither.

"November 16. Trench life. Intense cold, dryness, cases of frostbite.

"November 17. Frostbite numbers in lower extremities are up. Otherwise, we're living in the trench with man-hunting via gunshot, right in the middle of the war, open, legal, nothing to do with our enemy: These are men who shoot from a plateau at outliers, the uncovered, fatigue duty, guys using the latrine."[7]

Primo Farabegoli, farmer, was born June 25, 1891 in Formigniano. He joined the 6th Regiment rifle corps. He died on December 16, 1915, at the reserve hospital in Ferrara of pneumonia contracted at the front.

August 11, 1915

My very dear parents,

I am responding to your much-desired letter that I received just today, the one you sent to me on the 5th. I am pleased to hear you are well as is the whole family, as I am also.

Now I will tell you that on the 7th we were moved and they sent us even further from danger, where we were before,

---

[7] W. Miletti Farragamo (editor), *La Grande Guerra (1915-1918). Diario del tenente medico Fulvio Miletti*, introduction by Z. Ciuffoletti. Florence: Tip. Artigraf, 2010, pp. 43-44. Fulvio Minetti is born in Bonito, a town in the Irpinia region, in 1880. He enlists in the 136th Regiment infantry on October 1, 1915. His diary features a temporal arc that does from September 30, 1915, to June 11, 1916, when he leaves the front at Karst and is moved to the Trentine front. What he left are bare, essential notes.

and we are not resting because the battalion is infected [with cholera][8] because when we were in combat we drank water from the river Isonzo and the riflemen in our battalion got a great "visceral heat" [an intestinal infection], but nothing happened to me. If that illness doesn't pass it is probable that they will send us to the garrison, that is to Italy. Our battalion is made up of 461 riflemen, and at the latrine there are always more than 100 who are doing their business with great urgency. They say that the cause was the water from the Isonzo, because it's infected, because in it there are many dead bodies, some dead horses, and all the garbage from the hospitals goes into the river.

Dear parents, I will tell you that in combat I acted with great courage and never gave a thought to being in danger of dying. I will tell you that at home I was very frightened to see a dead person, but instead here I slept for three nights among cadavers that stank and that in taking part in the advance we threw ourselves on the ground not having time to dig a trench we hid ourselves behind dead bodies, piling them up on top of one another. And then on July 26 we went up to the top of the mountain and took part in three bayonet assaults and we managed to drive out the Austrians from their trenches. If you had seen dead Austrian soldiers, some of them were on

---

[8] In August of 1915 an extremely strong strain of cholera develops that ends up decimating the units of the two warring armies. Cfr. A. Sema, *Civili, militari e colera in Friuli, 1915-16*, in "Rivista di storia contemporanea," 1992, 1, pp. 109-142. Cholera, which hit the Italian troops hardest, did not however spare the Austrians. There are many accounts of it. Alessio Menapace, from Trentino, of the 2nd Regiment Kaiserjager, reaches Mt. San Gabriele close to Gorizia on July 31, 1915 and notes in his diary: "The heat was so excessive that for most of those of our kind it became unbearable. Most of the cadavers of the fallen as a result of the heat sent out a nauseating stench the impure air of those places, in short, infected our battalion such that when it was time to eat, no one showed up. More than that, all anyone wanted was water, water to drink; the battalion was infected with cholera and typhus. Throughout the whole battalion, no one was well, whether badly or less badly all were suffering powerful stomach illness, sudden headaches, also the officers were, in general, infected with this contagious sickness, and one today one tomorrow, disappeared, and we didn't see them again." Menapace Alessio, pp. 57-61.

their knees and in making the assault we trampled on them; others breathed out their last breath. I will tell you that I think more now than when I was in combat. You can imagine what someone's heart is like in those situations.

I will tell you that from the summit of that mountain you could see Trieste, which is as far away as Cesena is from Formignano, in other words about a dozen kilometers. Let me know if the planting has taken root well, if the medicinal herbs are turning out well, if the earth is in good enough shape to work it. I want to know if the corn is growing well, I want to know when you will have in the barnyard 1,000 pounds of hay. Tell me if you have bought or sold any animals; let me know how the pig is doing.

Dear Father, I understand that there's nothing left of the grapes on the vine. And I don't know if you will be able to persuade the grower that the vines should be cut, because we won't get anything out of them.

Many greetings to Giovanna.

Eugenio Ferrari was born in Soncino (Villachiara) in 1883. He was called up to the 26th Regiment infantry brigade in Bergamo. He died on November 29, 1915.

November 15, 1915

Dear Teresa

In sending you these few lines I am giving you news of my good health and I hope the same of all of you as well. I am in Santa Maria. I am fine, but I have a bad cold; it continues to rain and snow and we are always soaked and there is no building to go to for shelter, neither by day or by night. Those who are not still wounded are ill with bad colds and sufferings. I hope that this wretch's life will end soon and to be able to come home again. If I survive you would call me the luckiest man alive and wouldn't grieve for whatever troubles I had. In any case I greet you sending a thousand kisses to you and to the dear children, whom I remember always.

Forgive me my bad handwriting and for the slowness, but it's not my fault it's really that I lack the time. I wrote this letter with frozen hands; I can't really hold the pen.

Please write me right away and tell me everything that's happening in the family and of interest.

Here is my address again

Soldier Eugenio Ferrari
26 reg. Infantry, Company 15
War Zone

Greetings and kisses, dear, to you and the children

Your Eugenio

    November 19, 1915

I have been away from home so long and I haven't received any written messages, it's a sad life for me, here living in continuous suffering and without any news of my much-beloved family. Well, although I am certain that you will have written already, mind my urging and write always so as to let me be part of everything. I in the midst of this horrible life enjoy good health, and so I hope is the case for you and the children and everyone else. Please make them pray to God who sees always the wretchedness that here every minute is perpetrated. Let me know also news of all my brothers and something from the newspapers, because here in Santa Maria we don't know anything new, if they have decided to end this war or not if they don't end it I will die of this nonstop suffering. Cold and no sleep ever at night; always wet; and the terrible coldness freezes the clothes to our bodies. I write this letter between cannon fire in the trench on the front line, always in danger of death from one moment to the next. We are twenty meters away from the Germans' trenches and in between there are cadavers two or three months old. So you can imagine how hopeful one has to be of going home, because here if one isn't half dead or dead, one can't go home.[9]

Please write me and help me cheer up a bit, because I hate to tell you but my life in the trench is worse than those of our pigs.

I greet you dearly with the desire to come back home soon to kiss you and the dear children and the whole family. Warmest greetings to your parents brothers and sisters.

Please ask them to forgive me for not having written them, but it's not my fault as I have no time and then here there's no cards and this little paper I brought from home I am using to write to you; if I hadn't had this and the pen that you gave me I wouldn't be able to write.

When I was home they were saying that here the soldiers had cards for writing, chocolate and so forth that they had everything here but instead there's absolutely nothing and it's constant misery.

I'll quit writing hoping always to be able to come back home and enjoy again beautiful life in the bosom of my dear family whom I love so much. I send you dearest greetings sending

---

[9] The fourth Battle of Isonzo began on November 10 and ended on December 2 with 49,000 dead on the Italian side (including Ferrari).

you a thousand kisses pray to God for me, write to me soon yours forever your husband Eugenio.

Pietro Ferrari was born in Vaiano Cremasco (Cremona). He was called up to the 26th Regiment infantry, company 13. During the whole war he kept a detailed diary. On November 23, 1915, he was on the hill of Santa Lucia, a little south of Tolmino. In September 1917 he would be in the area of Monfalcone.

November 23, 1915

In the evening I had to go up to the outcropping to the place of the first lookout. On the way up to the outcropping I saw a dead man, completely black, sitting between two rocks. . . . I placed myself at the extreme left of a line of seven soldiers, and all of us together formed the guard of the advance line. Here being out in the open I use two blankets and two cloaks, of which one of the blankets and one cloak I found on the overlook, and I lay myself down in a little spot where to the right there was a wedge of stone and to the left where the mountain sloped down and where there were further down the trenches there was a meager wall made with some tables and branches. In front facing the enemy there was a type of barricade made out of dead bodies.

Austrians and some Italians, tables, sticks, rocks and little pieces of steel, abandoned by the enemy. Seeing as the dead had already been out in the open for a while, during the daytime they emitted an unbearable odor; many other cadavers lay around in the oddest positions according to how they were at the moment they were shot dead, and all of them were black and moldy.

At the sight of these abandoned and unburied dead I felt my heart ache, and I wept a little in compassion, and I said: Look at the point this modern civilization has reached; we don't even respect the poor dead, even after they die they're left in the field to rot and to be torn up by grenades!

The thought of my dear ones made me feel more alive than ever, and I wept over my unfortunate lot, and that I might not see them again. And here I vowed not to […] sin so as not to die in disgrace with God, praying that He would at least give me time to confess and then if I were to die I would be with him in paradise. I vowed to make the Holy Communion as soon as possible, and I swore to recite the rosary every day to the Holy Crucifix of my very blessed parish.

That done, an enormous peace and faith in God's powerful aid came into my desolate heart and placing myself entirely in his hands, I said: "In manos tuas commendo spiritus meos" I slept a bit, it being already nighttime.

But you couldn't sleep at night, you needed to always be on the lookout, lying down on the ground because in the slightest instant the Austrians shot at us, the rifle always loaded and ready with the bayonet attached, because it was a far-up location, very close to the enemy trenches.

I was there three days and three nights, and given that you couldn't move unless it was night and only in ones and twos, one suffered badly from thirst. . . .

Being these days on the outcropping without ever being able to move, my feet had become very swollen and they hurt a lot, so much so that when on December 7 at night they came to relieve us, on the way down I fell down at every step of the way, and because the trenches seemed to me interminably and it was very dark, I hid myself in a cave with a Calabrese guy and passed the night there.

Giuseppe Ruberti was born in Copertino (Lecce) June 14, 1890. After grade school he entered the seminary at Nardo and then went to the seminary at Molfetta. He was almost at the end of his studies when he was drafted. In the fall of 1915 he left for the front at Karst as a doctor's assistant. The little camp hospital where he worked from November 1915 to September 1916 was located close to San Martino del Carso across from Gradisca.

November 11, 1915

Incredible things. Bombings that never stop. I went to bed around 4 a.m. And was up at 5:30. They made the advance around 11 a.m. After an inconceivable bombardment. The wounded arrived continually. Always going here and there. Today is the day of San Martino, and it's always gone badly, very badly, for me. I frequently thought of home and at certain times I cried. So many wounded young men. Poor boys! Legs blown up, heads messed up, brains exposed, missing cheeks, broken hands, etc. etc. things that horrify and amaze. Poor boys! . . .

November 17

A relatively calm day and night, but always filled with fear. An airplane passed by, got bombed by us. Few wounded. Yesterday one of them, struck dumb, came. He doesn't speak, doesn't say anything. This may be on account of the blast of the grenade and partly because of a splinter of grenade in his left ear. Today another one of them arrived wounded in his spinal cord, totally paralyzed. Poor boys! Poor youth! . . .

November 20

Stormy day. Intense bombardment with many wounded and many victims of frostbite. For this reason I had to get up at

12:00 and go to bed around 2:30. Generals pass by all the time. Still a mess, but a moment of rest. Poor youth! Poor mothers' sons!

November 21

Another rough day. Bombardment even more intense. It seems like the earth is tearing itself apart. Mess, mess, mess, and fatigue. I don't know how it will end. The wounded say that it's difficult but they are making headway, our soldiers are heroes, they fight well and give proof of their valor . . .

November 26

Extremely tempestuous day. Continual bombings. We are looking around ourselves completely horrified. It was dreadful. The entire earth was shaking. My God, enough, enough; let's hope it ends soon and the blessed Peace comes soon. We got orders to break down the mobile hospital for the sick. Yesterday in the 31st section that was in Caselliano several blows of 305s fell and killed about six with many wounded. Where have I wound up, my God? But I can be glad that up to now the Lord has helped me. I hope in you, my Lord Jesus; in you I trust my care. Grant us peace for the sake of your sainted Crucifixion. Blessed Virgin, help me, ask your dear son for Peace. And you, my Compatriot and Protector, be my shield, preserve me from every evil . . .

June 29, 1916

Thursday. A memorable day. The enemy, annoyed by the positions that we've taken from them, has deployed suffocating gas and has hit the 10th infantry in particular. My God, what a time! Poor boys, they were dying before they even got here. The roads, the walkways were piled up with corpses. The gas was so strong that even the stars and the markings on the clock were almost made black or green. We had a good 350 of these soldiers in this state. Sixteen of them died, among them a lieutenant. In Castelvecchio and Fogliano more than fifty of them died, others died in the hospitals and in the trenches. The entire day cost us around 30,000 men. Besides that we saw our damages, but we haven't seen what the artillery did. The trenches were spilling over with Austrian corpses. What a massacre!

June 30, 1916

Friday. A day of nonstop action. We went to make graves for the dead. I worked a very long time with the spade. In the evening we buried them, while the enemy was attacking Selz and Monfalcone. My God, what a smell, poor kids! In one hole we put a good fifteen. Only the lieutenant we put in a casket. The chaplain is there, and he made the benediction. I began to cry seeing that mound of flesh. . . .

August 6, 1916

Sunday. The bombing goes on uninterrupted, inconceivably, unendingly, without pause. Bright rays in huge numbers, shells, shooting, bombs, etc. etc. Around 8:00 the bombing toward the front reached its height. I've never seen anything like it. It's said that they fired 8 million shells, no less than the Germans at Verdun. You couldn't see a thing; the front has disappeared. Huge columns of smoke rise up; shells everywhere. Impossible to conceive of it. Karst no longer exists, the earth shakes, sways, it's a constant earthquake. My God, my God! The Austrians barely respond. They say that during the night 200 cannon filled with Eritrean soldiers passed by. Also more than six other cannon loads of gas tanks. Is this still the world? Do we exist? Nerves are shaken, trembling, we're terrified of dying! I'm afraid of being sent up for the wounded. Dear God! San Giuseppe, my saint, my Blessed Protectors, help us, help us all, all of us. They are saying that today at 3:00 the infantry advances. To me that sounds like they've lost their minds. I took Communion. . . .

August 11, 1916

Friday. The Austrians have begun their retreat to the center on Castelnuovo, where I am located. This morning I had to visit the Austrian front line. It was me, Strauges, and some soldiers. I crossed our lines, I visited S. Michele, and Doberdo I saw nearby. Our lines were well constructed; the cannon were almost thundering; the bombing was without cease. I got to the Austrian lines, my God, not a single wire fence was standing, all blown apart by our artillery. The Austrian trenches had an incredible stink, there were in them very many unexploded bombs, maces, explosive gelatin, and mines. A huge number of caves. It was a real spectacle; I got out of there right away. What made the biggest impression on me was seeing our dead and theirs stuck in the wire fences. They were intact, they stank horribly, they were still armed, all dressed, it was pitiable. My God, my God! Bombs of every caliber were unexploded, including the 305s. Dead, dead, dead. We got lost on the way back while the Austrians were firing damnably . . .

October 13, 1916

The advance has slowed. Also the bombings. In the 102 there is an Austrian seminarian. I saw him, he wasn't delirious. We spoke in Latin. *Amatis me?* He said, *Sullevate, sullevate me.* He wasn't Romae. *Fratus sumus.* He might have died. . . .

Mario Ardizzone was born in Turin on May 18, 1896. He was called up in 1915 to the B Squadron of the 20th section of the sanitation assigned to the 20th armed corps. In June 1916 he was sent to Altipiano di Asiago with the assignment to bury corpses in small cemeteries.

July 12.

A memorable day because of the Austrian chocolate. Having finished Cemetery 5, my team look for a place to put Cemetery 6. We find it in a little flattened clearing close to about fifty bodies. We plant the stakes marking the site and start on the holes. Each hole can hold eight bodies, but digging it a little deeper you can fit twice that many. At around noon the infernal shelling starts its work against the crossroads and the provisioning: four men wounded and four donkeys killed; the cannon fire went on all day. We were witness to a lovely battle between a Caproni and a Fokker which machine-gunned each other flat out. Around 5:00 the shots from the battery were coming closer to us: They're looking for the provisioning corps, but meanwhile we hear them and see them a hundred meters away. Work goes on but with ears sharpened: Suddenly we hear a whistle that's louder than the others; it comes closer and closer getting louder all the time. The graves men threw themselves down one on the other and I who was on a higher piece of ground hopped up and threw myself on the dirt in the shelter of a pine. Just in time: The shrapnel arrived coming and going and with a horrendous blast the shovels all fell the partition wall between the grenades and the shrapnel close to Ferrando (al Raus). After the first moments of distress, you get up, pat yourself all over to make sure you're not wounded, and you check over your company. Orders to grab your tools and flee. Capt. Croso left even his precious pipe, sitting on a rock. An Austrian cadet is buried.

July 13

We move thirty corpses to Cemetery 6. I knew only one of them: It's Capt. Umberto Zangrando, 140th infantry. These thirty are heroes of the 133rd and the 140th infantry. After breakfast another two graves go in.

July 14

Thirteen soldiers are moved, of which five recognized: Lt. Gino Cristofanelli 140th infantry. Soldier Graziano Sanzilao 140th infantry. Soldier Michele Greco 140th Infantry. Soldier Giovanni Venturelli 542 Battalion Rifles Company 3. Soldier Giovanni Andano 5th Sharpshooters Company 7 24th Battalion (he's a guy from Turin with a lot of money). Needed to run on account of rain.

July 15

We fold our tents and get our stuff together in our packs to take ourselves to another town that's six kilometers from Marcesina. We'll go past Baricata (remember the two Italo-Austrian finance houses — the Italian one burned down) and we go into a valley. At the base of it we find the town, two shelters made of wood and called Lagosin, maybe for a little pool of water in a hollow: It's water that flows intermittently. Before arriving in this large municipality a terrible storm surprises us. A powerful hailstorm hit us for more than a quarter of an hour. The Alpini of the 8th regiment, real comrades, offer us a nice glass, which we accept gladly. We make our tents then and toward evening I am invited by the lieutenant of the Alpini to a lavish lunch.

July 16.

We leave at 6:00 in the morning and go to work: This time we find ourselves on Mt. Fin at 2,000 feet altitude. After ten minutes of walking you cross the old border and find yourself in Austria, actually in Italy, in liberated territory. After three quarters of an hour of walking you arrive at the job site, or really at the battle field of June 19. There the fourth company of the 134th infantry fought hard. The field still looks like it did after the battle: It made a terrible and terrifying impression on us. Above the summit of Mt. Fin was the Austrian trench with a line of fencing in front of it. Their trench is extremely strong and constructed in such a way that it can be defended by just a few soldiers. The slope of the mountain is quite steep and mostly dotted with massive rocks, twigs, and trees. The Austrians placed a machine gun every thirty meters. The heroes of the 134th go up to the assault on the evening of June 19 guided by the major and the adjutant general of the 1st battalion — the Austrians let them reach up to within sixty meters of the fence, and then they open an infernal firing on them with the machine guns. Our guys were really mowed down; the major falls, the adjutant general falls, a lieutenant, a cadet, four sergeants, and about eighty soldiers. And this was for me the first time that I see a battle field in all its horror; it gives me a feeling that I can never be free from for the rest of my life. . . . In a little open space for the coal burning we're making a grave: The work is hard and long because five hand-widths beneath the surface is rock.

July 17

A hard day for us: We bring to the dug grave fifty-four corpses: four officials, Maj. Alisieri Cavalryman Nicola, Adjutant gen. Enzo Ferraioli, Lt. Andrea Simonelli, cadet Pugliesi: four sub-officials Sgt. Bellavia, Pellegrini, Camusso, Bolla and forty-six soldiers. We disinfect the ground thoroughly and make the air breathable.

July 18

We work to improve the looks of #1.

July 19

We continue with the work described above and move to cemetery 2 made by diggers from the 134th infantry. #9 corpses of unknown soldiers: we even begin cemetery #3.

July 20

We finish cemetery #3 and put into it the corpses of three unknowns. We continue the hard work of moving earth and of improving cemetery #1.

July 21

We prepare the dirt and the rocks for #2: it's very hard and tiring work and that requires a lot of time.

July 22

We finish the wall of cemetery #1. We're going to dig up eleven corpses, but we have to stop on account of the intense bombardment, ours and the enemy's. The racket is frightening: This huge quantity of iron is dispatched to Summit 11, Summit 12, and on Mt. Chiesa. I've never seen or heard anything like it.

July 23

We transport eleven corpses to cemetery #2. The cemetery is thus filled, with twenty corpses, all unknowns.

July 24

It's raining. Mandatory rest.

July 25

We finish #1 and move nine corpses of unknowns to #3 making it full.

July 26

The section commander Lt De Alessandri comes to see the completed work; he is very pleased. The cemetery in fact you could call it perfect. It takes up forty square meters of land — the height of the dirt over the corpses is a meter and sixty centimeters. It's surrounded with two sets of fences: After you enter you see on the right the major's tomb and the adjutant general's tomb. On the left are the tombs of the other officials: These four tombs are in stone. They have a cross over them made of moss and at the head of each a rustic cross with the names written burned into a small wooden board. In the middle of the cemetery there is a passage and on both sides two rectangles with mossed sides. In the middle of these three more crosses of moss. At the end of the walkway is erected a small stone monument with an artistic headstone that bears the words, "To the heroes of the 134th infantry, the nation, June 19, 1916." More under twentieth disinfection subdivision. Behind the monument is a rough cross.

August 8

We're beginning a new cemetery. The hellish battery hits you hard on the road, and the shrill whistles pass us very close by and over our heads. Moresa and Croso are leaving.

August 9

We're moving six corpses into ten or so tombs; these contain a large number of Austrians. Given that they are dead, it's just as well that they are theirs . . .

August 11

We are moving twenty corpses: fourteen Austrians and six Italians. Two of the Austrians were wearing medals. I took one, and Capt. Della Giovanna took the other. One of the corpses is Rifleman Giuseppe Acuto.

August 12

We move seventeen corpses of unknowns. Sixteen Italians and one Austrian. In an Austrian tomb I find a rifle and a nice thermos, which I give to Lt. Tabusso?!?!

Francesco Giuliani, shepherd and laborer, was born in Castel del Monte (L'Aquila) in 1890. He attended the first years of grade school but then continued on his own, reading and teaching himself. Called up to the army on May 15, 1915, he was assigned to the 13th Regiment infantry. By May 24, he was already in the war zone. In May 1916 he would be transferred to the Asiago highlands. Giuliani was the author of a complete memoir, in the form of diaries, poetry, reflections and subsequent thoughts on the war.

This short descent from the trenches down to the ruins of Selz was completely abandoned and scattered with corpses, who evoked nothing but horror and disgust and to remember so many days of blood, so many that the new fear adds itself to the old. Where you saw a skull, a shinbone, a spine, a complete skeleton, and yet there was no one who thought to collect and bury them. There were still some pieces of Austrian fence from the defense of the first trench, and in the iron spikes you could see again entire skeletons snagged where the sun had dried them, like those insects that fall into the spider's web. The whole plain to the slopes of Karst, from Monfalcone to Redipuglia was a field of the dead, if each grave had had its own cross, it would have been an endless cemetery. Beyond the one at San Polo, at Ronchi, at Selz, at

Vermigliano, at Redipuglia, at Monfalcone: On the entire plain you found crosses that signaled graves. In the garden of a railway tollbooth by San Polo there were buried some of the fallen from the first days of the war, from the 13th infantry. Then when you see those tombs again and on the crosses some withered flowers placed there by pious hands.

The first dead can almost be envied because at least they didn't suffer; instead the poor survivors, rescued from a thousand dangers, suffering miserably, every so often remember and miss their old friends, and in the end who knows which patch of land was destined for our poor bones.

Alongside the last houses in San Polo by the side of the road leading to Aris, there were buried several who fell in the final days of June, and little by little it became a vast cemetery and each grave with its cross and all nicely laid out.

In those fields I encountered the graves of so many I knew and of friends fallen in the first phase, and then going over again the sad events my heart was pained.

In a vineyard in front of the military villa, in the space between the rows of the vines were buried the remains of fifteen fallen; on the crosses were written their names and the regiments they served in. A lovely garden in Ronchi was turned into a cemetery bringing together all those who died in a medical treatment facility. There were many sleeping their last sleep under those shady trees.

Nothing was left of Selz besides ruins, rarely someone saw a wall still standing and threatening to topple over. There wasn't a single day that the Austrians didn't fire. A walkway traversed the ruins, and when I had to walk along it, I was assailed not only by fear but also by the saddest memories of what all I had seen around those ruins.

Annibale Calderale was born in Monopoli (Bari) in 1895. He attended technical schools and went to work at the Italcementi company in Monopoli. In June of 1915 he was called up to service in the 4th Regiment rifle corps in Naples. On August 30, 1916, he was promoted to sergeant and moved to the machine gun unit. On May 1, 1917 he reached Karst.

May 24, 1917

Sometimes I have had the good luck to be able to rest in a tunnel, just below the front line, but it was a different suffering. Even if it was good luck to be able to stay sheltered from death, the heavy uniforms, all armed (1 pistol, a faceted dagger with three corners, ammunition), a gas mask, a rucksack with bombs, and all the other accessories, piled one on top of the other, impossible to breathe, that was an indescribable suffering. Sometimes not being able to go on, feeling like I was suffocating I thought about leaving the tunnel and going outside, but outside death was waiting in ambush and I gave up the idea. I was full of fleas, and these insects really bothered me. There were even so many mice (rats), I was about to say tamed ones, that would go back and forth among us; it was said that they didn't eat cheese and instead feasted on corpses. The food rations arrived every day between 10 pm and midnight. In the days it didn't make it, it meant that the transport carrying the food had been hit in the zone behind the front. The food rations consisted of a ration of pasta in broth cooked around 4 pm but arriving warm in casserole dishes hermetically sealed in a piece of boiled meat that arrived in burlap bags, a loaf of bread, a cup of coffee also warm, on occasion some pieces of cheese and a bit of wine, all of it just once a day: From time to time they would distribute some cigars and a few cigarettes.

The water ration consisted of a half liter a day. One time, in the containers for water that they use to cool the machine-gun barrels, there wasn't even a drop of water; it was all drunk. To avoid surprises like that they had to add gasoline to that water.

During my time in the trenches I didn't bathe on account of lack of water, never shaved, my uniform is in shreds, I am exhausted, discouraged, agitated I need absolute calm tranquility to get myself back . . .

June 14, 1917

A calm day.

The stench a corpse emits after sitting abandoned in the field five or six warm days is strong and penetrating. I've seen soldiers leave the trenches voluntarily, risking their lives just to move the corpses . . .

September 25, 1917

From position 144 we moved to the second line, around 200 meters from the front line, in valley just to the right of Comarie, a ruined village, there remained a little fountain which was very helpful for quenching our thirst. It's located in a valley facing Mt. Hermada; we told the 259th infantry battalion Major Murgie of the change. A rifleman from the province of Avellino was assigned to our company; he's about thirty-seven and has a large family. While we were getting used to the zone of operations he was complaining the whole time, he couldn't resign himself to his plight and, with his lugubrious way of talking he brought down morale that typically was high. At that point the second line was left undefended by troops. At the front there was calm, and everyone chose his post, without giving a care. The Rifleman right from the start distanced himself from the Group when taking care of his bodily needs: A grenade landed on our line, no one paid attention to it. On the next morning it was noted that that grenade had hit and killed the aforementioned Rifleman who was there in the combat zone for the first time. I have become aware that the fearful people risk their lives more than others because they miss the opportunity of calm times, they hesitate, they lose precious time before making themselves safe. After the first period, I never moved in the zone without first picking a new place to get myself settled.

Chapter 7.
The Assault

In war diaries and in subsequent memoirs, the assault on the enemy positions takes on central significance: It is the revelatory moment, it is the heart of the combatant's experience. Those who write about it give it the most tension possible, or on the contrary they fear its indescribability and decide not to write about it, in a contract of silence.

Filippo Animelli, for example, distills the descriptions of an assault carried out on the mountains of Asiago to a few lines: "In the morning of the 19th [of June 1916] at 2 o'clock I hear my name called in such a manner that my blood was already telling me everything that needed to happen in that moment having just woken up the head of the squadron calls his squadron and explains to us everything that happened and says cartridge rounds and reserve food rations in the rucksacks and loaded rifle and trowel in the belt and advance on tiptoes one at a time behind me, not even 150 meters after the first step we unsheathe our bayonets and attach them to the rifle. I was confused at that moment and then it occurred to me that the only thing it could be was an assault, my friends and I decided that at the shout of *Savoia* we had to act like we were crazed."[1]

The frontal assault, the decisive event of a strategy of driving stubbornly on offense, begins with the bombardment of enemy lines, which should demolish, at least partly, the adversary's position and open a gap in the dense fencing that protects them. But frequently the bombing doesn't cause damage that significantly affects the Austrian defensive system. Nevertheless the Italian infantry go on the attack in solid formations on disadvantageous terrain, usually ascending, under the fire of machine guns and cannon. They halt in

---
1 Animelli Filippo, p. 35.

front of the fences, regroup, and return to the attack. When they succeed in reaching the trenches of the enemy they need to defend them from repeated counterattacks. Other times they try to create a line of defense at the bases of the fence, or else they turn back to their own trenches. The action takes place with few variations until the depletion of the units and then recommences with new troops.[2] The obstacle of the fencing can also be managed by means of wire-cutting pincers, which oblige the soldier to come out in the open field and in broad daylight, or else with metal tubes filled with explosives dragged right under the prickly wire and exploded with a fuse.

"Now there are tubes of explosive gelatin," observes one of the veterans of Salsa. "But what difference does that make? The orders are still the same. You place the tubes at night. You think that they're bound to make the attack soon, right? In order to take advantage of the confusion and the shock. That's what you think! You need to wait until dawn in order to realize what the effects are and in order to determine a direction. By God, it takes a bit of order. So that the Austrians had all the time and opportunity in the world to place a machine gun right in the open gap, sure that it will be put to good use there."

The tragic experience of the assault has been amply recounted in war literature. This page from Emilio Lussu is rightly famous:

"'Ready for the attack!' the captain repeated again. Of all the moments in the war, the one just before the attack is the most terrible.

"The assault! Where did it go? They abandoned their positions and left. Where? The machine guns, all of them, lying with their bellies stuffed with ammunition, they were waiting for us. Who doesn't know those moments knows nothing of the war. The words of the captain fell like an axe blow. The 9th

---

[2] They are citing, indirectly, the volumes by Isnenghi and Rochat, *La Grande Guerra 1914-1918* cit., pp. 165-182, and of Fabi, *Gente di trincea* cit., pp. 59-61.

was on their feet, but I didn't see anything, they were leaning on the walls of the trenches. Two soldiers moved, and I saw them, one next to the other, fixing his rifle under his chin. One bent over, got off a shot, and crouched down, the other one imitated him and fell down next to the first. Was it cowardice? Courage? Madness? The first one was a veteran of Karst.

"'Savoia!' Capt. Bravini shouted.

'Savoia!' the unit.

It was a cry shouted out like a lament and also like a desperate plea."[3]

Augusto Gaddo, laborer, was born in Sardegna (Trento) in 1889. In August 1914 he was called up to the Austro-Hungarian army. In July of 1915 he was at Karst.

July 1915

The evening of the third day I go to the kitchens to carry a big empty cauldron and I see a group of officials who are talking; I listen a bit and understand that we will leave very shortly. On my way back I run into the first regiment of Landesschutzen[4] sent to the front. I go to my friends and say to them, "My dears, get ready for them to call us soon."

In fact, within an hour there came the yell, "Alarm!" We lined up, we got in a circle, and we put a priest in the middle, who gave a blessing and told us to do our duty as patriots.

It's an extremely dark night, they take us up via cliffs, piles of stones, across thorny bushes: All night we walk in the middle of those rocks. Around midday they take us down a road and close to 4 o'clock we cross our own artillery, and there begins

---
3 E. Lussu, *Un anno sull'Altipiano*. Turin: Einaudi, 2014, p. 105.
4 Naturally, nothing to do with the Alpinist troops in the Italian army; soldiers enlisted in the three mountain regiments of the Austrian army (*Landesschutzen*) were also called this.

a very steep road that leads to St. Martino Hill, between Gorizia and Monfalcone. Just as we are beginning the ascent the Austrian artillery starts to bombard the Italian. The Italian artillery on their side responds and gets some good results. Shrapnel hits a German right away, blowing him back ten meters. Our position was horrendous, luckily the road led to some country walls, so we threw ourselves under them and particularly for the shrapnel it was sufficient cover. Just then a company of Italian soldiers turned themselves in, quite happily, saying, "Hey, dammit! We killed our captain, we threw away our packs and our rifles and turn ourselves in."

In the darkening of the evening we line up again and the priest gives us a blessing; he gives us a short lecture and then says, "Soldiers, the position is horrendous; remember your oath."

Then for each two guys they make us carry a chest of munitions and they forward it to us close to the summit. Once we reach the summit, we arrange ourselves behind a wall, above which a road passed and below it was forest. They issue the command that that night we stay there, always ready to fight hand-to-hand.

All night the artillery continues to bombard and the grenades had a triple effect because each grenade sent a cartload of stones flying into the air.

In the morning we saw what our position was: To the right we could see below the city of Gorizia, but we didn't have time to look around very much because they were still bombarding. If it wasn't the grenades bothering us, it was the rocks. In fact every grenade that exploded, and some were exploding even twenty or thirty meters from us, after a few minutes from its exploding we'd get a hail of rocks on and around us.

> That Karst of Trieste
> Is the position of Cain
> Where a grenade explodes
> In the middle of the company and still isn't satisfied
> All that's left of the earth is a shovel
> For burying yourself
> Of thirst and bellyache
> By now we have to die.

It's true that all we get to drink is a half liter of water and even that arrives via mule from three hours away, and it doesn't even come every day. It's just a half-liter of water because during the journey the mules got hit my cannon fire and: so long, water. In our regiment cholera started appearing and the regiment's doctor advised the colonel to get us away from there, from that position.

Giuseppe Garzoni was born in Buia (Udine) in 1888, where he attended only the first two years of elementary school. He emigrated then to Germany, going to work in the brick factory. He was called up in May 1915 and was sent to the 6th Regiment riflemen.

Diary of the events of the army begun on September 18, 1915

In the evening of the 17th, the 1st, 4th, and 5th companies received the order to take up a position called Rovenichk, a position strongly held by the enemy, who controlled the entire wide plain where our trenches were. Because of a miscalculation on the part of our chief of staff, it was believed that the enemy forces were scarce, and as a consequence it was thought we could occupy the positions easily.

That night we came out of the trenches and advanced until we got to just below the fences, which were formidable and thirty meters long. The position was a summit that jutted out, 10,000 feet, formidably defended with three trenches forming a tunnel invisible from a distance. Also two mountain batteries, one to the right and the other to the left, we stayed nailed to the trenches, in the daytime I couldn't even lift my head.

Around 4 o'clock, the company having come up close, the enemy shone powerful rays of light down, which permitted them to see all our maneuvers. The first patrols with the explosive gel arrived below and placed the tubes beneath the fences, lighting the fuses. The tubes exploded thunderously, throwing into the air a portion of the immense prickly tangle. Then the officials gave the order to attack. With a formidable cry we jump up to ascend. But as soon as we got within a couple dozen meters of the enemy, who up to now had not given any sign of life apart from a few rifle shots, threw down on us tremendous machine gun fire, obliging us to pull back and look for shelter to get away from those murderous barrage.

With spades and fingernails we try to dig holes to shelter in. But we were too much out in the open, seen from all angles all around this extended plain, and our trenches were behind us five to ten meters, there was no way to retreat to them because the machine gunning was ripping up the ground.

The enemy, guessing our movements in the night, had positioned eighteen machine guns and our three companies were thrown into a real tomb that was impossible to escape from.

Immediately once the sun began to come up the desperate situation greeted our eyes. The officials encouraged us, but they were the more discouraged than anyone. Once it was properly daytime a terrifying spectacle could be seen. The wounded were writhing, begging for help. We couldn't move to help them. The Austrians in their trenches were on guard and if any of us moved he would have been immediately shot, and at that distance, there was no way they could miss.

It was a tragic and desperate situation for the 6th rifle corps, which for four months on the front line knew only victory. Around 6:00 in the morning on September 18 an Austrian soldier yelled in Italian, "Riflemen surrender." Our officials responded no. He said it again. Seeing that no one was surrendering, a tragedy commenced that in the minds of all who survived will last as an indelible memory.

The artillery and the machine guns fired flat out. In a short amount of time the number of wounded and dead became considerable. The Austrians stopped firing and said to us: "Surrender and take your wounded and bring them here. Don't die like this. You can see that there is no escape for you."

The wounded men began to yell, "Comrades, surrender! Otherwise there's no way out." These were piteous cries that would have moved even a heart of stone. Then began the surrender. We moved up, dropping our weapons, and bringing with us our wounded men. The Austrians came down with stretchers helping us and making sure that no one was shot. Lines of enemy soldiers and officials arrived and all of them gave us a hand, treating us in a courteous and gentlemanly manner.

One lieutenant wounded in the stomach being carried on a stretcher passed in front of an Austrian official. The official makes them put down the stretcher, and he greets the man with noble words. They give us cigarettes, cigars, and tobacco. And we, who didn't have anything to exchange for them, give them the feathers from our caps, our stars, and some canteens, that for them was cherished.

The evening of the 18th toward 9:00 we leave. After three hours of marching we arrive in a town where they hand out bread, cans of meat in jelly, and then they accompany us to a field all surrounded by wire and they leave us there to sleep. The next day they pass out coffee and then we march. Around 5:00 we get to the summit of the mountain where we find many Russian prisoners who were working on the road. We stop there and they give us bread and another can of meat. After an hour we leave again. We descend for another eight kilometers, arriving at Cronsi, where we find a train ready and immediately we depart for Villach. At midnight we get off the train and they bring us to a nice barracks where we stretch out on the straw. After four months of war it's the first night where we can take off our shoes and sleep on some straw. Then they give us some bread and coffee.

In the morning we get up and go to wash our faces it's been two months since I washed myself. Around 9:00 we quickly get together by rank and they bring us to the headquarters where there is a General Command and where many officials are, who speak with courtesy in a questioning way. Many of them had cameras and were taking pictures.

Having gone through the review, they bring us to a barracks where they give us bread, polenta, and cheese. An hour later, we leave and go to the station, where we depart for Klagenfurt. Once we arrive there, they put us in comfortable and well-made barracks. There was hay here too and with quite a few lice. I end here my writing and my report. I am a prisoner with all my fellows at arms hoping sincerely that this terrible scourge in Europe will end which throws into grief so many poor mothers and wives, etc. May peace come from which all peoples will derive satisfaction. Only then will we have the lasting and sincere peace that we all need and the world will return to its civil institutions of work and progress.

Carlo Franzelli was born in Roccafranca (Brescia) in 1895. He was called up to the 30th Regiment infantry. He died in a camp hospital on December 24, 1915.

From the trenches, December 9, 1915

Dear Esteemed Mr. Costanzo

Today with much pleasure and contentment I received the package you considerately sent me. I don't know how to thank you, because to tell you the truth those articles were as necessary to me as bread, because in this accursed place it is very cold and to tell the truth it is fifty days I've been in the line of fire and sixty days that I have been subjected to the damp day and night. Now every day we await the change, and I tell you the truth that a struggle like this not even a dog deserves.

My very dear esteemed Mr. Costanzo, now I will tell you a bit about what I did on November 20. On the 20th our colonel ordered us to advance, to go to the assault on a trench, and we went straight away, there were fifty-two of us and when we got to the position below the trench there only seven, while the others were all killed. We stayed there eleven hours under the enemy trench until my company managed to make a pathway out and saved me, but Soldier Franzelli is always brave.

Mr. Costanzo, before the war started everyone was yelling, "Hooray for the war." But now that soldiers are falling like flies we yell, "Hooray for Peace." But instead Soldier Franzelli never falters, always courage, and if I don't die I will get a medal.

When I go to shout, "Savoia" it's understood that the Austrians are afraid because I have a long beard like a giant, I have an iron cap on my head, I am muddied up to the eyes, I am covered with fleas like a pig. But what's left to do? Always, "Forward! Savoia!" Bye.

Having nothing further to say to you, I will simply salute you and thank you, and I sign myself,

One of your townsmen Carlo Franzelli

Forgive my bad handwriting and my bad letter and forgive me for not being able to make myself understood. Meanwhile, I salute you sincerely and thank you once again.

Always forward.

Please do me the favor of greeting Mr. Pepi Alfiere, the Bellinis, and Mr. Biggio Grumello.

Francesco Dotta, farmer, was born in Miella Belbo (Cuneo) in 1896. He was drafted in 1915 to the 34th Regiment infantry and, after a period of instruction in Turin, in March 1916 he was sent to the front in the Monte Sabotino zone. Two months later (May 12, 1916) he was at the front at Trento and took part in the offense of Monte Maggio. Here he was captured by the Austrians and deported to a prisoner of war camp in Sigmundsherberg (Lower Austria).

1916

They left us in that town until the 25th of April 1916 and then — grab your pack and go — we went three or more hours on our way to return to the Udine station. Here we boarded the train with the 201st, 202nd, 206th, and 207th regiments of the Sesia Brigade. They had switched fronts. We went back to Vicenza and then the railroad line changed and went to Asiago toward Trentino. The train took us as far as the station at Thiene, at the foot of the high Trentino mountains, and the train stopped there. We got off and started on foot again to a nearby town called Malo. There too was all right, but they didn't give us much time; the days seemed to shorten; the Austrians were preparing for an enormous attack.[5] And we were in that town just eighteen days waiting to leave for the front line. And so we get to the night of May 12, 1916. We started to be able to hear a constant sound when we were sleeping, and we'd wake up and say to one another, "What is that loud noise?" And

---

5 This deals with the Strafexpedition that begins on May 15 and overwhelmingly succeeds initially; at the beginning of June the Austrians advance north to Valsugana, to the center of the Asiago plain, to the southwest in Val d'Astico, Vallarsa, and Val Lagarina. Cfr. Isnenghi-Rochat, *La Grande Guerra 1914-1918* cit., pp. 188-194.

we couldn't sleep anymore and we had to spend that night worrying. On the morning of the 13th upon getting up and going outside we could hear from the direction of the front a sound that never let up of cannon and shrapnel and machine guns. And the trucks from that day were lined up like pearls on a necklace to come to the town and bring food and munitions and soldiers and to bring them to the front, and on that day the 14th and the night after the streets were filled with soldiers and trucks doing nothing but heading to the front. The enemy meantime raged pitilessly one more time. After various regiments of infantry, alpine soldiers, riflemen, and artillery had gone to the front lines on the morning of the 15th, before dawn also the 201st regiment, to which I belonged, was ready to depart. The trucks arrived in just a few hours, and then we ourselves were taken to the slaughterhouse, which is to say the front lines. And up there on those mountains at 3,500 and higher meters,[6] the only thing we could see was rocks and quantities of snow and we, who were not trained at all to defend positions and barely trained for war in any sense, we felt powerfully disturbed.

At the same time the enemy's large-caliber artillery were all going full force, and we had to take cover as best we could, behind rocks, but the day of the 15th, with a continual shaking in our hearts, passed without the order to fire.

You come in during the night, everything looks sadder, the enemy was advancing and we had to get in the trenches and get some shelter. And in that night there was not a minute of respite and the enemy lookouts were on the slopes, the artillery never stopped bombing, not even for a moment. Before it was even daylight the order came to move to the left some hundred meters and that position there was rather more cover

---

[6] The altitude in that sector of the mountains reaches almost 2,000 meters, but maybe seen from the plains of Veneto even these modest mountains can cause some fear.

and we saw with the naked eye in the morning of the 16th at a distance of about 1,500 meters the enemy infantry who were advancing on all fours in those rocky and snowy positions.

And before the sun got high in the sky a tremendous offensive began that lasted the entire day and the following night and they gave us the order to quickly fire one can say twenty-four hours without any interruption until the munitions arrived. And on that day we heard cries coming from every direction and cannon fire and machine guns, ours and the enemy's and we didn't understand anything that was going on, and I found myself there, after a few hours of combat in the middle of that slaughterhouse. I had just one friend in my company who was completely healthy, and that gave me courage and before the offensive had died down even he was killed close to me. At . . . that terrible point I found myself, you can't imagine the anguish that I had in my heart, but even sadder hours came later, toward morning, before dawn of the 17th of May, 1916, a day that I will remember until my head leaves my neck.

The offensive ended on that mountain called Monte Maggio, more than 3,500 meters[7] high. After some hours of silence I heard far away our captain calling our company, ordering us to fall back to the right, and I did everything I could but I couldn't do it in time because the zone behind the front were so filled with enemy soldiers that I would have had to go around the whole mountain before daylight.

Here, now we are at the saddest moment, the one in which I find myself in the first hours of the morning. Before dawn came I heard foreign languages and there were enemy soldiers who were going by slowly, place by place, slowly slowly over the whole terrain to see if anyone was left alive. They came

---

7 Mt. Maggio (1,853 meters), in the southeast Trentino, dominates the Val Posina in Veneto.

close to me; one pointed a bayonet at my stomach, others aimed daggers and pistols at me with the intention of killing me. They had disarmed me and after had taken me among them and after about a hundred meters of walking they had captured other Italian soldiers. We were then around a dozen and they put us in the midst of them and there those Germans, armed to the teeth, seemed all to be lions that wanted to tear us apart, one who tore off our stars, one our cloak, one who spat on us, one who hit us with his gun, all sorts of trouble, and as for us, we dared not speak. And the ugly thing was that we couldn't understand and as we went along the road little by little they gathered thousands and thousands of prisoners and took us down to the valley of Trento.

Antonio Graziani, manual laborer, was born in 1895 in Belricetto (Lugo di Romagna, Ravenna province). Recruited into the 114th Regiment infantry he was sent at first to Trentino: In May of 1916 he worked in Lagarina, between Monte Baldo and Monte Zugna. In October of 1916 he was transferred to the front of Karst. He died in circumstances that are unclear on June 7, 1918.

October 1916

At daybreak we get to a town called Redipuglia which is under the Monte Sei Busi. To take a rest, I sit down under a tree; just then it began to rain. During the day we made up the tents, and we understood we were there to take part in an operation. I looked around pretty well, and all I saw were cemeteries. And I went up to the top of Monte Sei Busi and went down into a trench that was filled with corpses already decomposing. I said to myself, "I've come to this place to end life." Several days of bad weather passed.

October 24 arrives and it's a beautiful sunshiny day. That was how the enemy discovered our encampment. Suddenly five or six cannon went off and wounded thirty-two Italian soldiers and killed five of them. I took off and for the rest of the day didn't go near the tents. During the night we changed the location of the camp.

The evening of October 31 arrives, we depart for the action. We walk through the night filled with the thought that we're on the way to death. We arrive at a trench over Doberdo in the third line; there we spend the rest of the night.

The morning of the Saints Day, November 1, the advance begins.[8] Between our cannon and the hits that come in, you can't understand anything that's going on. That's where we had the first wounded. At 1 in the afternoon the order comes to move on to the valley of Case Bonetti.[9] Then after a long trip we arrive to the place. But every minute I was expecting to take some cannon fire, because no one could tell anything that was going on, between the shots going out and those coming in.

I begin to see a vast number of wounded who look like they come from the regiments that were in the advance. Among them there were some with a broken arm, some with half a face missing, one was yelling one place another further on was looking for the medicine dispensary. I was gripped by fear. In the evening we had to go up to the front lines, up to elevation 208, relieving those few soldiers from the 141st Regiment still remaining. Upon arriving at the elevation but not yet at the position, hell broke loose. The adversary counterattacked our lines with a terrible bombardment; grenades were exploding and bullets from every direction, you heard the wounded cry out and some jumped in the air. I was running, walking over the dead and on top of those who were crying. I didn't know

---

8 On November 1, 1916, the ninth Battle of Isonzo began. (November 1-4.)
9 On the shores of Lago di Doberdò.

where to go to save myself. I'd lost my head. When I calmed myself a bit I reached the front line, the bullets were whistling, but walking down on all fours I felt a bit more protected. The enemy continued the shooting and bombing. The day of November 2, the Day of the Dead, at 11 a.m. they told us that at 2:00 we had to go on the assault. How sorrowful those three hours were! My heart was pounding, and I said to myself, "Now I'm in the world, but in a little while I'll be among the stones! At least it might happen that I'll get killed by a shot."

The officials had their watches synchronized on the assigned hour. At exactly 2:00 our artillery stopped the bombardment momentarily. We, with our bayonets already attached, were ready for death. The colonel was up, and we followed him at the cry of "Savoia!" I lost all reason, finding myself in the midst of the inferno. The colonel fell, wounded. We could no longer hear the officials. Soldiers were falling like pears. We got to the enemy trenches: Several Germans were giving themselves up. Their trenches were filled with corpses. We found we were very few of us and without any officers to command us. Then the enemy benefited from it all. We made a retreat back to our old lines. In the retreat the second line were shooting over our backs, the Austrians were returning the fire, and I didn't know where to jump. I passed by several wounded who were on the ground, wailing and they couldn't get up. Finally I reached our line.

Giuseppe Capacci, farmer, was born in Monterchi (Arezzo) in 1895. Assigned to the 8th Regiment infantry, at the end of September 1915 he was sent to the front at Trentino, to Passo del Tonale. In the spring of 1916 he is transferred to the eastern front. In June he was in the front line in the zone of Monfalcone.

Karst, October 4, 1916

We got to the third line, a covered trench; we set up there. "Tomorrow we'll see something!" That was my lieutenant. Later on, some others came looking for us; they were in the same trench; we got together. In the morning we went to Bertoiba, in the evening at 3:00 we were to go on the attack; at 11:00 the bombardment was to begin. While we were waiting, we were saying to one another that our company was the fourth wave: That cheered us up a bit. It's better to be the last than the first. . . . Then they call me, they call you two per squadron, they take us there to see the captain: They chose us as demolishers; they took the oldest ones. They gave us wire cutters, four bombs per each, our nine cartridge packs, gun, cartridge cases and a big shield against the machine guns. You couldn't even walk with all that stuff.

I said to myself, "Yes, I'm off to the attack; so they'll grab me by the bag!"

My mind was all upset, I was getting chills thinking that this awful job was up to me: I was positive I would not come back unharmed.

"If I have to cut the wires," I was thinking, "if the reserve troops aren't ready, just us few, we can't defend ourselves. Then there are four companies coming behind us. But we'll be the ones who go into their trenches first!" It seemed to me I was destined to end my life forever!

We went directly to the first line, crouched down, awaiting the bombing; the day seemed to me melancholy: There was no sun, everything was quiet. The machine guns were ready, the mine-launcher too. The colonel, the major looked over the positions and then the colonel went back to his command: Then they started the bombing, to our right, in front of San Michele, as far as the sea. They told us that first we would have to advance to there. We were waiting minute by minute for the bombing to begin there too; but 11:00 had come and gone. The weather turned bad, and then it began to rain hard. So, they were beginning to think, "We'll suspend the assault." We put cloths over our heads; I was crouched down on the banks of the river that went between the first and the second line; the water was rising. We needed to move, meanwhile I was totally soaked.

In those days one wasn't behaving like good Christians. When people had to piss, they didn't pay any attention to the river. Actually, it was a pleasure to piss in the water. But later when some others were thirsty they'd take these lovely glasses of murky water, full of all kinds of flavors. You drank it like beer; nobody cared about anything in those days!

Meanwhile, 1 o'clock had come and there were no shots in that location; then came the order that the assault had been suspended. The breakers went back to their companies. At those words I felt as though I were coming out from under an impossibly heavy load; I thanked the good Lord; I thought about my family, as though I had come back to life. I can't explain everything that my heart was feeling in that fatal moment: I felt like a condemned man and then like one who is pardoned.

Alessandro Amaduzzi, cobbler, was born on March 26, 1887 in San Vittore. He was enlisted to serve in the 2nd Regiment infantry. He died on November 2, 1918, in a camp hospital number 0157 after suffering from pneumonia.

August 14, 1916

Dear Wife,

I'm responding to your letter and I see that you are well as are your parents also and as I am able to assure you I am at present. Now I want to make sure you know that yesterday I wrote you a postcard where I told you that I left on the 9th and came to Monte Maio.[10] So, we got here the night of the 9th and immediately the next morning they sent us up to make the attack.

First, the artillery did some bombing and then they let us go up; it was actually our company who went up ahead, and even more it was our platoon that took the lead. So, we went up via a gorge with high rocks and we came close to their barbed-wire fences: It could have been around 5:00, and we still hadn't heard a gunshot. Then the order came to cut the fence to make the assault on their trenches, but as soon as we got there to cut the fences, the Austrians began to shoot at us and to bombard us with bombs that seemed to be 305s and that threw stones up that must have weighed 100 kilos each. Who could save themselves under fire like that? No one. At the moment of the great disaster, the soldiers jumped in the air almost all of them did it and those poor guys were left fucked up there; I threw myself on the ground hidden behind a small boulder and said to myself: "I want to stay here; so be it, if they fuck me." I raised myself a bit and I saw that not far from me there were another four soldiers, and they too were trying to think of how to get out of this situation.

---

10 Mt. Maio (1,499 meters) is on the left of Val Posina, to the northeast of Pasubio.

I looked at where I needed to go: Those men on the ground seemed to me to be all either dead or wounded. I said to myself: "Oh, God, poor Alessandro, this time I am not going to make it!" I didn't know what to do: I didn't want to go out in the open, but I had to leave because the Austrians had begun launching huge bombs that were exploding close to me. Suddenly I hear that they aren't shooting anymore, and so I got up and ran away, as much as I was able to run. They began shooting again right away, the bullets whistled around me all around, so much so that I lost any hope of remaining unharmed. But instead luckily I remained OK, but it will be difficult to always have such luck, let's hope I do. Anyway, there's nothing we can do: We're sold to the butcher shop and so we have to go to the butcher shop. What villains they are! To murder so many poor people in this way! Well, enough. Best not to think of it; if I think too much about it I'll be dead. As far as what you said about your brother: I understand everything you've said, but what do you want to do? You must always stay brave. Tell your father that he mustn't always think the worst, because if your brother is a prisoner it could easily take even two months to write, as so many others have been delayed. All that's left for me to do is to send you sincere greetings and kisses to you and to your parents, greetings to all, your Alessandro goodbye.

Pietro Ferrari was born in Vaiano Cremasco (Cremona). He was drafted into the 26th Regiment infantry, 13th company. During the entire period of the conflict he kept a detailed diary. In September of 1917 he found himself in the zone of Monfalcone.

September 4, 1917

This morning we're going to instruction, but an order brings us back to the camp. I, sensing something ugly, run to greet my friend Francesco Vailati. I tell him something's happening, he gives me courage, he tells me to go with him to eat our rations, that we should drink some wine together.

I get back to my company and see that everyone's lined up. I foresee bad things and, setting down my pack, kissing the photograph of my kids and then putting in the pack, I go line up with the rest of the company.

Around 10:00 we left, down the road we could see in the dry ditches many magazines of cartridges thrown there by soldiers along the way, we went through Ronchi and got to the piazza in Selz, we took the road going off to the right. The town was all dilapidated and where the roads branch off is where you know there is a piazza, and all that remains of it is a big plant, really just the massive trunk, because the branches were all broken off and contorted by cannon fire.

We go around the flank of the lake in Pietrarossa and at about 2:00 in the afternoon we get to the secured trenches of Velechi Debeli.

We are made to enter this trench, which extended just up to the low hill covered with rocks and brambles.

The food comes in the evening; we haven't been able to eat since before we left. It's distributed, and so we are able to eat. I lie down along the trench to see if I am able to sleep because I was tired. When, close to midnight, I hear that they're calling me, I see that they are distributing the portable bombs, of which they give me four, two ballerinas and two sipes.

Then we got out of the trench and in line one by one we proceeded again down the road and reached the sinkhole.

Here I smelled an odor of death that turned my stomach. Once we all came together well enough they make us walk around on the side of the hill, because on our left it was all protected by a low wall in the Greek style for protecting the soldiers from grenades that the Austrians continued to hurl before them.

I made this walk in jumps from side to side, moving at every grenade blast; the route was planted with the wounded and the dead. Along the way I encountered German prisoners who were calmly going back the other way.

Completely out of breath, sweaty and in pain, I reach a sinkhole where there was a tunnel or large cave where they were tending to the wounded, and outside there were corpses laid out on stretchers ready to be taken to the cemetery.

I look around there with sadness, and I think that maybe, who knows if I might be among those laid out on a stretcher as well.

We stop for a few minutes. I believed that we had reached our destination, but instead, we continued on. We went back to ascending the mountain, the Ermada, ugly and destitute and to see it at night throwing sinister shadows that arouse disgust. We went along a path that had been totally disarranged by grenades, and in the dark we lose our connection.

We stop for a little bit to reorient ourselves and, reestablishing our connections to one another, we proceed.

What horror! Walking on that trail so often destroyed by grenades, two or three times I stepped on the belly of poor dead soldiers who'd been buried by the landslide of the land, moved and moved again by the nonstop grenade fire that the living made to explode. Beneath the weight of my body, it having been a while since they died, several days, they burst and the step squirted me in the face, leaving me covered in an unbearable stench. At the end of the path we had to speed up because we were out in the open and we got to a little rise in the mountain, where there were little cabins made of wood and stone.

We stop here a few minutes, and I had already formulated the intention to stay the night there, counting myself lucky to be a bit recovered and fixed up. A buzzing and then some voices tell us to keep going. And so we do and speeding up a bit we find some soldiers from the 89th infantry and no sooner had we joined them than we took their stuff and they said to us that we were taking over, they returned back the other way. It was thus that I understood I was on the front line.

Chapter 8.
Killing the Enemy

The tragic circumstance of the soldier who, constrained to live in the chaotic landscape of battle, takes on the role of combatant, becoming a victim and butcher at the same time, is, as we will see, clearly present in memoirs and not only working-class ones. Also tragic are the limitations imposed by the officers, limitations that extended from direct control over the soldiers to a paternalistic or, depending on the case, authoritarian indoctrination.

The case of Captain Fracchia, related by Mario Puccini, one of the officer-writers most sensitive to the future of the ordinary soldier, seems to us illuminating for several reasons:

"Have you ever killed with this bayonet?"
The soldier looked at him without responding.
"A throat, a belly, have you gotten to know them, son?"
"Sir, no."
"Have you ever gone on an assault?"
"Five times."
"And the Austrians."
"They said, 'Good Italian' and raised their arms."
"And you?"
"I..."
The soldier didn't know what to say. There was, in that Virgilian hesitation, all the grace and virginity of the race. But Capt. Fracchia:
"So, your blade is still a virgin? And you think you've been in combat? The prisoner: What was he? A brother? A comrade? A friend?"
"An enemy."
"And you give quarter to the enemy? Offering him your bread because he said, 'Good Italian'? You don't know what's

going on inside him about you! He's thinking: the enemy, what a baboon! . . ." He concludes: "Let the locals in the rear offer bread to the prisoners! This steel, which the government has placed into your hands, is given for killing. And whoever doesn't use it one fine day will discover in his hands not a bayonet but a knitting needle, like your women use in Italy."[1]

The officer in Mario Puccini's example does what he is supposed to do; he tries to motivate the soldiers, to kindle in them aggressiveness, using also masculine pride so that, as it says in *Memento per il conferenziere di truppa*, "every one of our soldiers must, confronted with the Austrian, exercise the function of avenger and dispenser of justice."[2]

And the literature of war is full of these types of military spirits. Arturo Rossato finds it supremely ironic and can't get over the fact that the soldiers so close to the front line remain silent and resigned. "Who knows why, but no one makes a sound. I smell the odor of the blood that squirts like the must of a good wine from vein to vein, giving me the cruel flavor of joy and of violence: I think I make death mine the way you violently take a beautiful woman, and those guys, bent over like mules, with big ears like mules, clomp grotesquely on both sides of the street, without a shout, without a song. Why?"[3]

Maybe because, as Malaparte writes, those soldiers had "entered into the circle of war, heads down, cursing."[4]

And yet despite the very real distance between "convinced" and "forced," between militarists and those who are resigned, there are more than a few among the soldiers who take part in violence with a certain aggressive spirit, who take pleasure in killing, who zealously absorb the lessons taught by the officers.

---

[1] M. Puccini, *Caporetto. Note sulla ritirata di un fante della III Armata*, edited by F. De Nicola. Gorizia: Editrice Goriziana, 1987, pp. 37-38.

[2] In Fabi, *Gente di trincea* cit., p. 147.

[3] We are citing M. Isnenghi, *I vinti di Caporetto nella letteratura di guerra*, Marsilio, Vicenza 1967, p. 21, which in turn uses the citation from the complete edition of 1934 (A. Rossato, L'elmo di Scipio, Corbaccio, Milan 1934).

[4] C. Malaparte, *Viva Caporetto! La rivolta dei santi maledetti* (1921). Milan: Mondadori, 1981, p. 46.

Tullio Cavalli, in his book *Isonzo Infame* (Infamous Isonzo), wanted to stress this "tragic enjoyment" with some of his testimonials "because, with the distance of so much time, one prefers to imagine that our soldiers forgot the war and were looking forward to the moment when they embraced the enemy in the name of universal brotherhood: Unfortunately, it's not true. These same soldiers who had compassion for old women and children, as we've already seen, who took pity on the wounded Austrians and risked their skins to carry them far from the shooting, who shared their bread with prisoners, slew the men in front of them and didn't feel any sentiment of brotherhood for the enemy; the war had a horrible effect even on those for whom, according to their nature and tradition, violence was alien. We don't like to say it, but it's necessary to show the war as it was and not to sweeten it in any way."[5]

Domenico Moggia writes thus to his parents on August 30, 1915:

"Now I am writing just a little because I wrote in the trench close to the Chumps [the Austrians][6] and I never had so much fun as I have here in the war when you see a head and you take the rifle and then start to harass it a bit and instead of harassing it sometimes you give it a fresh hit but more often you get all six of them at one time."[7]

Giovan Battista Senestrari from Nave writes to his cousin on September 14, 1915, the same day on which he will die: "Now I will stop but soon I want to go check out if I can still kill a couple of Chumps."[8]

Domenico Novazzi: "Dear Mother, I write to tell you I have been a day and a night in the trenches if you could see how fun it is when some Austrian raises his head from his trench and we all of us together fire at him."[9]

---

5 T. Cavalli, *Isonzo infame. Soldai bresciani nella guerra '15-'18*. Brescia: Edizioni del Moretto, 1983, pp. 226-227.
6 An epithet used for the Austrians.
7 Cavalli, *Isonzo infame* cit., p. 225.
8 Ibid.
9 Ibid.

Luigi Fondrieschi writes to his father on October 8, 1915: "Let me tell you how I had the good luck to be able to shoot a Chump and see him fall to the ground in his own trench. On the night of the 7th I was commanded by my lieutenant who had eleven men at the post up ahead, in other words, I was in command of the advance element patrol for the regiment's security in case of an attack. I proceeded at night in silence right up to the enemy trenches twenty meters away and took position under a bridge where there was water and mud up to the level of my knees and I remained there for twenty-four hours. At the beginning of the morning a scout that I had alerted me that he could see an Austrian, at once I figured out where he was and, with his feet still in the trench he too was looking around to see if he could see any of us, I pointed my rifle at him and let off the shot and I could actually see him fall. I'm so happy I would have stayed there another twenty-four hours even with all the danger. I am in excellent health."[10]

However, as we will read in the selections in the anthology, killing isn't something one can do with impunity. The face, the body of the victim settles into one's thoughts, it comes back in dreams, as in the case of Nunzio Coppola who confides his unease to his father. A similar case is that of Giorgio Lo Cascio, officers in the rifle corps, on whose story Adolfo Omodeo lingers. In a letter from November 10, 1916, Lo Cascio confides to his sister Maria the tragedy of man: "I, Maria, on November 3 in a furious assault with the bayonet, slaughtered a man. . . . Maybe this action that ethically distances me from human beings is making my desire to be loved and to love more strong. . . . But why am I saying this to you? I don't know. To talk, to tell you that in terms of Italy and militarism

---

10 Ibid., p. 226. The letter Giacomo Zanotti writes to his mother on January 4, 1916, is a good example of the efficacy of the war propaganda: "Because you need to know that the war that we are fighting in now is a just war; because we need to avenge the thousands and thousands of innocent hearts, because the enemy whom we fight today is a vile and barbarous enemy, because he has no pity for anyone, he murders women and children." Zanotti Giacomo, pp. 33-34.

I like the war, but as a man—the hope of the twentieth century!—it horrifies me. There are moments in which you find within yourself a frenzied chaos of ideas, for which, while you want to advance with pistol aimed to destroy again, to mark another trench up ahead with the enemy's blood, you find inside yourself conventional inclinations and in the midst of these, the soul cries out to you (while your fleshly eyes remain without tears) over the infinite brutal and bloody madness, and you live in a delirium of wise and social ideas, because of which you seem to yourself to be the only rational one."[11]

These are reflections that we find repeatedly in the letters of young officers. In those of the twenty-four-year-old Filippo Guerrieri, already extremely young when he volunteered in Libya, they seem to assume a unique sincerity. He writes to his mother on August 17, 1915: "We follow the path of a little airplane in the sky, our bombs explode around him like so many little white clouds, they crown him like a saint and the three hundred pellets that rain down from every little cloud descend, jump onto him, envelop him, they close in on him, they squeeze him into a fearsome insidious circle. We down on the solid ground witness this, waiting until the aviator, once hit, plummets, we are there with vigilant eyes, like mastiffs, ready to finish the work, ready to intervene for a final slaughter, a final massacre. We didn't think that the guy flying up there could be a great hero, not of ours but of his own country, that he too was awaited at home by a mother, by a family; no, we didn't think of that, because we were no longer as before, happy and wanting to give aid, not the men of peace whom we are, but men of war, and in war, in'the recesses of the heart, in the depths of the soul sleep every pure and good sentiment, and all of them, in turn, awaken perverse, bestial instincts. We prepare ourselves, it's horrible to say, not to be men but to be wild beasts; to this extent modern civilization is false."[12]

---

11 A. Omodeo, *Momenti della vita di guerra. Dai diari e dalle lettere dei caduti, 1915-1918*. Turin: Einaudi, 1968, pp. 115-116.

12 F. Guerrieri, *Lettere dalla trincea (Libia-Carso-Trentino-Macedonia)*, edited by E. Guerrieri. Calliano: Manfrini, 1969, pp. 81-83.

And he comes back to the idea of the "brutalization" provoked by war, more radically and with dark sarcasm, in a letter from October 4, 1915:

"In general when one goes to lie down in the tent or on the stones in the lookout, one has a certain repugnance, a certain shame, shame of being men, of the bestial instinct that little by little we feel surging up in us, brutal and assertive. Because, you should know this, in war we become evil; we don't think of anything except killing in the end; everything gets reduced to what's in our sights, to a good hit and a bayonet thrust delivered at night between the shoulders of an enemy outlook surprised in sleep and silence, an outlook is a person like us with the same feelings and the same thoughts, who has a father and who maybe is a father himself, it becomes a great gesture, a noble act that makes worthy of reward, that crowns in glory him who effects it. And you in Italy in peace speak of morals and respect, of noble sentiments, all of it is ridiculous stuff that makes one laugh and laugh and laugh. . . . Poor laws and poor penal codes, how you are far from us and what vain things you are; murder is nothing more than a shot, an urge, a thrill; theft is a crime like that of property; killing is an obligation like that of living."[13]

Romeo Giudici is a native of Cremona. He was drafted into the 29th Regiment infantry.

July 11, 1915

Dearest sister, I come with this my little postcard to let you know my news, that I am perfectly well, and so I hope also are you, Angelo, and Claudio. Dear Anita, I will tell you that we have had a change, and I am located now in a nearby town, to have a bit of a rest, after forty days on the front line, I will tell you, dear sister, the risks that I have taken for the greatness of

---

[13] Ibid., pp. 94-96.

Italy and I am very happy to have served our Homeland. The evening of the 5th I was commanded to go and see an enemy trench if it was occupied by the enemy; I went on all fours so that no one would have even a glimpse of me and when I was about twelve meters away, I saw two enemy scouts under the fence, so I turned around, in the morning of the 6th about 9:00 I went another time and when I was close I was seen by an enemy soldier, so with the dexterity of a cat I was in our trench and understood that theirs was occupied, at midday I went with two hand grenades and when it was the right moment the fuse doesn't light and with much pain I had to turn back, I went to exchange the bombs and I returned with fifteen bombs, now angry like an animal I went another time and then I threw two and they had their effect after a quarter of an hour I went another time with a friend of mine but surprised by gun fire, we were blocked, in the evening toward 6:00 we went on the assault, I in the front with my bombs and I threw three of them. In the morning at 7:00 I and four volunteers went to place the tubes underneath the wire fences, under fire, enemy, and we made them blow up. So, dear sister, it seems to me that I have done my duty and I believe, as my companions say that I will be decorated with a medal of honor, or advanced for military merit, my lieutenant told me that it can be done as soon as they send me home on leave, let's hope, so I will go to Rome, now I will stop, and I say goodbye to you lovingly and accept a kiss from your brother Romeo.

A thousand kisses to Claudino and many greetings to Angelo bye.

Efisio Atzori was born in Cagliari, where he attended senior comprehensive school. He was enlisted into the Alpine corps, Aosta battalion. He fought on the Trentino front, from Mount Zugna to Pasubio. He died on the cliffs of Pasubio in the early days of September 1916.

Zugna, June 13, 1916

My dear ones,

For many days now I have done nothing but send you postcards with simple greetings on them. It's not my fault because these days I've slept during the daylight hours and marched in the darkness until dawn. Now I am in Zugna you can't imagine the kind of bombing they have done in this area. Yesterday they delivered more than 1,500 blows of small caliber, and this was a calm day. In a heap they shot for sixteen hours of the day on May 25 about 350 hits between 420s and 305s and around 40,000 hits of all calibers. Every five meters you find a hole four or five meters deep and about eight meters across. It seems impossible that we could still be here, but our resistance has been amazing. The Austrians were advancing with platoons side by side and banners raised, confident they wouldn't find any of us. But our cannon, which had up to that point been silent, opened fire on these men in formation; they slaughtered them. To give you a clear idea of these lost Austrians: In some places the Austrian corpses piled up to a height of a meter and a half. The Austrian command asked for twelve hours to bury the dead. Our command refused, and they responded: new bombings and new attacks. And we: shooting on and . . . enormous massacres. You can imagine that our soldiers were enthusiastic to see the Austrians riddled with shrapnel. Remember that my bunkhouse is situated right on the edge of a hole made by a 305 and it's the most secure place because during the bombardments instead of fleeing from where the projectiles are exploding, we go right down into the hole where surely (I say surely because up to now it hasn't happened) another hit won't happen exactly there.

Don't be afraid because the Austrians have captured some soldiers and here it's for sure they will take others. In our glorious 37th Division we have an old saying: They take some, and we give them something!

Please be reassured and happy. I am still the same, I am well and happy. You can't imagine the happiness we have here, especially when we eat. We sing, we drink (no wine) spumante and champagne, it's the only fun we have the whole day, eating, and when we sit down to it, I hate to mention it, but we eat so much of that food that you wouldn't believe it. We begin with antipasto and finish with sweet, champagne, and spumante. Our mess tent is just the kind you'd find in a town, no different.

With people eating, drinking, singing, laughing you can't do otherwise than be well, and I and my colleagues are. Therefore, you too be always happy. Don't think of the dangers of war, you can't even conceive of the indifference with which we hear cannon fire.

Today I received two letters one dated on the 7th and one dated on the 8th. Let me know if you have received a letter from the 24th that had pictures in it and some edelweiss found in a prayer book (which I kept) of an Austrian. I have written you using Austrian paper and an Austrian envelope.

Give my greetings to all and take the dearest kisses from your Efisio.

Zugna, July 10, 1916

My dear ones,

Finally after 31 days in the trenches after having taken part in the capture of majorly fortified trenches, after having rejected nine Austrian counterattacks and after having spent ten days under bombardment by 305s I am going down to rest. If I could tell you everything that happened from the night of the 25th to today, it would be enough to make you crazy. You should be aware that I am alone in the company, the captain sick a colleague of mine is dead and the other two have been wounded. I obtained it with five or six deep scratches that I got the first time I went through the wire fence at the moment of the attack. Thirty-one days without taking off my shoes and without sleeping more than two hours together. I wrote you every day (from the 25th) a postcard on leave telling you I am well, etc. but effectively I was exhausted, held up only by the holy enthusiasm I brought with me to the front.

My major who was wounded during the action sent me and a number of other soldiers from my platoon an alpine plume with a red tassel, behind the tassel a plate that reads, "For a good Alpinist."

Now effectively I am fine, I think about the happiness of tonight when I will go to sleep without shoes. All my soldiers confess that such bad days even Mr. Nero didn't have, and all the officials who have seen fourteen months of war agree.

Yesterday and today I had and have still the command of the company, I hope however that tomorrow or the day after my good captain will return (of four of the battalion's captains three wounded and one ill); even the battalion priest is dead. But I saw the Austrians fall at ten meters from the trench in which we mowed them down like cut grass, our machine guns, one of those that we took from them we used to massacre the enemy. They were so cowardly, they came to the counterattack, yelling in Italian "Cease fire" "Savoia." They were thirty meters away, and it looked like our line but we realized that they would have to deal with the Alpini from the Aosta battalion. During the next night during the occupation they came five times to the assault and left their trenches piled high with corpses. The thirty meters that separate our trenches from theirs are covered with the bodies of Austrian dead that stink horribly. Not being able to collect them, at night we throw lime over them, risking our lives to do so. The Austrians don't even raise their heads. They are almost all Hungarians still enjoying the ephemeral advance on the Asiago plateau, but now they are taking them everywhere.

According to news brought to me by a friend it seems that my good friend from Modena Nereo Sinigalia is dead. I didn't read anything about it in the newspaper. Poor guy!

Write to me again and at length because I need your news and to pass some minutes in joy.

I believe that now we can send packages send me a few sweets and some bottles of Oliena and Vernaccia wine.

About the wool, don't worry about it because it's warm here too. Up there I was at 1,600 meters here I'm at 200 meters so you can imagine the warmth. Even from the left side, everywhere. I kiss you all with much affection Efisio.

Giovanni Bussi, tailor, was born in Cossano Belbo (Cuneo) on March 15, 1898. He was called up in 1917 to the 255th Regiment infantry.

Now German troops have come to reinforce Austria. The other day, they tried to attack, I saw them and didn't recognize them on account of the spike on the top of their helmets. In the following waves they were in the front, poor guys, I think they were drunk and that they too gave their guys a drink, like they do us before going to the assault they give us a little cup of cognac, and they didn't understand what it actually meant to attack these exposed positions.

A corporal major machine gunner said to me, "Boy help me," and we took the gun off of the line, then I held his ammunition and he shot and he said, "li tragh zu tuc" : I'll knock them all down, and one by one that they came he mowed them down. He's from Parma and he too is a good for nothing. He's corporal major because of combat merit and he's in the machine gun section that's part of my company. We helped him liquidate those few who were advancing with the hand grenades and who had to stop and throw themselves down on the corpse-covered ground. The corp maj came down again and said to us: "You see that? Only the Italian infantry can beat their heads against the wall and make a hole in these infernal positions: You saw what happened to the others."

Nunzio Coppola was born in Pomigliano d'Arco (Naples) on November 20, 1885. He graduated in ancient literature in 1915. He was called up in 1916 as a lieutenant to the 138th Regiment of the Barletta brigade. He was taken prisoner on May 23, 1917 at Karst at Castagnevizza.

Mauthausen, July 1, 1917

Dear Father,

Now I must confess something to you. In the furor of the melee, when the enemy was body to body with us I had to use my revolver against one of them; I hit more than one, one who had aimed his rifle at Lt. Bellavista from my company and would certainly have killed him had I not shot him and the shot was diverted because he was staggering. But what impressed me more is the other one I shot almost at point-blank range while he was on top of me with his bayonet. He would certainly have killed me had I not been quick enough to empty my pistol into him, so much so that I had to throw it away because I didn't have any shots left and I wouldn't have had time to reload. He fell on me, getting blood all over my jacket, which I had worn, completely filthy, for an entire month since the 23rd when I put on a new one. The picture of that young man who my shooting caused to become white and who stretched out his arm, dropping his rifle, and in falling on top of me because I was somewhat lower down than he, seemed to embrace me without saying a word, is with me constantly, and many nights I dream about it. Many times I think of so many strange things, but I can never seem to get him out of my thoughts. I didn't know his name, and I will never know it. But I don't know why I can't stop thinking about the mother who is waiting for him, maybe he doesn't have a mother, the way I don't have one either, and yet if I hadn't killed him, he would have done the same to me and you would be the ones waiting in vain; even so, I can't get him out of my mind.

Even the other day during the weekly stroll I ran into a young boy who could scarcely control his legs, and who came up to us to ask for bread or money, in touching him on the cheek I thought about him as if I were his father; and yet he was Hungarian and an Austrian boy. You know how unprejudiced and unsuperstitious I am, but I can't forget this figure of the young man who came to die on top of me. And yet I've seen so many other kinds of death of our own soldiers, poor fathers of families torn up horribly by the grenades right before my eyes, dead bodies all around me, and none of them has left any real impression on me, and that one who was the enemy has. But maybe with time even this feeling will go away.

Chapter 9.
The Grand Hotel of Fear

In three different diaries, in the form of appendices, we found likewise versions of the text "The Grand Hotel of Fear," featured possibly as a leaflet, written probably by a caustic wit as were, sometimes, those storytellers who were popular at the turn of the century.[1] Already a residual text, it allows us to enter into the universe of what in the 1800s used to be called popular literature: songs, nursery rhymes, tall tales, nonsensical tales, enumerations, parodies, maxims, proverbs. In the years preceding the war, texts of this type in the "dead" time of military service wound up in manuscript notebooks that took on the form of catalogs and songbooks. In them, one could read "negative" texts about nostalgia and bitter leave-takings, of separation and of loss, of prison and of death that coexisted with journalistic crime chronicles, popular comedies, beer-hall songs, religious parodies, and thieves' slang.[2] Popular poets and storytellers were an important presence, they fell between written and oral texts, between folklore and populist writing, between revolt and resignation. With the war, storytellers' production on the contrary stiffens and bends to the needs of propaganda and military pedagogy which can't tolerate a foreign indeterminate, anachronistic, or opaque imaginary with respect to the valor of the nation at arms.[3]

The wide range of popular and folk types is offered to outline stories that are patriotic exemplars.[4] So it is that we find

---

[1] I refer most of all to the figure and the work of Arturo Frizzi, the prince of charlatans and storytellers. See *Arturo Frizzi. Vita e opera di un ciarlatano*, edited by A. Bergonzoni. Milan: Silvana Editrice, 1979.

[2] Cfr., Q. Antonelli, *Storie da Quattro soldi. Canzonieri popolari trentini*, preface by R. Leydi, Publiprint-Museo del Risorgimento e della lotta per la iberta, Trento 1988.

[3] Cfr., Q. Antonelli, Dai canti di guerra ai cori della montagna, in *La Grande Guerra. Esperienza, memoria, immagini*, edited by D. Leoni and C. Zadra. Bologna: Il Mulino, 1986, pp. 427-441.

[4] The reference is to the Bertarelli fund, settled close to the Museo del Risorgi-

the good-byes ("The Goodbye of the Soldier to His Family," "The Rifleman's Goodbye," "The Goodbye of the Conscript of '96"); the contrasts ("The Contrast of the Conscript and His Mother" or "The Contrast Between an Italian and an Austrian"); the laments ("The Young Girls' Laments," "The Reformers' Laments," "Laments and Regrets of Deserters in the New Jails of Brescia"); the letters ("Letter From a Soldier to His Mother," "Letter From an Italian Soldier Captured by the Austrians," "Letter From a Mother to Her Deserter Son").[5] We find regional folklore: the Lombary "bosinade" ("Patriotic Bosinada," "Bosinada a Sura La Guerra," "Bosinada del Rid de Giavan Sura I Areuplan"); the "zirudelle" of Emilia Romagna; the Neapolitan canzoni of Libero Bovio ("A' Guerra," "È Garibaldine d'o mare," "Tarantella d'o Guerra"), of E.A. Mario ("Patria," "L'Ardito," "Suldatielle"), of Califano-Cannio ("'O Surdato 'nnamurato").

The leaflets follow closely the unfolding of combat, they emphasize the attacks, the conquests of territory, the advances, and they celebrate the "hero's death."

On the "home front" they deal with the price increase for food, with dishonest shopkeepers, and, above all, with "shirkers" (*The Shirker*, for example, with words written by Quirino Ammonini, begins like this "I am a shirker/ I'm a bold military man/ I am of fear/ a splendid example/ When the war broke out/ I shouted loud and strong/ I want Trento and Trieste/ Or else I want death . . . I got a hernia/ insomnia/ anemia/ epilepsy/ nightmares/ and neuroses/ benign tetanus/ ear infection, heart trouble/ a bit of elephantiasis/ cystitis and a big tumor").[6]

---

mento di Milano, which features some thousands of leaflets. Cfr., L. Sorrento, *Canzoni popolari in italiano e in dialetto appartenenti al fondo organico Bertarelli*. Milan: Tip. Antonio Cordani, 1939.

5 The Lettera d'una madre al figlio disertore, by Pilade Soldaini of Firenze, begins like this: "How sad is my life!/ you are no longer my son/ because you alone are vile/ you have done nothing for your country!/ And I feel such pain/ that I can't remove from myself/ What life is this life of mine/ knowing you are a deserter!/ I feel my heart is wounded/ by the dishonor that you have brought to me."

6 Quirino Ammonini is also the author of the Pace Mondiale del 19 ... where we find the socialist if not the Utopian lexicon: "Tear down all your factories/ where

But it is the entire repertory of love songs that is privileged: from the popular, narrative ones based on the compositional scheme of "bitter leaving/distance/return" to those of the author always from the point "of overflowing with songs of grief and funereal self-pity in the collective diary of a generation."[7] "The songs," Isnenghi writes, "more openly concerned with manifesting be it consensus with or protest against the war, those that go beyond pain and beyond resignation, the songs of yes and those of no, don't really seem to belong to the space and time of the combat war of the common soldier. They are situated either before or after, in the environs, rather than in the center of the war; and rather among the spectators than among the protagonists and the extras in the theater of war, in everything that it needs around it, maybe even among the military themselves when they are still civilians or are returned, on duty or on leave."[8]

And yet the world at the front isn't so impenetrable: Leaflets and manuscripts penetrate it and are transcribed and passed around.[9] Certainly the "pessimist" songs (one thinks of songs like "Fire and Machine Guns," "Gorizia," and others less known) are works by a minority for the military minority but they take up and amplify that "moral revolt" that is so present in ordinary people's letters.

The text that will follow, this *Grand Hotel of Fear*, isn't per se a piece of protest writing; it's more like a bitter satire; it's the legitimate child of carnival literature, of parodies of testaments/wills, of sermons, of fake passports, of inverted

---

cannon were made/ build schools/ civic institutions/ make of your battleships/ peaceable places for commercial use/ as public toilets/ and not for vendettas/ Give to the defenders/ the individual borders/ the wild lands and remove them/ thus from squallor/ Think of the future/ of the orphans and those mutilated/ make just and prudent laws/ for the poor and the blind/ the field and the office/ the school will be the duty/ a pledge for all peoples/ for eternal civilization."

7 M. Isnenghi, *Le guerre degli italiani. Parole, immagini, ricordi 1848-1945*. Milan: Mondadori, 1989, pp. 96-97.

8 Ibid.

9 Cfr., C. Bermani, *Il canto sociale*, in *Gli Italiani in guerra*, III, t. 2, *La Grande Guerra. Dall'intervento alla "vittoria mutilata,"* edited by M. Isnenghi and D. Ceschin. Turin: Utet, 2008, pp. 838-856.

worlds. The front is transformed into a party, the bombs into food, the din into music, the advance into a stroll.

The three texts we publish present some differences, fruit of the passage from the written to the oral and the oral to the written and of the need to position the "party" at the real front of the writers (Karst, the Ortigara, the lower Isonzo), but substantively they work in the same way.

First of all, there is a dinner introduced by an antipasto of bullets given by the Krupp company (rendered as "glup" "group" "grup"); there follow various dishes: a plate of shrapnel, one of grenade splinters, another of incendiary bombs, and exploding projectiles conclude the lunch. This is followed by a dance organized by Madame Machine Gun with the assistance of Fence, illuminated by various glowing rays. One does take a stroll, naturally, among gardens blooming with barbed wire, accompanied by the music of a 305. The prices depend on the post occupied: The first spots cost "certain death," the last are reserved for "those who flee." The invitation is variously signed by Mr. Louse, Mrs. Hunger, and Miss Thirst.

Bartolomeo Baccalaro, farmer, was born in Fara Novarese (Novara) in 1894. He was enlisted in the infantry as a stretcher bearer.

Holiday on the horrible Karst plateau.

Grand Hotel of Fear, splendid banquet that will be given on the day of the assault on Trieste. Come, my dear friends, the cost is low, but the entertainment is grand, here one eats with fear and doesn't laugh, exquisite dishes at half price with antipasto of glorious bullets from the Krupp company.

First course: double-effect shrapnel with penetrating point

Second course: splinters of 305 asphyxiating gas shells

Third course: steak of incendiary bombs dropped from airplane

Fourth course: sweets and confections with spicy sauce of explosive shells sent from the award-winning factory Dum Dum.

In the evening, a masked ball with poison gas, tango with a bayonet. The dance will be hosted by Miss Machine Gun and the Honorable Wire Fence, the hall will be lit with luminous rays and by artillery fire and spotlights. Refreshments: Water from the holes of Mr. 305. On the next evening, a stroll in the gardens blossoming with Karst stones. Long boulevards of barbed wire, foxholes, fences with poisoned tips, walkways with hand grenades and mines and other lovely things. Music from Mr. 305, from Mrs. Campaign, from Miss Mountain, and finally Strength with all the famous musicians of the infected zone. Be advised that in addition one will hear even the sweet sound of the bombardments and tunnel mines. Also be advised that those who participate in the party are not guaranteed to return to their own homes. Prices for entry: Best Places, certain death. Second-rate places, difficult to avoid death. Third places, reserved for the wounded. Fourth places, reserved for those who escape.

Signed by Mr. Louse, Secretary Mrs. Hunger, Monitor Mr. Fear Little Happiness with Shivers.

Giuseppe Opreni, miner, was born in Bonate Sopra (Bergamo) in 1893. He enlisted in the Alpine troops, first in the Tirano battalion and then in the Stelvio battalion.

Echoes of war, June 10, 1917

Program for the party activities, Ortigara June 10, 1917. Begin. Day of Great Party at the Terrible Ortigara, Grand Hotel of Fear.

Splendid banquet which was made during the day of the assault before entering Trento.

Come, come, O people of Italy, the fee is small and the entertainment is great. Here one eats with fear and doesn't laugh. Exquisite dishes at half price with antipasto of explosive shells from the great Krupp company.

First course: splinters of grenades from the 105 shell.

Second course: double-effect shrapnel with penetrating point. Third course: bomb steak from flame-throwing airplane.

Fourth course: gelatin bombs with the spicy tone of hand grenades.

Followed by sweets from the award-winning factory Dum Dum, with masks and poison gas.

The dance is hosted by a Miss Machine Gun and the Honorable Wire Fence. The evening is illuminated by luminous rays and by artillery fire all night long. Refreshments of San Pellegrino water from the mouth of the 420.

Later the stroll in the Ortigara, long and frightening boulevards, foxholes and wire fences. Mr. 420 will speak with this holy voice and all the people invited to the Great Party.

Music from the 305 and Miss Mountain . . .

Prices for entry:

First place: Mt. Sinai 1.5 lire

Second place: Hard to hack it 1.00 lira

Third place: Reserved for the wounded .50 lire

The president, the illustrious Mr. Louse . . .

Monitor, Fear with trembling legs

Signed, Skin, Flesh, and Bone.

Best wishes to whoever reads.

The author, Penniless.

January 10, 1919.

Luciano di Nucci, breeder and shop owner, was born in Capracotta (Isernia) on July 5, 1883. In May 1915 he was enlisted in the 1st Regiment rifles.

Grand Hotel of Fear.

Splendid banquet and evening of honor. Come, come to this great party of which there will never be another like it 'til the end of the world. One eats with fear and doesn't laugh. I will give you an explanation of the exquisite foods that there will be at this great banquet.

There are exquisite fruits at half price: shells from the famous Krupp factory; howitzer of 305 with a side dish of 152 and many other foods of the best quality.

First course: shrapnel with penetrating points.

Second course: pasta with splinters from ordinary grenades.

Third course: steak with a side of poison gas.

Fourth course: gelatin tubes with spicy sand.

Fifth course: hand grenades mixed almond confetti 105s-75s-65s.

After having eaten and drunk, the play and entertainment commence: music and dance with the famous Bayonet Tango.

The food will be served by Miss Machine Gun.

The evening will be illuminated by the famous artificial fires with lamps, rays, fire, cannon, and gunfire all night long.

Then there will be refreshments but they will arrive at a later hour, of sky mixed with a bit of red and a bit of water from the lower Isonzo. At dawn then will be the stroll in the gardens blossoming with barbed wire accompanied by stretchers, weeping, and music from the 420.

The president of the concert who directs the spectacle is the celebrated 305. The play must take place between the wire fences and the foxholes and mines will begin.

Finally:

First place: death

Second place: cholera

Third place: Wounds and if it's possible with the employment of Mr. Old Trench we will be rewarded with an unknown condition. The party will last until next year and maybe even longer. We believe the public should be advised so they will come to take part in this great banquet. Sirs, you can be sure the play is beautiful.

Chapter 10.
On the Front of the Endless Winter

The Italy-Austria front that opens in May 1915 is, in large part, an Alpine-Dolomite front: a line that runs from Ortles to Adamello, from Pasubio to the Altopiano dei Sette Comuni, from the Dolomites of Val di Fassa to those of Cortina D'Ampezzo and the Pusteresi, from the Carniche Alps to the Giulie, and during all four years of war subject only to slight relocations.[1]

At high altitudes the soldiers experienced a very different war, fought on two fronts, because here they had to defend themselves also against a second enemy: one that the Trentino Kaiserjager Biagio Pisoni calls "the endless winter" ("Just at present we have our gun always on our shoulder 120 pieces of ammunition five hand grenades and on top of a freezing mountain hidden behind four cliffs we must wait until dawn under whatever temper the sky provides in this way we sit and spin and pass the long winter evenings").[2]

In order to resist the enemy assault, to adequately equip the soldiers, to house them, to feed them, to deliver to them, the mountain is set upon by the Italian army as well as by the Austrian one, with a technology probably hitherto never seen. The alpine area was transformed into an artificial space, criss-crossed by paths, mule trails, carriageways (2,500 km on the Italian front; 400 on the Trentino front alone), and then cableways, funicular and train railways, electric lines and telephone lines, water pipes; deformed by excavations and the construction of extended trench fields and of a fortified cavern system; occupied by gun turrets made of concrete and fortifications

---

[1] Cfr., D. Leoni, *Guerra di montagna/Gebirgskrieg*, in *La prima guerra mondiale*, edited by S. Audoin-Rouzeau and J.-J. Becker; Italian edition edited by A. Gibelli. Turin: Einaudi, 2007, I, pp. 237-246.
[2] Pisoni Biagio, c. 7.

of various types, shacks made of wood and stone, aqueducts. Diego Leoni writes, "The war in the Dolomites was the maximum extension of mountain combat, of the processes of interaction between man and his surroundings and of replenishment, on the part of the urban civilization, of the interior of the mountain. From this point of view, the war represented absolute fullness: full of men, of technology, of construction, of constructive and destructive potential. The mountain soldier goes where the mountain climber has never been, using spikes, ladders, digging in the rocks and appropriating it for months and years: not a lone conqueror but one of a tribe that boasted tens of thousands of members."[3]

Tribe is a significant word. It returns us to self-definitions like "primitives" "troglodytes," "eskimos": because regarding the accelerated human and technological intervention in the alpine landscape, the living conditions of the soldiers necessitated extreme forms of regression. The diaries and letters constitute an extremely vivid testimonial of this process that causes the writers to prove with a kind of incredulity to what levels of deprivation and misery it's possible to sink.

Andrea Pistoia, confined on Mt. Pizzac di Arabba in the winter of 1916-17, repeats despairing words that we have read elsewhere: "Poor Pistoia, how you have been reduced to these great miseries." Words of self-pity that in the field hospital at Passo Pordoi will quickly become desperate in letters to his wife on June 18, 1917, which we will presume to approximate here: *don't think about me too much, consider me gone, I am nothing anymore, I no longer exist, I don't even hope any longer to see you again.*[4] For everyone, the conflict, this clash with the enemy, who in some cases remains invisible, is always in the background. Firstly there's physical exhaustion, the suffering, the cold, the unbearable conditions. The diary of Celeste Paoli, of whom we bring back a few pages, is nothing but a

---

3 D. Leoni, *La montagna violate. Note sulla guerra, il turismo, l'alpinismo nelle Dolomiti*, in "Materiali di lavoro," 1989, 3, pp. 12-13.
4 Pistoia Andrea, letter from June 18, 1917.

sequence of nighttime voyages up and down the mountain with boards, wood, bread, without a moment of peace. These are "beastly lives," he comments. The days are aggravated by military exercises, guard shifts before the invisible enemy. No tree, not a flower, not a blade of grass or a bird to give a bit of comfort, writes Antonino Cella, confined on the mountain Adamello, only "us, who bear no resemblance to humans, dressed in white, always with our masks on our faces in this ocean of ice, outside the world, outside all the things of this world."

Snow, ice, avalanches.

"The snow is a weight that threatens to crush you at every step," writes Fritz Weber in the winter of 1916 from the peaks of Pasubio. "From summit to summit the roar of the avalanches falling into the valley echoes. The numbers of the victims is growing. Every day a new catastrophe. In the course of the winter the mountain that we're on has taken the lives of 8,000 men. Only very few fall at the hands of the enemy: The great majority end up in crevasses or else have limbs freeze and die from exposure. There's no fighting the snow. It's like a subtle and mysterious scourge that strips you of every power of will and robs you of life like a slow poison."[5]

In just three days, from the 10th to the 13th of December 1916, on the entire arc of the alpine theater, there are a total of 10,000 deaths on both sides from avalanches. The tragedy that occurred on the Marmolada Massif has been related in many books, but it's worth talking about it here in this brief introduction as well. "After the heavy snows, between the 12th and 13th December 1916," recalls Heinz von Lichem, "the Fohn, or favonio, wind began to blow, a warm wind from the south, making that night the most catastrophic in the entire war on many mountain fronts. All over there were disastrous avalanches of never before seen proportions, burying friends and enemies without distinction. At dawn on December 13th

---

5 F. Weber, *Tappe della disfatta. La fine di un esercito*, Italian translation by R. Segala. Milan: Mursia, 1973, p. 86.

the favonio wind reached its maximum power, bringing the horrors of the night to a climax. On the Punta di Penia also a mass of snow accumulated that was calculated by Leo Handl to be at least 150,000 tons that demolished the shelters of the Gran Poz, destroying everything and killing in one blow at least 300 soldiers."[6]

Giuseppe Capacci, farmer, was born in Monterchi (Arezzo) in 1895. Enlisted into the 8th Regiment infantry, at the end of September he was sent to the Trentino front at Passo del Tonale. Here we find him in December of 1915. In the spring of 1916 he would be transferred to the eastern front. In June he would be in the first line of the zone in Monfalcone.

The 8th of December was over, but we were even more tired and worn out, without being able to sleep: In the little trench carved out of stone, among the rocks, there was no comfortable place. It was covered with boughs, wood, and a bit of earth, but the snow made a good roof; the bottom of the trench was always covered with water and our feet were martyring themselves to the cold; you could be still just a few minutes and then you had to keep stamping your feet constantly!

"Who can hold up another three days?" we asked among ourselves.

"It's no use!" the corporal major himself said who was always in there.

We mounted a guard for two hours outside the trench, looking out over those tall mountains. Your neck got stiff, the ears and face froze, your eyes couldn't stay open. How long two hours seemed!

"Who will do five nights of it?"

---

6 H. von Lichem, *La guerra in montagna 1915-1918. Il fronte dolomitico*, Italian translation by G. Richebuono. Bolzano: Athesia, 1993, II, pp. 228-229.

Among seven of us there were just three overcoats: the corp. maj. kept one, and two were for those standing guard. When you came back in, you had to give up the coat to whoever was mounting the guard, in order to handle the cold better. In the other trenches they even had stoves, that way they could warm up when they came back in.

The ninth day toward 11:00 the fog had lifted, from the trench you could see the crests of those mountains where the enemy was perched, you could see some smoking stoves, you heard close-together gun shots. Just then behind Monticello you saw appear our soldiers who were bringing the food rations. When we heard the bullets they threw themselves in the snow to take cover, but the enemy had already seen them and when they got up they were a sure target for a burst of gun fire: Being afraid of getting hit they paid no attention to the cold. Around 4:00 a bit of fog came back, which protected them, and they finally were able to reach us. They stayed almost four hours in the snow: Let's consider their suffering; their clothes, their overcoats were frozen; they couldn't even walk. They suffer the cold and we suffer hunger. The rations were a cold rice that had become like glue, the grains were all one mass; but notwithstanding all this we didn't mind and we ate with such gusto!

The next day, at the same midday hour, our captain came; the Austrians saw him too, and some shots came from on high. The bullets came so close to him that his legs were shaking; he couldn't defend himself, he threw himself down in the snow. From our trench we saw him, but we didn't know who it was; when he got to us, he didn't want to talk; it was the first time that he'd been exposed to that kind of danger: He was still recovering.

Getting himself together and making himself comfortable in the shelter, he said to us:

"You saw your captain in danger, and no one came to help?!"

"Captain, Sir. There was no use. We couldn't have helped you."

The corporal major then said that he couldn't spend another night there: "I have soldiers who haven't slept for four nights now; the cold is all with us; three coats for seven men; how can anyone go on like this?"

The captain asks, "Where's your stove?" One soldier from Reggio Emilia says to him, "Here it is, Captain, Sir!" And he indicated a big stone that they hadn't been able to lift out of the trench. We all just had to laugh.

He said: "I can't change you from this post; I will send up everything you need and recompense you with addition time off when you come down." And in fact, that evening more coats arrived and the stove and wood; so it was possible to spend another twenty-four hours much better.

Antonino Cella enlisted on April 20, 1915, the Tolmezzo battalion, 6th company, 8th Alpines with the grade of corporal trumpeter. From the beginning he was sent to Karst, then in the spring of 1916 he reached Mt. Adamello.

March 1916

Twelve days passed (sufficient for the necessary preparations), and we've come to Mt. Adamello, at 3,545 meters above sea level. Five hours of marching into icy eternity. Our shelters in this position were those of a polar bear, and so a hole in the ice for each three or four men and there one was certain not to be able to close one's eyes for the cold and also wanting to sleep there was the risk of freezing over, having only the camp blanket and the cape or an overcoat, but that was no match for such a cruel enemy as the cold and the endless torment of being in this position. And it was for this reason that every morning some soldiers left, being taken to the infirmary or to the hospital, some with frozen feet, other with eye problems from the reflection of the ice, which can make you almost blind, even though you always wear colored glasses.

In this rigid place that doesn't lend itself to reheating food, one lives on cans of meat, cheese, and chocolate, and bread (all of which were completely and permanently frozen); you can't unfreeze anything except if you do it between your knees in order to be able to eat it. So it's necessary to be strong not only in spirit but also physically in order to make it in these positions.

The holiday of Easter of 1916 was more painful than other past holidays, because we were in the advance on Dorson di Genova Lobia Alta. It was 11 at night when we began the advance on the enemy trenches. The Val d'Intelvi battalion was in the lead and we followed them, all was calm, it seemed that the enemy was sleeping and that we were lucky to have a position of surprise. The formation of the battalion in the lead was admirable, all ordered and you couldn't hear anything above a minimum sound on the snow, but just when were a few meters from giving the assault, the enemy opened murderous machine-gun and bomb fire, mowing down almost the entire Val d'Intelvi battalion. It's a sure thing that the enemy was waiting for us and picked the perfect moment to inflict the most damage.

The rest of the night we worked transporting the wounded fallen on the ice, transport we made with stretchers attached to skis.

As far as the eye could see, it was impossible to glimpse a patch of land, a tree, a bird, nothing like that; we were alone, we who didn't bear any resemblance to humans, dressed in white with masks always on our faces in this ocean of ice, outside the world, outside all the things of this world and not even those closest to us would have known us in with our faces blackened by ice, with any recognizable feature obliterated by the suffering endured.

Emanuele Calosso, store clerk, was born in Finalborgo (Finale Ligure) on December 6, 1894. He was drafted on February 23, 1915, to the 1st Regiment Alpine, Pieve di Teco battalion. On May 23 he arrived at the mountain front line of Carnia. In September of 1916 he would be at the Trentino front and later the following year in the battle of Ortigara where he would be taken prisoner and sent to the Sigmundsherberg prison.

March 12, 1916

Dear Mom,

Yesterday I got your letter of the 4th and I see that you are telling me to write you often but I hope you have already gotten my letter where I explain to you how things are going here, in other words that I write to you when I know that letters can get out, because on account of the huge snow, that since February 22 hasn't stopped for a single day, the duty truck hasn't been able to come to bring us food, and so it can't take letters either. You can imagine how much snow has fallen and continues still to fall, because we are forced to eat tins of meat with crackers that make us very thirsty so we have to keep eating snow.

Did I hear, here where I am, on Mount [...], that my friend Biundin died; is it true? Let me know. And please also let me know anything you can about my companions from Finalborgo who are at the front.

Let me know if Cousin Lelo is enlisted, yes or no. I'd be very happy to be able to see Renzo a bit dressed up for the infantry; it should be really funny.

I'm happy to know that Berto da Centa has a herniated disc, at least he won't be sent back to this "crazy place" and won't hear anymore the dear thundering of cannon and the crack of gunfire. If only that would happen to me I would be really happy.

You don't have to be afraid for me because now in the place where I am guns won't reach it and cannons can't either because we are behind the huge peak of the mountain, which hides us perfectly and also the Austrians don't even know we're here because there's just thirty of us soldiers who are here just for transporting food rations to our guys who are up on another mountain.

The only danger consists of the fact that when we go out on the detail little avalanches can fall, and all we can do is cover ourselves, but when we know this danger exists we don't go out, and we stay under the covers in the shelter to warm up the lice that keep us company.

Our lieutenant tells us that when we run out of food we'll make a nice lice soup and live on it for several days.

I received what you sent about my friend Tortarolo. Please send me what I asked you for in my last letter in the next letter you send, all the more the tobacco and matches because those really help. For now, that's all I have to tell you. My greetings to everyone, relatives and friends and a hug and a kiss to you and my brother from your forever son E. Calosso.

Look, this writing is done with the blood I got from the lice I killed.

Celeste Paoli, cobbler, was born in Denno (Trento) on July 18, 1897. He enlisted in May of 1915 in the Landesschutzen Regiment Innichen Nr.III. At first he was sent to Val Pusteria and then, in 1916, to the icy Mt. Marmolada. Wounded on the Asiago plateau, he died December 15, 1917.

July 12. Set out. We went through Moena, Vigo di Fassa, and at Pozza we received food rations and stopped until the morning of the 13th. After departing, we went through Perra, Mazzin, and then at Gries[7] we stopped until after midday on the 14th.

July 14. We left in the midst of rain and we climbed up and up until we found snow. Having arrived there,[8] tired, wet, frozen, they put us into a shed built to contain fifteen people and instead they had put forty in there. Once there I rested a little but it was cold. Laden with snow, I arrived at a shack situated beneath the peak which is some 3,259 meters of altitude, there I slept a bit, but my teeth were chattering and I was shaking like a leaf, on July 15.

July 16 Rested a little. From the evening into the nighttime I had to go shovel snow. Cold wind. It was snowing.

July 17. Today also I worked shoveling snow. There's nothing but snow.

July 18. My birthday. I spent it very unhappily, filled with sadness, with a stomach ache. In the evening I worked shoveling snow.

July 19. Still filled with sadness, I didn't know whether I should cry or what to do, seeing myself there on a snow-filled

---

7 Moena, Vigo di Fassa, Pozza, Pera, Mazzin, Gries (hamlet of Canazei) are towns in the Valle di Fassa (Trentino).
8 Paoli gets to Marmolada, we don't know if it was under Cima Rocca (3,309 meters) or Punta Penia (3,343 meters).

mountain, perilous, at the altitude of 3,259 meters, in the middle of people I don't understand; I was the only one who spoke my language.[9] "Patience, Celestino," I said to myself. "Trust in God and always have faith that one day even this hardship will end." I continued praying and appealing to the Blessed Virgin and to my Guardian Angel that they protect me and keep me safe until the end of the war.

July 20. Still cold and sad.

The night of July 21 I did an hour of guard duty: snow, furious wind, cold on July 21, July, July, July!

The night of the 23rd we descended. The descent was torture, weighed down as we were; a bit on our feet a bit on our butts we got to the huts. There was no room there, so I went to the roof; I was totally drenched, but because of how tired I was I slept anyway a couple of hours. When I woke up I was so cold I was trembling like a leaf, on July 23rd.

July 24. I rest during the day and also at night.

July 25. I rest during the day. In the evening I had to carry tables up the mountain. The trip was long and hard. Having gotten there, we had to work another hour shoveling snow.

We got back at 3 in the morning on the 26th of July. But they didn't leave us in peace, they made us do maneuvers with our guns and then they made us carry rocks. In the evening again I had to carry rocks and then shovel snow.

July 27. The same; they don't give us a moment's peace.

The night of July 28 thank God they let us sleep. During the day I worked, the evening I had to again carry tables up.

---
9 Paoli is the only Italian speaker in his multinational unit.

July 29. Slept in the morning; the evening again up the mountain.

July 30. During the day I worked; I brought a beam up.

July 31. During the day I worked; in the evening thank God I was able to go and sleep.

August 1. I was very sad, thinking that I've been through two years of war, two years during which I haven't seen my dear brother. And it's still not over, and who knows how long it will go on, this war, but then hope comforts me a little. In the evening again, four hours up in the snow, the ice, to transport munitions, patience.

August 2. I was blessed to be able to attend Holy Mass. In the evening again to transport wood.

August 3. In the morning maneuvers with arms, then I worked. In the evening again carrying a sackful of bread. It was heavy, I was sweating and suffering from the cold, patience.

August 4. In the morning I worked, in the evening up again. I began to cry seeing that fate, apart from my health, doesn't seem to favor me. When I returned it was dark, you couldn't see where you were walking, on rocks bathed in rain you always are slipping. All in all, wretched living! But anyway, patience, I told myself.

August 5. In the morning maneuvers with arms. After midday I came down from the accursed Marmolada and we came back to Pozza. The journey was painful, I got back to Pozza in the evening, I was dead, my feet were killing me!

Francesco Giuliani, shepherd and day laborer, was born in Castel del Monte, in Aquila province, in 1890. He attended the first years of elementary school, but then he continued on his own, teaching himself. Recalled to arms on May 15, 1915, he was assigned to the 13th Regiment infantry. On May 24 he was already in the war zone. In May of 1916 he was transferred to the upland plateau of Asiago. Giuliani is the author of a complete memoir, made up of diaries, poetry, reflections and further considerations on the war.

The Asiago Plateau, December 14, 1916

Finally this morning as was expected and to the great satisfaction of everyone, three soldiers, the oldest ones in the company, left on leave. To those not fortunate and those who believe themselves more favored, this event made them envious, but at heart we are all happy that sooner or later we all get to go.

In these days our only occupation is to move the snow from the roads, we go out early and come home in the evenings in the dark. So many times when we return in the evening and it has been snowing all day, we find the tents heavy with snow and we have to clear them, and sometimes they don't hold up and fall to the ground, and then with the patience of Job we have to remove the snow and put them up again if we want to spend the night with cloth over our heads. It's more than a week now that the weather doesn't know how to do anything other than snow, and the snow is almost three meters high, and the danger is lessened. You still suffer terrible cold and it's been about ten days since we were lucky enough to see the sun.

It may not seem possible to you that here I don't see the sky or the earth, only the snow and the old fir trees of the forest. We can't complain about the snow because it lowers the danger.

Both sides' cannon are mute, and I hope that they stay that way until the end of the world. Now that the danger doesn't menace us, and that I am not seeing dead or wounded, I don't feel like I am at war, but rather am living someplace I don't know. The May sunshine will take this blessed snow from us, but until then we are very sure not to bother and not to be bothered.

Yesterday the 13th was unforgettable, a blizzard was raging and we had to remove the snow from the road. Just as the storm was at its strongest, and the shovel was falling from our numbed hands, we ran to take shelter under the roof of a shed. It was then that the news began to be passed around that they'd made peace. Finding ourselves high in the mountains surrounded by so much snow, starving and exposed to such cold, if peace had really come it would have torn us away from such suffering and so the good news brought us a huge comfort. No one was silent; people were laughing, joking, jumping up and down trying to dispel the cold. But, oh well! That joy was more than brief because the news was quickly proved to be false. If peace had really come, how welcome it would have been.

Only a few days ago the company I belong to has had the good fortune to stay in a shack, but even in it you're uncomfortable, we're packed too tight, and you have to sleep on a bare tabletop like in a prison; the few woolen items aren't sufficient to keep us warm at night.

Francesco Laich, clerk, was born in Rova del Garda (Trento) on April 2, 1895. Enlisted in 1915 into the Austro-Hungarian army, he went into the musicians corps behind front lines of the Royal Imperial Tirolese Cacciatori. In the summer of 1916 the music corps was sent to Mt. Pasubio and then later taken over by the department of health.

Pasubio, December 10, 1916

Dawn had barely broken on December 10 when a laborious alarm, which overcame the roar of the storm, woke us suddenly. Coming out into the open, forcing the door, which was semi-blocked with the new-fallen snow, a skiing soldier announced an avalanche, really an enormous avalanche with many victims. Quickly equipped with shovels and wooden spades, we ran to the place, where we were greeted with a terrible sight of destruction. An avalanche, of about four-hundred meters, had detached from Mt. Bisorte, stopping in the valley and crushing every built thing in the course of its way.

Half of the station and the cableway warehouses were destroyed; all you could see were beams, pieces of tar paper, and various debris that was sticking out of chunks of muddy snow that looked like a stormy sea that had suddenly frozen. All the shacks, and with them their inhabitants, no longer existed! A desolate picture with a mournful effect. The salvage job was extremely difficult and almost fruitless. One long shed, shelter for youth or the elderly no longer obligated to fight but still working for the military guiding horses with carrying their loads, had disappeared and was discovered at the bottom of the valley too late to save any of the three-hundred poor wretches. Horrible scenes presented themselves to our view! The victims, semi-nude because surprised while sleeping, were laid out in such a way that it was clear they died consciously and in agony. Some of them, their fingers stiff and sticking through their ribs of their chest, others with mouths open wide and looking like they were gasping the air that now they were lacking; others crushed by a beam and surrounded by blood reddening the snow! The few survivors, saved by vigorous rubbing with snow and alcohol, were telling their horror stories like crazy people. Then hundreds of dead were buried in the same snow that so recently had massacred them.

Giuseppe Aspesi was born in Busto Arsizio (Milan) in 1895. He enlisted in the 3rd Regiment telegraph sappers, 3rd company. In the winter of 1916-1917 he was at the Trentino front, in the mountains of central Lagorai, just below Malga Ziolera at 1,926 meters.

December 5 [1916] Today is terrible weather again and it's snowing. I work a bit and as a result despite the weather time passed; Filippini went from here to Malga Zigolera Alta and I went there too—O what snow, what positions—they're frightening—Sleeping again under the tent.

December 6 Today the Marshall came back. Weather still the worst. Also today he went up to Malga Zigolera but I didn't feel like going. Actually today I am warming up and melting the snow at the entry to the shack where I'm going to sleep. A bit of work.

December 7 Today I spent the biggest part of the day fixing up the shed. It is still snowing, and in the night because I was under puffs of it I am cold today.

December 8 It's still snowing and I keep myself busy repairing the shed. There's not much work, but there will be more of it because the captain is giving me some.

December 9 This morning I get up early and go to accompany Toni who is going on leave. It's snowing and is cold out. Filippini goes back down and goes to Fiera.[10]

---

10 Fiera di Primiero was occupied by the Italian army until June of 1915.

December 10 It's begun to snow again and I am still keeping busy with the shed. Filippini comes back up and also a line repair man because the lines are down.

December 11 This morning I get up and for a while I can't leave the shed because last night a good meter of snow fell; given that the roof doesn't seem to be too secure I began clearing it off and so warmed myself up a bit—at midday it was very calm, but then it clouded over and that means that more snow will come—those poor guys up at the high altitudes, how do they do it up there?

December 12 All day today I kept working at getting rid of snow. We've been hearing from up higher avalanches and something wretched is sure to have occurred. I work here carefully.

December 13 Even today it's snowing incredibly—at the high altitudes they got avalanches and a bunch of those guys there escaped. Filippini and Murra went down to Fratazza.

December 14 It's blocked, and we've started talking about going into the food reserves. Our guys could still manage to bring the rations. We can't communicate because all's interrupted because trees fell and brought down the line.

They brought twenty soldiers here for an emergency who were extracted from avalanches. Two rifle companies were buried, and there are some men they couldn't get out. They vacated the new office and, given that we weren't able to get the line working again Lt. Vignali, threatened to write us up in a report.

December 15 Today was my turn to go up toward Malga Zigolera to reactivate the line, what a disaster. Avalanches, fallen trees broke all the wires. I was working to fix it a bit, but then it's necessary to stop—here too at the field hospital trees fell on the medicine sheds, on Manzella's shack, and on the military dormitory. Trees were threatening to fall also on my shed—I sure hope they don't fall and do me in.

December 16 Today it's cursedly snowing again. Greco and the others got to Malga Zigolera, but they couldn't fix the line—my new one was broken—I fix it.

December 17 In the morning it seems as though the weather has settled down. Again they go up to Malga Zigolera and reestablish the line here at the field hospital; some riflemen come to cut down some trees and they cut down the one that was leaning over my shed. More wounded and frozen soldiers come.

December 18 Last night again it starts to snow, but then an intense cold sets in and it stops snowing. This morning the weather is again beautiful, but the line breaks down again and so I go to fix it. There's sunshine, and the Austrians immediately interrupt the calm with gunshots and cannon fire. At Frattazza they show me a flier from the General who orders that military personnel from the class of 1895 need to be transferred to the front line. If they do this also for us telegraph workers, I need to go into the infantry; that would be the height of this catastrophe because I am too scared to go into the trenches—it would really be the end of every hope—I hope that doesn't happen because I would die before I'd go into the trenches.

December 19 This morning they woke me because the line's down. Sure enough, trees fell and broke it, but the others fixed it. Today the weather is a bit windy, but it's not snowing. There's a rumor going around that there's an armistice, but I am sure it's not true. What does seem to be true is that the young guys have to go to the infantry; this for me would be disgraceful. It's sure to come, but as long as it hasn't happened it's good: Let's hope always for the best.

January 16 [1917] This morning at around 9:00 a huge avalanche came to Malga Zigolera that covered and took down the centurions—about fifteen wounded and five killed and more lost. At the same time an avalanche at Passo Rolle killed another six. In Val Zanchetta another avalanche luckily with no victims. Even at Col Bricon avalanches but it seems without victims—they allowed some soldiers for rescue here luckily and nothing is happening, but if it keeps snowing something will happen.

[from February 4-27 there is a period of winter furlough]

April 2 As it snowed all night, today is the day for avalanches—at Passo Rolle it took away the telephone exchange; luckily no victims at Malga Cis, an avalanche buried some riflemen—two companies sent to rescue them were crushed by a second avalanche; of those saved they pulled out just a few; it's said there were seventeen killed. Another avalanche at Malga Zigolera buried a skier—this avalanche was a kilometer wide and twenty-five meters deep—

While they're out rescuing some who'd been overtaken, a fire breaks out in the servicemen's quarters. Tosi and I were able to put it out. It burned some things but if we hadn't gotten there in time, it all would have burned. It stopped snowing.

Chapter 11.
Giuseppe and Maria

Some thousand meters from the trenches began the zone behind the front, with command centers, hospitals, warehouses; still further away in the cluster of villages sat the military operations' tent cities, with health services, the prison camps, the kitchens, and animal housing. The small towns that made up these "war zones" appeared, to the astonished eyes of the soldiers, crowded, filled with traffic, bustling with life.

Giuseppe La Scala, a no-longer-young Sicilian corporal, a Methodist and an enthusiastic supporter of the war, gets to Asiago on April 25, 1916: It's an entrée into what is, for him, a marvelous machine.

"Circling the airfield we arrive in Asiago. It's the first time, after having gone through it to get to where I am stationed now and after the fleeting trip today, that I am setting foot here.

"It's a nice town. It has all the characteristics of a small city. Pretty streets, a magnificent piazza with an arcaded fountain in the center; nice houses, banks, public baths, libraries, many cafés, the best hotels, stores stocked with everything under the sun. You can find anything here, especially everything a soldier needs during wartime: from uniforms to rubber pads, from field cots to portable canteens, from shoe oil to hiking hats, from fur collars to waistcoats. But all you see are soldiers, from every branch of the service, and every kind of man. The civilians must see us like whiteflies. Crowding the streets and the piazzas, invading the cheap restaurants and the cafés: You could easily say that life in Asiago revolves completely around the military bases. There's the command of the 34th Division, which is to say provisioning, the police station, field hospitals 004 and 007. The horse veterinarian, the photo-electrical area, the airfield, trucks, trains, wagons by the thousands. There is a huge military movement. One sees trucks driving everywhere, interminable lines of trains or of mules coming and going to and from the front. You can't understand why there is so much confusion; but certainly every movement, every operation corresponds to a precise end in the full strategy and in the organization of logistic services for this terrible and yet marvelous machine called war!"[1]

Furlough behind the front lines, after the permanence of the trenches, was something soldiers dreamed of and remembered after they returned to their lives. Even if, as Lucio Fabi writes, "the so-called rest away from the front ended up being mostly tedious, regulated immobility in the encampment and prolonged repetition of military exercises,"[2] even still there was the possibility of diversion, of having some encounter, some gratifying experience. In the front-line city there were "soldiers' houses," theaters for puppet shows and movie houses, mobile libraries. Notable persons would make lecture tours there: writers, poets. So it was that some soldiers were able to see D'Annunzio, for example, or Father Giovanni Semeria, the illustrious orator of the 3rd armata.

Giuseppe Ruberti had the chance to hear a lecture by Agostino Gemelli, of whom he made a little written sketch, which ended up being unintentionally a bit grotesque:

"I made Communion in the parish church. For three days I have had digestive problems. Terrible diarrhea. Around 2:00 in the afternoon while I was on guard duty Padre Gemelli arrived. He was an impressive figure. Tall, slim, in military dress, a medic captain. At about 9:30 a torrent of people were in the church. There were very many generals, officers, and soldiers. Padre Gemelli spoke eloquently, a beautiful lecture. He spoke about patriotism and our duty in war. At the end he was applauded. I was feeling sick from the diarrhea. Later, he himself blessed everyone in the name of the Holy Father.

---

1 La Scala Giuseppe, pp. 78-79.
2 Fabi, *Gente di trincea* cit., p. 294.

When we left all the officers of every grade surrounded him. He is a real great mind, a genius, but not a terrific speaker. He swallows his words when he talks."[3]

For his part, Pietro Ferrari heard in the Basilica of Aquileia, after the "soldiers' Mass," a lecture by Don Celso Costantini. Ferrari, a foot soldier and a practicing Catholic, remained very impressed by the talk's efficacy: a real and true "meta-storical ideologicalizing overlay of incidents in the midst of war."[4]

"After the Mass Don Celso Costantini, who I knew was here, spoke to us from the marble pulpit. He greeted us in the name of our Roman forefathers who before us trod this earth spreading civilization. He greeted us in the name of the defenders of our faith against Atila, flagellum Dei, who should be opposed with stubborn resistance. He told us that the Holy Evangelist sent disciples of Jesus of Nazareth to Aquileia to preach and that St. Mark on the way healed a paralytic, a proof that made many people embrace the Holy Religion, and that under the very threshold here were buried the bones of many martyrs who gave their lives for Jesus Christ.

"This earth was now crowded with you soldiers of Italy; it was at one time crowded with your Fathers and their bones trembled with holy passion. Many soldiers have come this way, he told us, many prayed in this basilica and then died on Karst for their country Italy. May their bones be like a crop in the field that, trampled and believed to be dead and destroyed, beneath the earth germinates a new life and renews one hundred for one. In that way fulfilling your duty and with the

---

[3] Ruberti Giuseppe, note from April 9, 1916. On Father Agostino Gemelli, doctor and military chaplain, intellectual charged with upholding the reasons for the war, and psychologist convinced that the diminishment of a soldier's mental life actually improved that soldier's capacities as a combatant, see the extremely informative profile by Sergio Luzzatto, "*Un chierico grande vestito da soldato,*" La guerra di padre Agostino Gemelli, in Gli italiani in Guerra, III, t. 1, La Grande Guerra. Dall'intervento alla "vittoria mutilata," edited by M. Isnenghi and D. Ceschin. Turin: Utet, 2008, pp. 452-462.

[4] The expression is used by Mario Isnenghi in a comment on the diary of Pietro Ferrari. Cfr., M. Isnenghi, *Muniti dei conforti della fede, in Il soldato, la guerra e il rischio di morire,* edited by N. Labanca and G. Rochat. Milan: Unicopli, 2006, pp. 95-105.

help of God who always champions the just cause, you will triumph and return victorious to your homes, proud to have occupied each one of us your posts for the cause of justice and of Christian civilization.

"This talk made a big impression on me because it was given by a great artist, and it rekindled in my heart the feeling of duty and of the good of Italy."[5]

Of course, the majority of the soldiers were looking for other kinds of encounters in the front-line city, very different occasions from those offered by patriotic orators and celebrated propagandists. The soldiers went to taverns, did business with civilians, courted (more or less respectfully) women; there they frequented brothels born of the initiative of war economy and tolerated by the military hierarchy.[6]

Popular letters and diaries are fairly cautious on this topic, as a rule, if not downright reticent, while they abound in references and descriptions in the literature of war in the memoirs of officer-writers. The mildest pages are those, very famous, of Giovanni Comisso[7]; the worst, possibly, those of Mario Muccini:

"Two steps away from the encampment, there's the house of an obscene woman who has a nasty blonde daughter barely fifteen or sixteen years old. The soldiers go there and, after hours some of the artillery and engineering officers haunt it also. The woman sells wine and cooks stuff people bring her; anyone who wants the daughter can have her. Once I saw our quartermaster, a rotten syphilitic, go in there.

"But in a farmhouse on the big Piano D'Arta street, before the bridge, the fun is much better. There are six or seven girls with their old parents, and every evening Capt. Masoni goes there with some of his friends to eat polenta and make some hoopla. The oldsters sleep and the girls let the guys grope and

---

5 Ferrari Pietro, note from February 9, 1917, p. 67.

6 Cfr. F. Franzina, *Il tempo libero dalla guerra. Case del soldato e postriboli militari*, in *La Grande Guerra. Esperienza, memoria, immagini*, edited by D. Leoni and C. Zadra. Bologna: Il Mulino, 1986, pp. 161-230.

7 G. Comisso, *Giorni di guerra*. Milan: Mondadori, 1980, pp. 66-69.

spank them. That scoundrel told me about it yesterday while I was settling up a bet, and he laughed until he cried."[8]

The history of rifleman Giuseppe Filippetta and the peasant Maria Ors---[9] is completely different and qualifies, in a way, as one of those relationships that begins with a simple exchange of services. Giuseppe was looking for milk, and Maria, who was milking a cow, was kind enough to sell him some. But then the rapport evolves, becomes a habitual reciprocal understanding, an extremely respectful friendship.

The context is Valle del Cismon, in the region's center, the village of Fiera di Primiero. The valley, from which the Austrians had withdrawn in the night of May 22 and 23, blowing up the access bridges, had been occupied on June 5 by the Italian army, which installed itself there to hasten the administrative business as a civil commissary.

In Primiero their reception was fairly cold: The local population watched the Italian troops' installation anxiously, viewing it as a military occupation, but most of all because it interrupted the correspondence with the enlisted men of the Austro-Hungarian army, combatants in Galizia or beyond the front.

So, the disenchantment of the Italian occupiers changed, exactly as it did elsewhere, into a kind of open diffidence, and the conviction of being overtaken by an extended web of spies multiplied randomly the practices of internment to some of the most remote and desolate locations in Southern Italy.

The motive of chilly patriotism by the inhabitants of the valley is one of the themes of the exchange between Giuseppe and Maria: Giuseppe who doesn't get it, and Maria who explains that, all told, under Austria the Italian minority was respected, the schools were Italian, and the taxes reasonable.

---

8 M. Mucini, *Ed ora Andiamo! Il romanzo di uno "scalcinato"*. Milan: Garzanti, 1939, pp. 82-83.
9 Filipetta, out of fear or having forgotten it, doesn't write Maria's entire surname; given the initials, it might have been Orsega, Orsingher, Orsolin, all regional names.

In conversations with Maria, Giuseppe learns not to trust the government's propaganda.[10]

Giuseppe Filippetta, shepherd and farmer, was born in Moricone (Roma) on February 10, 1890. In 1912 he emigrated to Canada; he came back to Italy in 1914. In May 1915 he enlisted in the 2nd Regiment riflemen, 17 battalion, 8th company. In the spring of 1916 he found himself at Fiera di Primiero, in Trentino: the zone, bordering with Belluno, was occupied by the Italian army in June of the preceding year.

In the middle of the spring of 1916, my regiment was sent for rest to Marostica. A friend and I stayed in Malga Toraro, working for the division's food service. After about a month, we too were sent to the Marostica regiment, and there I was assigned to the command of the regiment and charged with evacuating the post.

After some days, we left for a new destination across Bassano. Then, on the march there, we went up the Brenta valley; at Primolano there was a bit of rest, then we started back up for Fonzaso, so, we went again through Fiera di Primiero. The front was quiet. Our battalions went back up into the mountains to relieve an infantry brigade. Our line was immobilized at the Passo Rolle, and the troops were entrenched there under a slope of the mountain about 3,000 meters high, above St. Martino di Castrozza.

I stayed in Fiera, with the transport and the trains. The captain of provisioning gave me responsibility for the feed warehouse and it was necessary to distribute the rations for the mules for the entire regiment. I had a pretty nice life there,

---

10 On the Italian occupation of the Valle del Cismon, see Q. Antonelli-G. Bettega (editors), *Il prete, il podestà, la guerra. Primiero, 1915-1918: I diari di don Enrico Cipriani ed Enrico Koch*. Trento: Museo storico in Trento..

without too much discomfort, and I had a bit of free time also. And I was sleeping on hay and so wasn't cold. Often in the evenings, even though it was forbidden, I'd walk around the town.

Maria Ors---

One evening I asked someone from the area who could sell me a bit of milk, given that the ration wasn't enough for me. He told me about a woman who was in a nearby stable milking a cow. I went there, and she politely told me to go and get a mess tin. She filled it up halfway and wouldn't accept any payment for it. She told me to go every evening at the same time. I went for a few nights, but then I told her I wouldn't come anymore because she wasn't accepting any payment. She told me she didn't want to accept payment because I was a soldier and she liked giving me the milk; anyway, the milk was only for her family's use, and they had enough of it. Then she told me I could come to her house and get the milk more easily. So, I asked her her name and she told me it was Maria Ors---.

I was happy because I had found a woman who could help me out, but I was also uncomfortable that she wouldn't take any money for the milk. The next evening, I went to her home, she was there with her two children, one six years old and one eight. Maria made me sit next to the chimney, where a nice fire was burning. "Warm up," she said. And then she asked my name. We chatted a bit, and then I asked her why I hadn't seen her husband. She told me her husband, when the war broke out, was in the colony[11] and had been interned by the English on account of his Austrian citizenship.

---

11 It's not certain why Filipetta talks about the "colony." It's much more likely that Maria's husband was one of so many emigrants who found themselves in England when the war broke out and who were interned as subjects of an enemy state.

I didn't know what else to do. While talking, I told her my fear: I didn't want to cause her any trouble by my presence in her house, in case it were misunderstood by her neighbors or her family; it could be an offense to her distant husband.

Maria at first seemed surprised; then her expression became very serious; then it changed into a smile, and she said, "This is silliness, Giuseppe, we are a little different from you southerners: where we're from there isn't the kind of jealousy as there is for you. If I bring you into the house, it's not offending my husband, and my neighbors don't think anything of it either. You can come whenever you like; I'll do anything I can for you, the same as I would hope some family would do for my husband, who maybe like you is suffering because of the war."

Those words comforted me, and I started going almost every evening to Maria's house. It was very cold, and I would find her close to the fire, knitting socks or patching some old garment, together with her two kids. I sat close to the fire also, and we spoke about all kinds of things: about how it was living in my part of Italy, about how they were living under Austrian rule, and things about ourselves and our families.

One evening I asked her why, when we took Fiera di Primiero on May 24, we found the town deserted, doors and windows shut, as though everyone had left.

She replied saying that Fiera's inhabitants were terrified, including Maria herself. They hid themselves in the most hard-to-find places because they had been led to believe that the Italians would rape the young girls and loot the houses. When they realized that none of that was true and that the Italians behaved civilly and respectfully, they came out of their hiding places and resumed normal life.

I made sure she knew that our press and our propaganda worked very differently; they said, in other words, that Italian subjects of Austria wanted to be liberated and were just waiting to be reunited with Italy because they could no longer suffer the tyranny of Austria.

"It's not even remotely true," Maria said to me. She continued: "We don't want Austrian schools because we feel ourselves to be Italian. But we know that the Italian government takes advantage of you, that you have to pay heavy taxes, also that you are not doing well economically, and that if we are reunited with Italy our lot will be the same as yours. That's why we want to remain under Austria, which treats us well economically, but we want to remain Italians with our own schools and our own language."

I was surprised, amazed, confused. From then on I have understood how governments use propaganda to fool people, to push them toward war. And from that time, even reading our press, I have not believed what governments say, but I have sought always to understand with my ideas and my experiences.

One evening Maria asked me how I sleep in the warehouse. I told her I slept very well, with my jacket as a pillow and two blankets, while my fellows were sleeping on the summits of the mountains, beyond Fiera. But comparing my situation to that of my fellow soldiers didn't convince her because she wanted to force me to take a down pillow to lay my head on while I slept.

Some months passed. I was still in the warehouse. And the friendship with Maria Ors--- became even closer. Almost every evening I went to see her in her house. But one evening the order came to depart to an unknown destination. For me it was a harsh surprise.

That evening I went to Maria's with more haste than usual, I gave her back the pillow and told her I was leaving the next morning for parts unknown. She was very unhappy. We spoke of many things, especially of my departure while she went through my linens, which she had washed and ironed for me. I again tried to pay her for the milk and for all the things she had done to help me. She refused decisively and asked me to give her my news, no matter where I was going, wishing me good luck. I was very emotional: I gave her my hand, I gave her a kiss, and I fled. I ran through the dark streets to the warehouse, I threw myself on the straw, but I was unable to sleep all night.

When it got to be day, I prepared my few things and my knapsack. The mule troops came to load up their provisions. We were gathering in a small piazza outside the residential area. I found the battalion already lined up, and I took my place in my company. While we were waiting some minutes, I was thinking about good Maria who had helped me affectionately like a sister. And while I was thinking these things, and I could hardly do less, I saw her coming ahead of the battalion; she had a white handkerchief in her hand with something in it. Her eyes sought me out and quickly found me.

"Take this," she said. "It's five fresh eggs. Drink them during the march."

You could hear a murmur among my battalion; my companions watched and whispered. We said an affectionate goodbye. And then Maria, heedless of the stares and the murmurs, with her head down but with a confident step, went from one platoon to another and disappeared.

The order was given, and we began the march.

Chapter 12.
A Painful and Heartfelt Nostalgia

Reading the letters from French soldiers imprisoned in Germany, Romain Rolland could do no less than remark on "the strength and beauty of family feeling." He writes in his diary: "I am deeply impressed reading in hundreds of letters saturated with the painful and heartfelt nostalgia for the small family circle. These pour souls never leave it, they don't see anything outside of it, nothing to interest them, no other reason for living; outside of it, they feel themselves lost, all they hope for is to speedily return to it, to close behind them doors and windows and so never to know anything that happens outside it."[1]

Rolland is talking about prisoners' letters and the warm family life that seems to him particular to the French. But the substance of this opinion doesn't change if we take into consideration letters and diaries of Italian soldiers—"imprisoned" "hidden away" in chains, deprived of freedom, confined in a world dominated by fear, they look at family and home with unbridled nostalgia not only as the site of their emotions but also of humanity and civilization.

Antonio Graziani, a Roman infantryman, writes at the end of a winter furlough: "As it came time to leave, I began to think where I should return to. Up to the last day that was a problem of the past. Thinking how happy I am here and yet I can't stay. And what I am going to and not knowing why. Above all else, I had to leave my family with little hope of returning again. If that day I had found myself close to a butcher's, I don't know what I might have done out of

---

[1] R. Rolland, *Diario degli anni di guerra 1914-1919. Note e documenti per lo studio della storia morale dell'Europa odierna*, edited by M. Romain Rolland, translated into Italian by G. Bonchio and M. Rago. Milan-Florence: Parenti, 1960, I, p. 172. Note from January of 1915.

anger. The moment came when I needed to leave. What pain I felt, leaving my family! Saying: Will I see them again? Filled with thought I went to the station. Saying goodbye to all the neighbor families. Following the road with a pair of buddies. Getting there with an hour before taking off. Spending that hour drinking with some of my friends in the café. But for me it was a useless drink. When the time came to leave, I got sweaty hands getting on the train, leaving friends and hometown. . . . When the morning came, I dressed like a murderer again, taking the blanket, the cartridge cases, and rifle, armed with ammunition. And I take the path walking as a butcher of human flesh. Within just a few moments on the path, one begins to hear the cannon fire, and I begin to know what fear is again."[2]

The gaze of the soldier who writes is turned, more than on the theater of war, on the world of the family; he evokes in a compelling way images of the wife or the children or parents.[3] These come back in dreams and live again in waking hours and take on, by means of photographs, physical substance.[4] More precisely, as Leo Spitzer writes, the photograph is a "surrogate for the physical presence," an object of emotive investment even superior to letters.

"Ah, dear Ugenia," writes Nello Lorenzi, "as soon as I got your photograph, I went off by myself to be alone and enjoyed kissing you, you and our dear daughter! I believed in that moment that we were together and the whole evening I held your hands and so many kisses I gave you, and I spoke to you; but you stay silent. But I believed, Ugenia, that when I

---

[2] Graziani Antonio, pp. 41-43. Note from January 1917.

[3] We note in passing the prevalence of the love song in the wartime repertory finds its reason in this mental horizon of the soldier. As Gian Luigi Beccaria writes, "The themes of the war song that have confirmed popularity are the 'metonymy' of the private, of the sentimental sphere. The country soldier or the one from the mountains is that one set apart, who doesn't live for the war, for heroism and for his actions, but for memories of home and his feelings by which he is torn up." G. L. Beccaria, *Convenzionalità linguistica e alterita ideologica nella letteratura degli ultimi. La canzone poplare narrative*, in "Sigma," a. XI, 1978, 2-3, pp. 3-40; cit., on p. 30.

[4] L. Spitzer, *Lettere di prigionieri di guerra italiani, 1915-1918*, Italian translation by R. Solmi. Turin: Boringhieri, 1976, p. 104.

look at it I would go insane. Now I feel better; at least I have a memento of you and our dear daughter, and I can enjoy kissing you both and hugging you; now that I can't hug you in the flesh, I hug you on paper. Ah, this vile war, how can you have made us despair! Only war could have desired to make us so miserable, we who love each other so much."[5]

Similar despair in the words of Antonio Grazioli:

"Dear Teresina please don't think bad of me for I am well but Dear Teresina I Am Unhappy because you haven't sent me your Photograph look if then send it to me Also yours Soon write to me Soon write to me write to me Dear Lover I love you so Dear Teresina You Know my Heart weeps for you Dear Teresina..."[6]

Luigi Pasini, a week before his death, writes:

"What I regret is that my children, who are small, haven't had time yet to know their father's love, but I never forget them 'til my last breath. I would like, if you can send the image, Maria, that photograph of my children when you can, if I can't see them at home, the dear ones, to kiss them on paper."[7]

Also packages, with food sent from home making survival on the front possible sometimes, strengthening ties with family and bringing the combatant back into the domestic circle of familiar traditions, possibly lost forever.

Letters from farmer soldiers, in particular, are filled with questions about the weather, the progress of the seasons, the crops, the various rural tasks, accompanied by advice and recommendations.

"Dear Wife," writes August Tonetto, "can you tell me how the vines are doing for this season and if there are still tomatoes and if the beans are good and if the oats are coming up well like in other years and tell me if the vines are pretty with the leaves and if there are many grapes like there used to be."[8]

---

5 Lorenzi Nello, pp. 183-190.
6 Grazioli Antonio, letter of June 26, 1915, p. 69.
7 Pasini Luigi, letter of July 20, 1915, p. 71.
8 Tonetto Augusto, letter of June 13, 1917.

As has already been noted, the exchanges of letters strengthened relationships with daily life of the past and served to imagine the future, without letting it be overshadowed by the present.[9]

Antonio Gibelli writes: "The sight of the house, the anchoring to domestic things, to emotions and family ties seem like the only refuge in a completely alien and precarious situation, almost like the only source of identity in a disorienting situation for one's own connotations of his perceived surroundings. [...] In certain aspects, then, a letter presents the character of therapy, becomes a means of self-preservation: Writing home and getting mail are first of all ways of alleviating the pain of separation and the horror of the present state, recomposing in some sense the elements of an identity that is powerfully at risk."[10]

If this is so we understand better the promptness with which one writes home, the anxiety with which one waits for a reply, the numerous expressions of joy and of being overcome that accompany reading letters from home (it's like receiving "communion," writes an anonymous soldier with an expression filled with mystical significance). And one understands also the irritation with late mail delivery to the front of letters to and from home, and the delusion provoked by letters that seem too short or too evasive.

Of the charged situation for illiterate soldiers (37.6 percent, according to the census of 1911), we report in the anthology the testimonial of Ettore Travostino, who acted as a scribe.

The ritual of the mail, lived with the same intensity whether one was upper-class or lower, is rendered here with particular humanity by Filippo Guerrieri, a young infantry lieutenant, in a letter addressed to his parents on June 29, 1916: "A block of concrete that on one side is flat and smooth was suddenly turned into a small table, from the knapsacks and rucksacks

---

9 Cfr. G. Procacci, *Soldati e prigionieri nella Grande Guerra. Con una raccolta di lettere inedite*, Bollati Boringhieri, Torino 2000, p. 108.
10 Gibelli, *L'officina della storia* cit., p. 55.

emerged a sheet of paper, a pen, and everyone is writing, and in writing relaxed because in remembering all of you, in telling you about our life, it seems that fatigue goes away, it appears that every word that is written can take away one of our many pains and when the letter is finished one feels a sweet sense of well-being, one breathes more freely, I would almost say one begins living again. It's for this reason that every free moment is dedicated to those who are far away and that writing a postcard, and when possible a letter, is not a bother but a joy; it's the best way of passing time, the only one that is blessed for us. In those moments one is removed from all that surrounds us and that is never beautiful, one is no longer under a stone, hidden in a rock, one is no longer in danger, no, no, one is close to you in the same peaceful house that knows only peace and we're talking about a million things and the weather is fine and the wine is good. We know it's an illusion, but even that for now is something, it helps us to live with a certain happiness and with a certain faith.

"So then when your letters arrive it's an explosion of joy, it's a rush of hands out into the night, because they come to the advanced positions always at nighttime, divided and sorted by company, and all night they are with us, held tightly from the minute they're dropped off, and when the dawn makes it possible to read, every one of us gets out of the shelter where we were hiding and grabs their precious envelope bearing their precious address. You know that the selection is made in a moment, you can see it from a distance, even in the pile of letters, who wouldn't recognize the envelopes from his own family and the handwriting of his dear ones even from far away? Everyone would. Your envelopes are bigger, grander than all the other ones, and that helps me because I spy them quicker than the rest, I pull it out quickly and rush over behind my rock, which is my palazzo. We rarely curse, almost never, because we are all used to and resigned and don't get angry if it rains and we don't have dry clothes to change into, if the food doesn't arrive, if the gunfire flares up, one knows: We are at war and it has to be like this. But if the mail doesn't come! The wrath of God is loosed on us. We understand why the Austrians shoot us with all their, for them, optimism and, for us, pessimism, but if the mail doesn't come, no: That we don't understand and then the curses go forth in the thousands and fly out to all those elements of the postal service from the smallest and most modest ones to the highest director, to the most civil Civil Minister."[11]

Faustino Pinelli was born in Montichiari (Brescia) in 1889.

September 6, 1915

Dear Wife,

Now I am here with my news, letting you know that I still am in good health, and so I hope that the same is true of you and our little boy.

Now, dearest wife, I will let you know that I received your card and I heard that you sent me 10 lire. I thank you for your good heart that you use to take care of your husband, but in the trench we don't need money, so go right back to the post office and get the money back, which will be better.

I am waiting for your photograph and also one of the baby. This is very important because if I go missing at least I will be able to see you again. You tell me you expect me home again soon, I too would come willingly home but I'm afraid that it's all over for me and that I won't be able to see my family again.

My courage is gone. While I've been writing a grenade went off close by, killing many of my company and wounding others. I am sorry to explain such things to you, but I don't

---

11 Guerrieri, *Lettere dala trincea* cit., p. 140.

always want to be telling you I am well when in fact I am not well at all. Some days are a bit better, it's enough if the sun is shining, otherwise we're pretty bad off. You need to keep in mind that we are always wet day and night.

Of course, it won't seem that way to you all, you believe that trenches are like houses, but really we are making so many holes in the earth as if we were mice.

I am sorry to explain all this to you, but if I don't explain myself I won't be able to find any comfort. Therefore I believe that you have understood. One other thing I have to tell you: that I am thinking about you, if you see that I don't come home this winter I won't be back at all and you can find another house close to the town, otherwise it's sure that this winter you will suffer from the cold. Let me know what you think about that once you have read this letter.

Here we have stones for pillows, for mattresses we have rocks, and for blankets we have the sky and then there's nothing for this winter when it will snow and rain every day.

I have made peace in my heart and think that if we don't die from grenades or rifles it will be from cold and hunger. So, be strong, since you have at least the baby to console you, but [...] I don't feel anything any longer, because it feels as though my heart is telling me I will never see my family again. So pray to the Holy Virgin for your husband that he may maybe come back home. I pray to her also and I cry out to her in my mind and say always, "Holy Virgin, help me!"

Nothing left but to say a heartfelt goodbye. Your husband who always remembers, F.P. Kisses, bye, a kiss.

Celeste Paoli, cobbler, was born in Denno (Trento) on July 18, 1897. He enlisted in May of 1915 in the Landesschutzen Regiment Innichen Nr.III. At first he was sent to Val Pusteria and then, in 1916, to the icy Mt. Marmolada. Wounded on the Asiago plateau, he died December 15, 1917.

November 21, 1915

My very dear parents,

Since I have time and am not on duty, I want to write to you a little letter to let you know that, thanks to the Lord and the Blessed Virgin, I am still in good health and I hope you are as well. Looking back today on the past months I discovered it's been six months. Six months seem on the one hand like six days and on the other like six years, from the day that saying goodbye and kissing you, weeping, I left my own roof to go far away to unknown lands, to a place where I don't even understand what they are saying,[12] and then after three months in the field where often it was very dangerous, now these times have passed and I am still whole, so let's pray to the Lord that he preserves and protects me from danger as he has done up to now. Therefore let's hope, hope in these times is the only comfort for each poor military man who finds himself in these places, hope of being able one day to return, each one of us, to his own home.

So, let's hope for the best. When you write to me let me know something new: how you are, how things are going with you, what you're thinking about, if it's snowing, if it's nice weather. You never write me anything. You always send just a simple postcard, but you don't give me any of your news. My sisters don't write me either, if they weren't able to, then I'll be patient. But that's their job is writing. So, write more and write more often, because when I get one of your letters it

---

12 An allusion to the fact of finding oneself in a multi-lingual unit, where the orders were given in German, a language Paoli didn't know.

makes me feel better. I have so many things to tell you about if you'll permit me, but I would never stop. So, I will tell you only that I am still in the same place amid the beautiful whiteness of snow, on this deserted mountain. At the beginning of the month they said that by the 20th we would be relieved and we'd go for a bit of furlough, which is to say in reserves, but the 20th came and went and no one said any more about it.

But here's what I think: Later on we will go on leave, and then after that we will come back to this mountain. For now I will say goodbye and send you kisses from my heart and also on behalf of my dear friend (he's still here). With the pen I leave you, but in my thoughts I am always with you.

Greetings also with kisses to my dear sisters, now your dear company.

Greetings to the rest of the family and friends and my companions if they are still there; help out M.L. and tell her to pray for me, as I am sure she will, poor thing. I have her in my thoughts always, together with my companions who were her students. Again I wish you goodbye and I kiss you with love your

Unforgettable son Celeste.

Greetings in the name of my friend Nini Braito to his family.

Greetings in the name of her brother, my dear colleague, to Mr. Parisi's cook.[13]

---

[13] Giuseppina Paoli, the sister of Celeste, responds to the letter from her brother on November 28: "My dearest Celestino. Today I received 3 postcards dated 22-24-25 yesterday the letter that you wrote to Papa, we hear very happily that you are still healthy as we are all as well. You complain that we don't write to you often and we do so briefly, regarding the writing we write you quite often either Luigia or I but at length, no, because what you write is only unhappiness, and nothing else. So, you have enough of that yourself. I will write you everything honestly, but since they are things that instead of cheering you up will bring you more unhappiness than anything else, mamma says it's better that I keep silent."

Augusto Della Martera was born in Ginestreto di Pesaro in 1892 into a family of sharecropper farmers. His profession was worker in the brickwork ovens. In May 1915 he was drafted into the army and enlisted in the 121st Regiment infantry. He died in the highlands of Opacchiasella on August 15, 1916.

November 28, 1915

Dear Anna

I sent you two photographs and today I sent you another one and in the next few days I will send you some copies that I will make of them and I think you will be very happy to see at least me and if I am able to come back it will be for us a great memento.

I had the chance to make these photos, no one else has this luxury; maybe they won't be of such high quality but they're just for a great memory. When you get them let me know. After I send you these, all together, then you will give some of them to our parents and to the closest relatives. But then I hope to come back in person; this is my constant thought, if God helps me. I hope to be relieved soon and there will also be furlough. And when will that good day come? A press of the hand to you and the warmest kisses coming from my heart and kisses to our Irma . . .

If you don't hear any news from me, don't think the worst; it's that the mail doesn't come, but I am still reassured that every day I give you my news . . .

Luigi Gottero was born in Bibiana in Val Pellice (Piemonte); enlisted in the infantry, he was sent to Karst; he died in October 1916 during the ninth battle of the Isonzo.

December 14, 1915

Esteemed Angela,

Just having read your dear letter; I wished so much to know your dear news, you can't imagine dear the pleasure that I enjoy reading your letters because here it's the only pleasure and as a consequence I beg you to do me the favor of writing more often.

Dear Angela, I must tell you that today I received with great pleasure a letter from Maddalena and she has given me news of your dear family. So, dear Angela, I wrote you several postcards that I hope you have received, in which I tell you to send me boots, two salamis, and two handkerchiefs. Therefore dear Angela you want to know how I am, you must know dear that I am not living well here, but patience. From the moment that I have the good luck to have health I am forever content.

Tomorrow I go into the trenches, I don't know how it will be, but I will make myself brave and hope to return. Enough, my dear. Watch and see that I will write you every day and you must do the same, that way we can know the news.

On these mountains where we are going there is a lot of snow, but I hope to have enough clothes, and so for now please send me just what I've asked for and if by chance I need something else I will let you know. I only ask you to write to me more often. Forgive me for asking you to write more often, I know that I don't have much time either, but make the sacrifice, have patience.

Dear one, I am writing you always and always, every day, I let you know my news and I leave you with the prayer of giving so many greetings to the Beltrano family from me. I leave you with a thousand kisses for our dear children and a huge kiss for you. I finish my letter, since I can't continue for the tears and a stomach ache that comes to me when I think of you. I am yours forever,

your Luigi Gottero

Many kisses to father and all those who ask after me. Bye, bye.

Ersilio Gregorich was born in Trieste on July 11, 1884; a typographer, he married in 1910 Stefania Novach, with whom he had two children, Bruna and Nerina. In the spring of 1915 he was enlisted into the Austro-Hungarian army, 2nd Regiment of Landwehr Infantry. He was killed in June of 1916.

May 8, 1916

Dear Stefania!

I share with you that I am in good health, as I am happy to read that you all are also. But, my Stefania, why do you give me such little news regarding your family? Why don't you ever include in your letters anything that seems useless to you? You know how much I enjoy reading your letters; it's like talking to you, like being near you, even if you are repeating the same things ten times, I read it with joy! And then tell me all about our little girls, I dream all the time about Bruna, I dream that she's grown up, but what joy I would have to see you all, if I could after all this time hold you, because you know that I never forget you for even a single moment, always always I think about when we would go happy and contented to the osteria, to the café, because in one word: I think of you minute by minute. But who knows if I will have the joy to see you again? Or will I end up like so many others? But I hope not because I have come close many times and yet I am still alive! I never thought I would be strong enough to survive, and let me tell you that of those guys who went out with me on July 28 of last year only a few are left still in the camp, everyone ends up here or there or in the realm where they remain forever still and mute! But I have either a devil or an angel who protects me. The other day talking to an old man I told him some of my adventures, and the poor guy said to me: "Your wife and children will pray for you!" I didn't say anything because I know you think about religion about as much as I do. Unfortunately I don't kid myself about anything, and those rare ones who will remain can say they handled it well and I beg you that as long as you know I am alive to love me and not to forget me. As you can see from this letter, I received the package of 35 decagrams containing nine Virginia cigars, postcards, and a half packet of chocolate[14] and other candy, also two newspapers with the description of that event; poor children and women, victims themselves of those assassins. With that I say goodbye and kiss a thousand times you and the dear Bruna and Nerina. My greetings to your mama and sister and father and may God keep you well! Goodbye your affectionate Ersilio.

Quintilio Cantini, a clerk in the post office, was born in 1888 in Tizzana (Florence). He attended school up until fourth form. Enlisted into the 83rd Regiment infantry, 12th company, he was stationed in Trentino for battle, in Valsugana. He was injured, goes into the hospital, and is discharged. In January of 1916, he returned to the front.

January-February 1916

The train whistle blew, and it began to move slowly, slowly leaving the station behind, then it picked up speed and, puffing, began the rise into the hills of Pistoia. It was then that I began to miss more and more my family, the dearest things to

---

14 The package of 35 decagrams contained nine Virginia cigars, postcards, and a half packet of chocolate.

me. I was returning through the endless snow of the Alps, up there where the cannon would have continued its homicidal thundering, up there isolated from the world, from humanity. Through the doorway of the train car the gaze ran down there, far from the high plains and the surrounding mountains. I was thinking, meditating, remembering. I felt afflicted, alone, without any physical force as a man, and I wanted to weep. My companions on the trip and in destiny were also dejected, with darkened and fixed expressions staring at the infinite, looking for some person they had left crying and miserable.

What a difference between then and fifteen days earlier! So much happiness, so much noise in the wagons! So much yearning to arrive in that place where many people were awaiting us! And dad, mom, the wife, the kids, the brothers and sisters, and then so many other people who it seems we hadn't seen in a million years. Thousands of hearts were feverishly beating and wanted to leap from the train as soon as possible. What joy when we reached the halfway point, what tears of consolation! And there were fifteen days of free living, of amusement, of happy pastimes!

The monotonous "ta-pum" sound of the Cecchino had stopped but we heard it in our uneasy sleep. Then the furlough ended and we found ourselves together on the same train for a departure that was more melancholy for our destinies. And the black monster ran, ran and panted dragging us along behind like a supernatural force and uttering its cries into the countryside it seemed to say to us: You had fun, boys? Let's go, let's go back to war, to the other companies who are waiting to go on leave themselves to their families, just like you did. No one said anything, some dozed, some were thinking, someone was nibbling at the food that loving hands had carefully filled up his haversack with. The train ran and ran and panted up into the grass of Appennine Tuscany. The day was already dark and one's gaze still fixed on that point of sweet memories, I sent a last goodbye to that blessed land that had given me so much time and that maybe I would never see again.

Farewell, native land that saw me as a child and made me a man under your beautiful pure and tranquil sky. Farewell enchanting mountains, charmers of things, grandeur of nature, spectacles of creation. Farewell gentle hills of Tizzana where I have sat many times on your fertile soil, looking out on the green mantle that the spring gave you again.

Goodbye olive trees gracefully drooping that remind me of enthusiastic moments of some journey in the most beautiful seasons; goodbye little church, only comfort for my afflictions, in my suffering; O, how many times in your temple did I feel myself growing happier, how many times have you given me serenity again and peace! O Divine mother, who on high surrounded by your Immaculate Altar you have seen me so many times at your feet invoking you and asking for your help, don't abandon me for even a moment in this dark and gloomy hour; make it so that your name is always with me in the trenches and in the fields of battle. Now maybe I won't see you again o little country church but I will preserve your immortal memory even in the cold tomb of the Alps if it's there that I must find death. Goodbye Catena, place of my journey from the first years of my infancy, farewell the walls of my home that have preserved me as a safe haven, farewell, farewell![15]

---

[15] The reference to the Manzoni page of "Addio ai monti" is clear. But one must add that the re-use of the interjectory and vocative structure, always very personal, can be found also in texts that are more socially recognizable than this. The leaving of house and home is frequently described by Trentine women, refugees in the more internal provinces of the empire, going back to Manzoni's words. It's the case, for example, of Giuseppina Filippi Manfredi, a worker from Rovereto, who writes in her diary of her exile, "Really the last words were those written to our house. Farewell, house, dear furniture so useful at one time. Farewell the home of our father where he hoped we would pass out last years; farewell my native land, holy field where the bones of our ancestors rest, and those of our little girl. Farewell! church where we were made Christians and where adults we swore faith at the altar! We have left it all, and maybe forever!" A more general reflection with many other citations can be found in Q. Antonelli, *"Io ò comperato questo livro ..." Lingua e stile nei testi autobiografici popolari*, in *Pagine di scuola, di famiglia, di memorie. Per un'indagine sul multilinguismo nel Trentino austriaco*. Trento: Museo storico in Trento, 1996, pp. 209-263.

The evening had already laid its sad mantle on the horizon and the night was bringing its dark shadows. The train ran, ran, and panted. Finally it came into the narrow canyon of the Appenines and bending closer to the other soldiers who dozed and snored stretched out messily, I tried to do as they did, while that miserable bed moved into the breast of the mountain. Mt Setole, close to Valsugana, February 1916.

Ettore Travostino was born in Gattinara (Vercelli) in 1887. He enlisted in the 76th Regiment infantry. In 1917 he moved to the machine-gun section in the role of quartermaster. The battle area he described is Carnia, the place was positioned on the Udine-Pontebba line and "precisely on a high ground that looks over this little town, now abandoned, by some 400 meters."

December 10, 1916

My very dear ones:

Maybe you are not wrong to chide me because I write so little. But I don't know what else to do. I believe I have responded to your letters and cards, and maybe some others besides. What else do you want? I can't make up stories for you, so as to have some reason to write more often; and anyway, I don't like the way others do, who every day repeat the same exact words. All they are doing is copying the card from the day before, and daily send the same greetings and kisses to their parents, to the wife, to the children, to the brother-in-law A., to Cousin B., to their godfather R. etc. etc.

And heaven forbid if one single time they forget the name of the last member of the entire family! They're suspicious right away and imagine a spat or argument. This happens a lot with southerners. They're wretched enough to be pitied.

Maybe I haven't told you that I am in the trenches, that I sleep in shelters dug out of the earth, lying on tables nailed to the trunks of trees, always dressed, with my cartridge cases on my back and covered with lice? That at night I stand guard and during the day I work to repair paths and walkways, to fix trenches, to cut tree limbs and carry them to the shelters so they can use them for repair, or cooking the winter food? That every week I get to wash my linens, that almost every day a button falls off my clothes, and I have to wash my mess tin after every meal?

And this is my daily life, from the time I got up here, and there's surely no chance of it changing. Every day is just like the others. Do you want me to repeat the same song to you every time? Let me know. Do you want to know if I have taken part in any combat yet? And that if I had, that I hadn't told you about it? No one in my entire company has shot a gun in four months, unless it was taking a shot at some airplane. We haven't had any deaths or any injuries. And it's lucky because the Austrians fire frequently over our trenches with artillery and with guns. But we can't even respond. They are on the peak of Paralba, hidden in trenches, at an altitude higher than ours by some 1,000 meters.

They only get a response from our artillery. We're here on guard to make sure they don't come down. Anyway, you have maps and you read the newspapers. You haven't heard of any military action here. Should I invent one for you? I am not, certainly, a teller of tall tales, to make up attacks and advances every day and to make myself out a hero. So? What should I write you if nothing ever happens that's new? Tell you every day I am healthy? Will that help me somehow avoid misfortune? If one day I do die, what can I do about it? I'm not going looking for it, for sure. But the news I ask from you all, on the other hand, are really interesting for me and have to do with things I don't know. Whereas I haven't asked you to send me gossip from town. I've never wanted to know anything about who was being born, who was dying, who was lucky or disgraced, who's doing well and who's not. Some pettiness doesn't tempt me a bit. Anyway, I gather enough of it from the other Gattinara guys here with me. I don't want you all to be telling me that stuff.

And it's not laziness on my part. Every day I spend hours reading the papers and writing. I have a lot of military friends, who send me cards all the time and who I have to reply to. Not only Gattinara people but also people I met from Lecco, Palmanova, and St. Daniele. They write to me when they are sending greetings to the other guys from the '86 and '87 class who are in this company, and I always reply to all of them. Also there are some here who only know how to write a little bit. If they get letters from respectable people and they want to reply in the proper way, they come to me and dictate their replies. It turns out there is really a multitude of illiterates, it seems almost incredible. It's already humiliating enough to have a stranger know your personal business and to ask them for an answer: but for these guys it would be worse still if they couldn't find someone to help them in similar circumstances. And I, when I can, can't refuse.

As you see, I don't have a lot of time to waste in idleness. If you really want me to write you every day, even if I have nothing new to tell you, let me know right away, and I will do it.

Affectionate goodbyes from your Ettore

Agostino Tonetto, greengrocer, was born in Cavallino (Burano, Venezia) in 1883. He was enlisted in 1916 into the 87th Regiment infantry. His last letter was from October 22, 1917. In the days after the rout of Caporetto, he was missing.

February 19, 1917

My very dear wife:

Now I will give you my news: I am in excellent health and so would like to hope that you and our five dear children and entire family are as well.

Dear wife, what can it mean that from January 31, when you wrote me that letter with the address of the hospital, I haven't seen another letter from you for eighteen days?

You can imagine how unhappy I am not to see another letter from you.

I am going along thinking that something bad has happened to you or to one of our darling children or to someone from the family. If someone is ill, write to me right away, because I want to know what is the thing that's keeping me from getting your letters.

Dear wife, do you want to know about the conditions I am in now? I am fairly well. I got to the company on the evening of the 14th. And now I find myself on the peak of Mt. Nero which is at 3,000 meters altitude. If you only knew how tiring it is to get up here, particularly for me, who am used to walking on the plains. You can imagine, though it's nothing real: It would be worth my skin to be able to come home and see you and the kids and the whole family. I would love so much to see you all, but I have no idea when that blessed day will come because there are so many older guys than me here at the front, and they too need to go home on furlough. One or two of them go a day, but not every day, and so it's going to take a while. If only you could come for Easter holidays!

About coming, I will come if God gives me the grace, but I don't know when it will happen for me. Let's hope this painful war ends soon.

Dear wife, when you write to me, do me a favor: Send me paper and stamps because otherwise I can't send you letters. In positions like this one, we can't get them; we are too far away from the places where one can buy them, but first speak to Gildo who won't charge you the penalty because maybe the package will be too heavy.

So, again: Send me a bit of paper or either postcards so I can write to you. I hope some letter of yours is en route, and that it will get here soon. I will write to you right away once I get it. My dear wife, you want to hear about the food here? For now, it's not so bad. Given that we are too far from the kitchen, we go to get the uncooked food and then we cook it ourselves, there are twelve of us, and we eat fairly well. Maybe it will stay like this. Then, at night, we stand watch for an hour and then take two for rest because it's too cold. For now, there are more than three meters of snow. But I have to tell you I thought it would be colder, and instead it's like home is in the winter time. Also there's a wind, because we are high up here. But for the rest of it, it's not too bad. As far as the bombings go, the Austrians here are bombing less than they were where we were before, in Gorizia. Be sure to give my little girl a kiss!

Nello Lorenzi was born on May 16, 1888 in La Cella in the community of Pian di Sco (Arezzo). He didn't attend public school and learned to write on his own. Like his father, he was a bricklayer. He married Eugenia Tognaccini in 1911. In 1914 their daughter Annuziata was born. He enlisted in May of 1915 and was sent to the Karst plateau.

War zone, 9/8/1917

Oh, my unforgettable Eugenia

I'm replying right away to your letter with your picture in it, which made me so happy. As soon as I saw it I felt so much better; I had been waiting for that letter many days. Ah, my dear Eugenia, as soon as I got your photograph, I went off by myself and was so happy kissing you and our dear little girl! Please believe that in those moments I felt like I was with you, and all evening I held it in my hand and so many kisses I gave you and I spoke to you, but you were always silent.

But believe me, Eugenia, when I look at the picture I become crazed. Now I am calmer. At least I have a record of you and of our darling child and I can make myself happy by kissing and hugging you both. Until I can hold you in the flesh, I will hold you on paper.

This despicable war, how it's separated us! It took the war to separate us, who love one another so much.

But dear, my dear Eugenia, after having kissed you so much last night, tonight I dreamed of you and the baby and I felt like I was holding you and I woke up and found myself here, in this miserable dump.

Ah, dear Eugenia! Dreaming of you I spend beautiful moments and feel happy that it seems like we're together, but then how awful it is when I awake, and I don't feel you in my arms and don't see you.

But patience, Eugenia, and courage; this war will end! And then no one will ever separate us until death and we will be able to enjoy our happiness and remember times past when we were apart.

Ah, it's terrible to be so far away, for us who love each other so much! But let's hope that soon the day will come when we can embrace again, and so we will live more happier and calmer. Ah, my dear, but when will it come? We hope and pray that it comes soon, we've hoped for it so long. But believe me, Eugenia, I can't wait for the moment I can have you in my arms again, to soothe my heart and soul, for I think of you night and day; your image never leaves my mind. Hope and courage.

In your letter I see that Sunday was the day of Forgiveness, but I didn't even know. But it sounds as though you didn't receive my postcard. I don't know what is happening with this mail: I send you something every day either a letter or a card, and now I discover that you aren't getting my mail. I don't know what to do; I write all the time, some days I write even two letters to make sure you hear my news every day.

Now I see that you didn't want to send me the picture because you look bad in it. But you know this means nothing to me; it's no one's fault, not yours, not the machine that photographed you. Dear Eugenia the machine takes people as they are. And you Eugenia are unhappy because you're homely and you want to be pretty in photographs. It's impossible, don't you think? The baby is beautiful in the flesh and beautiful in the postcard. But I am happy. You know, Eugenia, I am saying these things to make you laugh; don't get offended, you know, Eugenia!

Now I hear that your sister isn't getting my news. But I wrote to her many times and she never wrote back; I wrote her at least three times.

Today my uncle wrote to me and told me he was resting and that he's well and told me to give you his greetings, to the whole family.

Dear Eugenia, I can hardly talk to my comrade here, because they arrested him right away and gave him eight days of prison. I can see him but I can't talk to him. He came back two days late.

Now all I can do is send you my goodbyes and many kisses, to you and to our little girl. I kiss you and I want you in my arms so much, and I sign this your unforgettable Nello Lorenzi.

Greetings to Mrs. Ricciolo and to whoever asks about me.

I kiss you, I am thinking of you, I long for you, I remember you, I want to hold you, but you are far away.

Chapter 13.
The Moral Revolt

Next to the letters overflowing with heartrending nostalgia for home and country, filled with exhortations and prayers, with farewells and wills, we have, since the beginning of the war, letters that express, in addition to distress and terror, also a growing rancor focused on two objectives—"one, close by: one's own superiors; the other, further away: the executive class that wanted the war. With regard to these, the rancor seemed to come with a lack of esteem, be it for their capacity to run things or for their not behaving fairly."[1]

The most evident reactions of scorn were directed to the press: don't trust the papers, don't believe their prattle, write in unison soldiers, relations, and friends all of whom were offended by the dramatic contrast between the reality of the front and the stories spreading through the country. Omodeo commented on this reaction also: "The bitter and contemptuous note toward the war comes back often in the letters from combatants," he writes. "Above all the falsification of their psychology is what embitters the soldiers, the idea that during wartime they enjoy themselves and pluck satisfaction from it, no more or less than one does with a sport. This seemed to be an offense to their suffering and their pain, and almost an invitation to those left behind to forget them."[2]

---

[1] Procacci, *Soldati e prigionieri italiani nella Grande Guerra* cit., p. 126.
[2] Omodeo, *Momenti della vita di guerra*, cit., p. 4, note 1. In the letter from a certain Bepi addressed from Santa Maria La Longa, February 21, 1916, to an Antonietta, we find, on this topic, a significant passage: "Reading a lot in the newspapers things about the life of the soldier, who from this life is quite distant, one would form the conviction that war is a great exercise gym where the soldier can develop his muscles with many different acrobatic exercises! But unfortunately, in modern war either you're moving too much or nothing! What is true is the humidity, it's the water that swells up the soldiers' legs and fills the hospitals! And what is even more true is the arrival of a projectile, the explosion of a grenade that has the soldiers continually with their nerves tensed and thinking about death a thousand times

The soldiers' resentment also turned on the "sirs," the interventionists, the students, the ministers, the profiteers, who wanted the war but who subsequently went into hiding in the offices behind the lines, leaving at the front just the "poor workingman."

"We want with us here," writes a soldier on March 6, 1916, "those who one day said those cursed words long live war but who from May 24 are still in Italy and have only seen the war in the movies; here it's necessary to see what the word war means, to see the exhausted work of the cannon and the poor houses completely destroyed and massacred."[3]

The motives for this bitterness and for discouragement are provided frequently by the harshness of the discipline and the senselessness of many of the punishments. There are doctors who don't recognize illnesses, officers who punish just to establish the hierarchy, to say nothing of the risk of firing squad if one refuses to take part in a suicidal action.

Giuseppe Ruberti, assigned to the field hospital, notes how "forever unforgettable" was the day of September 9, 1916, "on account of being unjustly punished with two hours in irons, tied to a tree while the bombings were raging. Here's what happened. In our ambulance there is no barber, and because we are required to shave, the centurions' barber was called. He came and began to cut my hair. While he was finishing and I was washing up Col Cannas saw me; because I finished my work in an hour, he punished me. And I even had permission to get a haircut. This fact bothered me very much and really depressed my morale. I didn't have to wear irons because they didn't have them and I was under the tree for two hours from 4 to 6 while the grenades were going over our heads. I felt like crying and would certainly have done so in other circumstances. This too passed me by. In my whole time in the army and in fifteen months of war I have never been punished. I had to come here to get put into irons."[4]

---

a day!" Cited in Procacci, *Soldati e prigionieri italiani nella Grande Guerra* cit., p. 411.
3 Procacci, *Soldati e prigionieri italiani nella Grande Guerra* cit., pp. 414-415.
4 Ruberti Giuseppe, note from September 9, 1916.

Other soldiers noted, in later memories, the arrogant and contemptuous ways of many officers. Pietro Ferrari, taken out of the first line with swollen and semi-frozen feet, tries uselessly to report sick. He writes on December 8, 1915:

"Morning came, and also fatigue duty, I went down with a lot of trouble, and, once I reached the main street, which went to Volzana, I was walking like a 100-year-old man, and I said to myself: Just look! Look what the war's reduced me to, a man who's good for nothing anymore.

"Once I got to the town piazza going slowly slowly with a walking stick, I stopped at the fountain, and I was so thirsty that I drank two pails full of water and I took another full pail into which I dunked, under the usual portico, my half loaf of bread. And I ate the whole thing, which felt like a balm. Under the same portico I found Sconfietti, who made me a bit of broth and then he took off the way the company had gone. I ate really well, and then I rested a bit, and then I walked on, barely making it, to see the doctor. Here the doctor told me he doesn't visit those from other battalions, and he wouldn't see me. I asked then the carabinieri where I could find my company, and they told me that they had gone from Capella Slemme to Casa Dugo, and I got back on the road.

"I kept walking and since that road is very mountainous, it brought me a lot of pain. About 3:00 in the afternoon I got to where the company was, camped in the midst of the mud. Here I did my best to find a place to spend the night and later I found a spot in the mule stables. It was nice there because they kept the fire going. Here I was in good company with Donida Angelo from Bagnolo Cremasco. One day my feet were so bad I went to report sick and the doctor said to me quite meanly: Go away, away, peasant! Here the company was doing fatigue duty every day, going to get tables or other things in Rochino, but I didn't go. Once I went, but no sooner had I started off than I found I could barely walk, and Maj. Giuseppe Porta came up behind me on horseback, grabbed me by the jacket collar, and slapped me twice, throwing me to the ground and said to me, Get going, you do-nothing, by God! I said under my breath that that wasn't the right way to behave, that he needed to be more polite. I went back with difficulty and without looking behind me, because it was impossible to go with the others."[5]

Another thing that caused soldiers to be disdainful is the fact that officers were issuing orders with their pistols in hand, threatening to use them. Also it seemed unjust to the soldiers that there was a difference in how troops were treated compared to the officers above them, whether on the front lines or behind them.

Virginio writes from the front line in a letter of April 5, 1916, and intercepted by the censor: "Our poor brothers seem ground down as though they were the flesh of wild beasts, how are we supposed to have the courage to go forward seeing these barbarities perpetrated on our beloved youth?! Our good officials are in their caves as though nothing was for our inconvenience; they send little notes to initiate operations and with them nice and safe it would never occur to them to run any risk themselves, and we with a cadet or under a lieutenant go straight in to face death."[6]

During the course of the conflict the feelings of adversity did not die down; on the contrary, affirms Bruna Bianchi, "it's actually the letters written in the last year of the war that have the most exasperated tone, the most violent expressions of rancor: 'God dammit, they do well to give out moldy bread, so that the war will finish quickly! And am I happy, you cuckolded and beaten down people, that you want to keep the war going? Why don't you just rebel, kill all the officers, and it will be over!' "

A twenty-year-old cadet affirmed, "I am constrained to be an officer, and I didn't want the war and I almost came to

---

[5] Ferrari Pietro, p. 35.
[6] Letter from the front, April 5, 1916, addressed to Grottammare (Ascoli Piceno) and brought up in Procacci, Soldati e prigionieri italiani nella Grande Guerra cit., p. 425.

blows before the war with students who were staging interventionist protests. The ones who wanted the war are two or three groups of scoundrels."[7]

Sometimes the bitterness finds a way to transform itself into a more open-minded reflection, on the nature of war, on militarism, on peace and the way to achieve it. Reflections of this nature, which obviously would not get by the censor are the work of militant socialists, who are capable, more than others, of giving form to the diffuse feelings of hostility.

B. E. Udine, twenty-eight, a soldier of the 54th Regiment infantry, condemned to four months for writing a denigrating letter, on August 27, 1916, writes to his father, "How can one adjust oneself to this horrid life once one has embraced the holy idea of justice? How can one go along with this war that, more than even being barbarous and stupid is of a grotesque and colossal stupidity and want to make it seem civilized like a struggle for rights, when instead it is a pile of greed and of the interests of the few to the damage of the people who suffer and who pay with their own blood?" He affirms in closing that in order to overthrow "this unhealthy society" it would be necessary to move from law-abiding socialism to anarchic socialism.[8]

Others, like the Trentine Pederzolli, reflect bitterly on the absence of God's love and, in contrast, the power of the "divine and great idea of socialism" which has no enemies or limits ("the world, all nations and languages should form a single family, which, in labor, for the progress of society, produces, not destroys").[9]

---

[7] B. Bianchi, *La follia e la fuga. Nevrosi di guerra, diserzione e disobbedienza nell'esercito italiano (1915-1918)*. Rome: Bulzoni, 2001, p. 476.
[8] E. Forcella-A. Monticone, *Plotone di esecuzione. I processi della prima guerra mondiale*. Rome-Bari: Laterza, 1968, pp. 82-83.
[9] Pederzolli Giovanni, p. 247.

Stefano Manclossi was born in Ombriano (Cremona) in 1891. He enlisted into the 42nd Regiment infantry. He wrote a letter to his brother-in-law, secretary for the Socialist section in their town, so that he would refer it to the group.

September 13, 1915

Dear Brother in Law

I am sending you these couple of lines to let you know our news, up to now we are enjoying excellent health as we hope all of you do too, we received the postcard that you sent me. As far as the building goes, I leave it to you who are at home to decide.

You, as secretary, tell all our folks that I didn't write directly to the society because there was no paper; I hope they won't take it ill.

Dear Agostino, we've heard from some of our fellows that in many towns they are giving something to the families of those called up again, but I am not talking about the government subsidy. There are army committees for the families of those called up again who are needy; let me know if in our town there's such a committee.

Dear Agostino, I heard from some of these soldiers who just came here that in the area of Crema that they say that we at the front have all we need. If you hear anyone talking like that tell them in my name: that we sleep on the dirt and that now we are full of lice and that we are still wearing the linens that we had on when we were called back again. They are also saying that here we have wine, in fact it's been four months since we saw any wine. As far as eating goes, for the last two months they've given me a "loaf" a little piece of meat, less than they give in the military garrison, and a little piece of cheese that you can eat just before going to communion and a half a cup of coffee, cold also, and nothing else. But more than all that we're treated worse than animals. I've got other things to tell you, but I will let you know later on. See if you can make it so these words get published, that way people who think we're doing great here will understand that this is the "great."

If you get this letter, respond to me soon.

Primo Farabegoli, a farmer, was born June 25, 1891, in Formignano (a community in Cesena). He was enlisted into the 6th Regiment rifles. He died on December 16, 1915 at the reserve hospital in Ferrara of bronchial pneumonia contracted at the front.

November 20, 1915

My dearest parents:

I received your much wanted letter so happily, and I am very happy to hear that you are both well and that the whole family is also, and I may assure you the same of me.

Now I will tell you that the 11th corps of arms took over for us and we will be on leave for three months. Now I will tell you that to our division of the armored corps they have begun to give furloughs from fifteen to twenty days, but to our division up until December they're not giving them. I understand that Zoffoli's family have had news of him; in fact I wrote a postcard to them myself.

I've understood everything about Ciretti I wrote him a card specifically about that so that he would know and when I come on leave I will tell him in person also that I was happy that he would try this life for himself. Because he wanted war and instead of going voluntarily he did everything he could to be declared unfit. Those of us who have managed to survive this war will be making another one with the interventionists who wanted this war. I would be happy to let them see what we have conquered in this war, that the Austrians are still coming into Italy with the cannon fire. And I would like to make them see the massacre of this poor youth.

Dear parents, I beg you don't worry about me, because I am well and we are stationed in a farmer's cottage and they say soon they will send us to Italy. Afterward, I will need some money because when we get to Italy they will take away our military benefits and therefore one gets only fifteen cents.

I understand that you have received all the cards I have sent you from the front; you aren't complaining like Zoffoli's family, I hope? I tell you that the season is lovely, but it's starting to become cold and there is a frost. I tell you also that today they gave us woolen garments, socks, a hood, gloves, underwear, and a shirt and tie. If I had known it would be like this, I wouldn't have asked to get clothes from home.

My dear parents, I will stop writing by telling you to be brave and that we will see one another soon and spend some happy days together. There's nothing else to say. So, please accept the warmest goodbyes and kisses also for my little sister Iolanda, and a kiss for my wife and the little ones.

I am your son, Primo Farabegoli

Many greetings to Giannina, to Faedi Colone, to the Casandars, to the Brasinis, many greetings to everyone we know. Greetings back to Battistini's family "det piensen."

Let me know when you pay the penalty to collect my letters, if you have to pay a lot I will put some stamps on. Let me know if Giannina intends to stay with us next year also.

Cesare Menghi, manual laborer, was born on January 11, 1892, in Casale di Cesena. He was enlisted into the 120th Regiment infantry. He died of an illness on April 23, 1917 in the military hospital of Pavia.

October 16, 1915

My dearest parents:

I come with this my letter to let you know my news, I am fine, as I hope you all in the family are. In these days many soldiers have arrived of third rank as reinforcements for our regiment.

It's five or six times they have reinforced the regiment; first we were all from Romagna, now we're reduced, and there's none of us left.

I'm glad everyone is enlisting, even those who were rejected, because they will know what war really is.

Those who have arrived are crying and asking us how we've managed to survive five months living life like this. But really you have to cry day and night so as not to go insane.

They're always talking like this; so much chatter! And were living always with a good hope that the weeks and months will pass. It's not at all true what they say; it's all chatter.

Keep in mind something I said to you once, that before this war is over they will have drafted even you, dear Dad. You will see I am not far off.

But anyway, let's hope not, be brave and be happy and I bid you goodbye from my true heart and kisses to Mom, to Dad, to Vittoria, to Aurelio and all of you in the family.

Greetings also to Alessandro and to the other friends and neighbors.

Farewell and I sign

Your son, Cesare Menghi. Farewell.

Greetings to the Bonandis.

The weather here is nice.

    August 5, 1916

Dearest Sister

I am fine and so I hope you and the family are. I will tell you that I am not able to take a photograph and now the Germans have got me with the toxic gas. But I will say to you that if you send me your photograph that will make me happy. I won't add anything further, except to send you goodbyes from the heart, greetings to your boss and I am your brother Cesare Menghi.

Tell me something that will make me happy. If you only knew how tired we are!

    August 15, 1916

Dearest Sister

I am fine and I am sorry to have worried you. It's my fault for having told you certain things. I am sorry. I understand you're unhappy but that's how it is. Don't you see that they have no intention of ending this war? My fear is that it has too many supporters. Understand, we here are consumed with anger to hear that they are making parties to celebrate taking Gorizia and ringing bells! They should be ashamed!

I send you my goodbyes from my heart, and be happy for we will hope for the best. I am always your brother, Cesare.

August 16, 1915

Dearest Father

I am well like all of you in the family I hope. I am sorry to have let you know what happened because I heard it made you very unhappy. But I have to tell you that for us soldiers on the front line it gave us great displeasure to hear that you all in Italy were having celebrations and ringing bells because they took Gorizia. Remember that they are never happy and that the war isn't ending. Who cares about Gorizia if you never get to see your dear sons again!? If those who were celebrating were in our place they would leave Gorizia too! If only we can avenge ourselves with some people!

There's nothing left but to bid you goodbye from my heart, all of you in the family. Also I tell you that I received the money.

Your Cesare.

[September 19, 1916]

Dearest father:

I received your card, and I am happy to hear you are all in excellent health, as I am now also. Indeed, I am not writing to Esterina. You know that I was fighting for three nights that we have gotten mixed up with the Austrians several times, and I don't know what I did to save myself. And she was trying to talk to me about victory! I know that in Italy a lot of people make themselves happy like this, but it kills our hearts to see such things. Now they have invented bombs that are creating slaughter. Don't think that it will be easy for us to come home; it will be very difficult. Rheumatism, bone pain, lice that devour us, the snow is falling. I am sorry to have to tell you all this, but I feel like I am losing my mind.

Francesco Giuliani, shepherd and laborer, was born in Castel del Monte (L'Aquila) in 1890. He attended the first years of elementary school but later went on to become an autodidact, reading and teaching himself. Called to arms on May 15, 1915, he was assigned to the 13th Regiment infantry. On May 24, he was already in the war zone. In May of 1916 he would be transferred to the upland of Asiago. Giuliani authored a complete memoir, made up of diaries, poetry, reflections, and later meditations on the war.

San Lorenzo, March 10, 1916

It seems that the nice weather was quick to leave. Almost a month of more human life has gone by and maybe the day is near in which one must make penitence, and with this I believe one doesn't gain indulgence.

From the place where we are now, we can see and hear the war and because we are outside we don't think about it. But when one thinks that the day soon will come when it's necessary to go back to the trenches or even that it's time to start talking about it, then one stops feeling good, and worry and fear grip us again.

After having escaped from danger so many times, one loses one's courage to trust it will happen again. And then to keep going back to a place where one has suffered so much, and with everything we have seen, it can be said that it is very painful. All of us who are condemned to take part in this damned war I am sure yearn for peace.

I shouldn't speak to you about war, my dear, so as not to keep your pain present; but you know how it is, it's like when someone is ill, all they can do is think and talk about being free from it.

I have sought always not to be vanquished by fear because when one is in a dangerous situation it can be damaging to lose the light of reason. I can say that I am neither cowardly nor courageous; several times courage has not left me, but I haven't abused it uselessly. I am not ambitious to raise myself by acts of valor; I am happy staying at the lowest level. It will be enough for me if I save my skin. I have neither sympathy nor esteem for those who are courageous heroes. In wartime, all those who distinguish themselves as heroes are assassins. The real hero is someone who puts his own life at risk to save others.

I don't see the Austrian as the enemy that they want me to believe him so as to make me chase and kill him at all costs. I think that in his village he's left his dear ones from whom he was plucked as I was from you. In my heart there is no urge to kill; I think everyone's life is dear and that every dead soldier, be he friend or enemy, leaves a mother without a son, or a wife without her husband, or children without a father.

Man shouldn't be like a dog to be wound up and set on someone; from nature he has the gift of a brain, he needs to try to understand everything, to think and to ponder, and when he is urged to what is bad he should take care not to do it.

Maybe my dear you will say that I am wandering too much into these things that you think are no use; you would rather I pay attention to what's going on at home, but for some time now I have put them aside on account of not being able to take care of them. I have completely regained my health, and you can relax about it.

Vitaliano Marchetti, a shopkeeper, was born in Ancona on June 8, 1892. He enlisted in the 13th Regiment infantry, 1st Diggers.

War zone, December 18, 1916

Dear Attilio

I have what I need to send this letter to let you know a bit about what kind of life one lives among these redeemed lands. The interventionists went about making their propaganda, speeches, all for taking what, then: mountains and mountains, kilometers and kilometers of rocks.

Attilio, here all you find is great rocky mountains and nothing else. This is what we get from all the great speeches that Ancona's interventionists made. If I am lucky enough to be able to return to you all—and all day long all my thoughts are turned always to you—I will have something to say to those guys, and some of it I will say under my breath to them privately.

One goes on living—luckily I have been only a few days in the trenches—really a pig's life. We sleep in shacks that we, when we're on the first or second line, have to construct as best we can because they don't give us proper materials. It feels to me exactly as if I were sleeping in a pigpen; if only one could have a little pen like those we have in the country.

Attilio, the first six days, from the first to the sixth of the month, I slept in a shack where the rain fell inside, and under my shoulders I had tree branches. But, patience; at least I could bring home this toughness! Ah, if only we could get to that point. Last night we relieved the third unit of diggers and we had to bring blankets, haversacks, and other things and with all this stuff on our shoulders, we had to go work on the first line, actually even further up than that. Toward 10:30 we were making two gun emplacements for the machine gunners, when the enemy began to unload on us: not only rifles but grenades and shrapnel. Just imagine it to yourself, we were about two and a half kilometers from the enemy: What a lucky spot I picked! Am I right? But that would have been nothing because the enemy doesn't only fire in the front line but also in the second and third, where the bulk of the army is coming for reserve support. But the fact is they were shooting from the sides; that was the tragic thing. Luckily, with my sergeant and other soldiers, old guys with lots of military experience we found a good little spot and we pulled our hides into it. I got hit by a stone in the arm, but that's all over with.

This terrible bombardment from both sides continued until 2 in the morning. I forgot to tell you that grenades were coming at us on the side on account of the fact that where I am the front is like a strip, and it's for that reason that we were getting "pills" from the sides.

The bombardment having ended, we left at around 2:30 with all the stuff on our shoulders, en route to a small hill, like going up to Mt. Paterno. We got there with our tongues hanging out at 5:30 in the morning, but even there sometimes some "pills" would come on our flanks.

It took me two days of lying flat for my bones to begin to feel better. But patience, patience. At least, I repeat, I might be able to bring some of this toughness back home.

So, listen. If I had to live the life of a córporal and major corporal who are with me, I will tell you frankly that I would prefer to die immediately.

Be mindful that this letter doesn't get into Mama's hands, because if it did I think it would be the death of her.

I'd have many things to tell you about, but if I am lucky enough to get furlough I will tell you some other things. Now I am thirty kilometers from the front, but I am always anxious because at any minute they could send us either to the line or for rest, where I have been from the 6th to the 11th. You're all day under the shrapnel fire and under the pieces from the 305. One of these fell on the Opachiesella armory, and it made such a blast that I believe they could hear it in some Italian cities. Terrifying!

Affectionate goodbyes and a kiss to you

Vitaliano

I am tired of writing; I will have so many things to tell you. Kisses to Caterina, please remember. Then you can also tell me something about the bearer. Excuse the handwriting and any errors.

Antonio Graziani, bricklayer, was born in 1895 in Belricetto (Lugo di Romagna, Ravenna province). Enlisting in the 114th Regiment infantry he was sent first to Trentino: In May 1916 he would be working in Val Lagarina, between Mount Baldo and Mount Zugna. In October of 1916 he would be transferred to the front near Carso. He died on June 7, 1918, under unclear circumstances.

January 1917

As the departure approaches I began to think about where I should return to. Having reached the last day, that was the destruction of the ones passed. I was thinking about how I am well here and yet I can't stay here, what I am going up against without knowing why. Above all I had to leave my family with little hope of coming back. If on that day an official had come to me, one of the butcher class, I don't know what I would have done to him, out of rage. The moment comes where I have to leave. What pain I felt leaving my family. I said to myself, "Will I see them again?" Consumed with thought I made my way to the train station, greeting along the way all the neighbor families. I went along the road, with a couple of my friends, I got to Voltana with an hour to spare before the train came. I spent that hour drinking in the café with friends, but for me it was a useless drink. The time came when the train arrived, and my heart palpitated, leaving my friends and my town . . .

I get there the morning of January 16; I put on again my assassin's costume. Taking the blankets, cartridge case, and rifle and fully armed I take the path going as a butcher of human meat. After a few minutes of walking, I begin to hear the first cannonfire, and I begin to know again what fear is.

    Vermigliano, January-February 1917

The 27th of January they sent me to work at the usual post. It's necessary to work because the cold will freeze you otherwise. You can see some wretch on the ground rotting for some time. At nine, about, four grenades landed just a few steps from me. Completely frightened, I took off running. What a terrible job, being a rifleman! That evening was in a little shack, and there was a bit of a fire; several comrades were warming their shirts and their underwear to lessen the torment of lice. I spent the 28th and 29th working on a walkway in a terrible cold; it was unbearable; we were working with overcoat, gloves, and balaclava and we still couldn't take it. I've been here twenty months suffering these discomforts! As I am writing this I can hear cannonfire coming in and bombs, as happens every evening, and on this account six or seven wretches die every night.

The 30th they sent me to work in the trenches; I spent the day hidden in a cave from fear of being hit by the cannonfire. In the nighttime I was sleeping in a hut, but a sudden blast that a nearby hit made, throwing stones and splinters over the shack, I woke and spent the rest of the night terrified and waiting to flee. I stayed there with my ears open listening for the shells, waiting for them to arrive.

The morning of the 31st I was working on a walkway, every so often I heard grenades pass over me; suddenly I heard a shell that exploded directly over my head; I was sure I was going to be wounded. After that I took off and was left completely powerless from fear.

The first day of the month of February I spent working quietly.

The day of the 2nd I spent in the same way.

The 3rd I went into the trenches, after spending sixteen days of extreme sadness.

Vermigliano, February 11, 1917

Today the 11, festival day, I spent remembering what a miserable soldier I am, wandering and never finding peace, seeing the chain I am linked to, with my thoughts always turned to the freedom I used to enjoy. The barbarous government dragged me from civilization, in order that I might follow this infamous life. I am depressed, depressed seeing that this life never ends . . .

May 25, 1917

At 2 o'clock the orders that the attack will commence at 4 o'clock. To me it was as though they said: You're dead! What heavy hours those were! There are situations that will drive you crazy, and many did become crazy. Four o'clock came. The officials with their revolvers in hand. And with a single cry: Out! I didn't understand anything anymore; I was in hell;

cannonfire that fell from all sides, rifle shots and machine guns that were mowing men down. It was all the yelling of the poor guys who had fallen on the ground and you could see so many wounded and mutilated, it was incredible. Thankfully, I was wounded in my left hand. I left everything behind, I took the only course I could, climbing over piles of dirt destroyed by the cannon, rifle fire whistling past my ears, the cannon palpated the terrain. After a kilometer on the road I arrived at the aid station.

Chapter 14.
Impossible Flights

More than a few writers communicate from the front as prisoners, as detainees, as "lifers": condemned to immobility under the ever-present threat of death. The image of freedom is associated with the image of prison; but realistically what were the possibilities of flight available to soldiers? Antonio Gibelli writes of this question that there were four: "Draft-dodging, which is avoiding enlisting, backing out before the enlistment; desertion, which means fleeing when one is already enlisted or going toward the enemy or making oneself unavailable when behind the front; sickness, understood particularly as mental illness (mental illness is a form of flight, a way of removing oneself when the soldier's practical, intellectual, psychological resources don't offer any other way); and finally physical illness such as self-inflicted and faked, what is called self-lesionism or self-mutilation. These are the four flight possibilities of taking oneself out of the score-driven logic of the war, the imperative of massacre on an industrial scale. These are different modes that have different quantitative weights but that all point to this same line of tendency."[1]

From May 24, 1915, to September 2, 1919, those who refused to enlist in the Italian army numbered 470,000; of these 370,000 were Italian emigrants who decided not to return. Also among the Italians in Austria the percentage of draft dodgers is rather high: 34 percent of crimes prosecuted by the war tribunal of Trento regarded "the failure to present oneself for mass conscription."[2] And even in this case we're

---

[1] A. Gibelli, *La fuga impossibile. Autolesionismo, simulazione, follia*, in *1914-1918. Scampare la guerra. Renitenza, autolesionismo, comportamenti individuali e collettivi di fuga e la giustizia militare nella Grande Guerra*, edited by L. Fabi. Ronchi dei Legionari: Centro culturale pubblico polivalente, 1994, pp. 27-34; cit. on p.27.

[2] P. Pedron, *In nome di Sua Maesta l'Imperatore d'Austria! Il fondo "Processi di guerra 1914-1918" dell'Archivio di State di Trento*, in "Materiali di lavoro," 1985,

talking about emigrants who had already become part of the various nations of Latin America.

Desertion however is a more complex and multifaceted phenomenon. For now, the numbers: "the charges for desertion were 189,425; in the course of the conflict, 162,563 cases were tried, and 101,685 sentences were issued. Therefore if in the four year arc of the war one soldier out of twelve went through a court proceeding, one soldier in twenty-six appeared before a military court to respond to the charge of desertion and one out of forty-one were sentenced."[3] Very few deserters went to the enemy (around 3,000); the larger part of them simply went toward home, and those who overstayed their furlough were counted among these or who went away from their unit temporarily or who, after an action, went off track and wandered without any landmark.

The punishments were extremely severe: Desertion "in the face of the enemy" was punished by firing squad; domestic desertion with various sentences from three to fifteen years, depending on aggravating circumstances.[4] Apart from the tribunals' punishments, a refusal to advance, mutiny, or involuntary deviation also led to summary execution. Approved by the high command, camp executions reaffirmed subordination of the troops, strengthened the hierarchical relationships, and imposed a climate of terror.

An anonymous soldier writes on June 5, 1917, in a letter intercepted by the censors and that never reached its destination: "We are all here subjected every moment to barbarous death (killing) like so many beasts at the slaughterhouse; daily there is an enormous number of wounded and killed, the selfsame grenade killed three people from the 159th infantry, one of the Engineers, and several others wounded — just yesterday a grenade wounded seventeen of my company, and several of them badly. Here we are penned up in the woods,

---

1-3, pp. 3-113.
3 Bianchi, *La follia e la fuga* cit., pp. 160-161.
4 Ibid., p. 164.

there's no longer a hole to hide in, demoralized in an extraordinary way, so that even the officers are losing their minds; it's not death that demoralizes, because we already know we have to die, but the extraordinary cases that reveal the slaughterhouse—the massacres, the suffering, and then the ill treatment—the cruelty that unfortunately was dearly paid for toward Brig Col F. and Cav. Temistocle, himself killed, the two running from an enemy grenade, executing in the presence of all of us four soldiers—two of whom because they were thirsty and got permission to go for two hours to the Isonzo to get a canteen full of water. Let me come back to saying that I, we, have been three days without even a drop of water. So, therefore let's hope for a nice wound or a cursed death. Ah, if I manage to get home what a thug I want to become, instead of being part of civilization and progress."[5]

Aside from the deliberate desertions, there are also those that are not deliberate. There are soldiers who wander without a destination, confused, regressed into a childlike state; men who flee without knowing where to hide, obeying a deep impulse that pushes them far from the front. They go into field hospitals, often after long and bloody periods of action, shocked, paralyzed, having lost the use of their voice and their hearing, lost their memory. Others, agitated, seem obsessed by the memory of their families, convinced that they are ruined like everything else is on account of the war. Others, hit by the shock of bombardment (shell shock) are tormented by nervous tics and take refuge in a total lack of involvement.

In the diary of Don Primo Discacciati, chaplain in the field hospital of Storo, just before the front line of the judiciary sector (Trentino) we find more than a few annotations dedicated to soldiers traumatized by experiences in the trenches.

"February 3, 1916. The poor injured Forti died dreaming of winter furlough. Another 'dreamer' was locked into the security room. He says they killed his entire family and they want to kill him too. He keeps his ear cocked to every sound

---
5 Letter cited ibid., pp. 179-180.

and jumps out of bed. This evening he was locked in with a key and the infirmary guard put his cot up against the door. The crazy man, who came from the artillery, smashed at the door with his shoulder. If they hadn't jumped on him and put him in the strait jacket he would have calmly gone through the door with his shoulder.... April 12, 1916. They're saying that our guys took twenty-some prisoners at the outcropping of San Giacomo. A 305 exploded at the entrance to a farmstead where they were entrenched, and they were all taken like moles. Three were gravely injured; they were taken to Ponte Caffaro. The action goes slowly and roughly in those parts. Some positions were taken, lost, retaken. In addition to the wounded an authentic insane man was brought to the hospital. He is pitiful; he keeps praying and saying the war is God's punishment, that his mother was killed in the field along with all of his brothers and sisters, and that he is damned because he wasn't killed along with them. Etc. etc. Fear has caused a turn in his brain. It was necessary to put him in a strait jacket. He doesn't eat, doesn't drink, he just keeps talking like a whirlwind.... May 21, 1916. Eight wounded have arrived from Monte Sperone. Five of them were injured by a single bomb while they were taking shelter in a cave. The bomb went off right in the mouth of the cave. One of them, a cadet, had his right arm almost torn apart. Probably they will go ahead and amputate it; the best hypothesis is he will be left with a shriveled arm. His elbow is gone; the bones of his forearm are mangled. Another typical case. While a soldier was sitting with his gun between his legs, a 105 grenade smashed the butt of his gun and fell at his feet, without exploding. The poor devil, he was so stunned by the impact of air that hit him, he hasn't said a word for two days. Then he has started little by little to get his breath back but he still has a nervous tremor so strong that he has to be hospitalized at our facility. He is constantly agitated by a powerful after shock; we're moving him to Vestone. They'll have him for a while."[6]

---

6 Discacciati Primo, pp. 69-87. Bruna Bianchi writes in the essay "Psichiatria e

The phenomenon of traumatized soldiers besieged all armies. Italian soldiers who went through mental hospitals numbered about 40,000: an official figure that's an underestimate that one should accept with great caution.[7]

But the record of the man fleeing from the daily risk of death is long and made up of all kinds of atrocious and repugnant forms of self-injury.

"The war tribunal has recently condemned to five years of military imprisonment a soldier who was rapidly processed. He drilled his right eardrum with an iron nail from a horseshoe; and twenty years were given to a condemned man who rubbed the gonorrhea excretions of another into his eye."[8]

The breadth of behaviors by those self-injurers is inexhaustible: abscesses obtained by subcutaneous injections of gasoline, petroleum, or urine; dermatitis produced by preparations of buttercup flowers; conjunctivitis brought on by smoking or copper sulfate or by tobacco powder; otitis obtained via an application of irritating substances; bronchitis provoked by protracted inhalations of smoke. Those more desperate chopped off their hands with their field spades or let themselves be smashed by large boulders; still others shot themselves at point-blank range in the hand or the foot.

The texts that we find in the anthology tell of some of the means by which soldiers try, almost always uselessly, to take themselves off the front line, away from life in the trenches, away from the order to advance. They are tortured paths, sometimes unaware, almost always desperate. And at the same time they show, by means of the efficiency of officers, judges, doctors, and psychiatrists, the repressive force of the military machine.

---

guerra," found in the already cited volume edited by Audoin-Rouzeau and Becker, *La prima guerra mondiale* (1, pp. 309-325; cit. on pp. 319-320): "The repeated attacks, the lack of respect for the turns in the trenches, the canceled leaves, wore thin the possibility of survival, added to the fears for the future and the soldiers lived with the anguished certainty that they would never see their loved ones."

7 Bianchi, *La follia e la fuga* cit., pp. 63-64.

8 A. Frescura, *Diario di un imboscato*, in *Tre romanzi della Grande Guerra*, edited by M. Schettini. Milan: Longanesi, 1966, pp. 41-292; cit. on p. 184.

Mimo Genga was born in Colbordolo (Pesaro) on August 18, 1894. A bricklayer like his father, he emigrated to the United States at a very young age. He went back to Italy in April of 1914. He was recalled to arms on December 13, 1914, and enlisted in the 37th Regiment infantry.

Zagara, October 30, 1915

Having gotten to the hole, I couldn't decide. For several minutes I considered the fate that so many of my companions faced. What to do? And yet I had to move forward.

Even if the journey were short, it was nonetheless dangerous. I made my resolution and took off on the way, no sooner had I reached the hole than the corps was ready ahead of me, the Austrians made a volley that lasted four or five seconds. All the bullets came close to my face; then for several seconds the gunfire ceased. I said to myself: I am saved. And I took off running at top speed. But there was another volley; the bullets were hissing like vipers, one hit me in the left flank where my bag saved me, a second one hit me in the row of buttons on my jacket and a third got me in the hand holding my rifle, and I was wounded. God, what happiness!

I abandoned the weapon and all the supplies I had with me and ran off like lightning, the bullets whizzed by endlessly but I never let up on my way. I got to Plava and collapsed from fear, it was all a murmur of shells; one didn't know where to hide. Groups of prisoners were going down into the town. The joy was enormous, being off the front line, but the fear was just as great. Having reached the aid post, there was a major doctor, fairly bad, who asked me where I was wounded. "In my hand," I replied.

"You shot yourself?" he asked me. I, hearing this, was about to faint because I knew that many had been sent to trial and declared traitors to their nation.

Trembling, but still with some courage because I was sincere, I held out my hand and he unwrapped it and looked several times at my wound and didn't say anything to me. He bandaged it up again and made me wait till the truck could come and take me away. I stood close to the tent where a lot of wounded were waiting for the transport; so many poor guys died on the stretcher, even before getting any medication. Some were moaning over here, some yelling over there. You'd have to have a hard heart not to suffer listening to them. Even though I was wounded, my wound was bearable. I didn't think about my pain, since those of my companions was much more serious.

Duilio Faustinelli was born in Pezzo in Valcamonica in 1893. He was enlisted into the infantry in the 13th Fusilleers Pinerolo Brigade. He wrote his memoirs in 1953.

Toward the end of July we had a shift change again, we descended first thing in the morning, we crossed the Isonzo on catwalks, then we climbed up Mt Sabotino. We were wrecked; we didn't even seem human anymore, humans of this world. Just at that moment we passed next to a unit of locals, and I heard one who said, "Is there anyone here from Ponte di Legno?" Someone said, "Yeah, there's Faustinelli."

And so we found ourselves at the front, and this was Sebastiano Longhi from Prescaglio, but I didn't know him because he was older than me. So we left each other and we went each of us to his destiny. Here we are taking a couple of days of rest at the Cusana again, not far from San Martino di Quisca.

Here, at this point, there is a rumor going around that an assault is scheduled soon on Monte Santo, and I hear that this time we're leaving our "skins" leaving our lives, and so I was trying to think of a way to save myself.

Inside my tent, where no one could see me, I took a big stick and hit myself in one of my ankles with it. I took off my shoes, I put a blanket over it, and then I hit. At every strike I said to myself, "So bad, so bad!"

I was crying not only for the pain but also for the suffering that I was causing: "Look what a young guy has to do in order to save his own skin."

My foot had gotten very swollen and in the morning I go to see the doctor. They gave me some medicine and a bit of a tincture of iodine and let me rest. The second morning I was marked to be seen again, they gave me more treatment there at the encampment, but there went my chance of going to the hospital . . .

Then we leave again; it was August 10 of 1917 and they are talking about a great action, that in effect happened on the 16th. Many artilleries of large and medium caliber began and the bombardments that were placed at the foot of Monte Santo. Everyone switched their shooting on the enemy lines. That morning the rations arrived for everyone after midnight, and no one knew when the next would get there. For many of them, it would be the last.

They had showed me how to add the powder from the cartridge to soup and drink it, and I did just that. I emptied six cartridges into the broth, a whole clip, and I drank it. They said that this concoction would bring on a fever of 104 degrees or 105 and that if it worked, you could get to the hospital. In this way I could save myself from the imminent action; it would keep the fever up three continuous days, until the dawn of the 19th, which was the day of the assault. But that powder didn't have any effect. So, nothing worked. More patience; even in this case one has to submit to one's own destiny.

Tullio Nicoletti was born in Trentino in 1896. In 1916 he enlisted into the Austro-Hungarian army. In the spring of 1917 he was on the highlands of Lavarone and Asiago. He kept a bare-bones diary: the weather, the work, the bombardments, aerial duels; also the diary kept record of a growing anxiety and loss of self.

3/16 In the shack almost buried in the snow in the middle of the forest on the right side of the wide road to Vezzena

3/26 Service; pandemonium all day long

3/27 Lively combat around Cal Sugana

4/14 Work, powerful mortar fire

4/20 A half hour from Asiago

4/21 up to 4/27 usual work Italian Caproni airplanes, fight in air, bombardment, cannonfire thundering continually the whistle of shells and the explosion

Piero and I sheltered under a pine tree, a piece of grenade just a step away

5/23 Morning 11 and a half shells of large caliber Italian grenades pass above our work and go 2 or 3 hundred steps up the mountain, the terrible explosion. The blast of mine and the fear of being discovered the shells go by over us with a sound of a thousand screeching cats and of rusty irons.

5/29 Usual work, rainy

6/6 Nice weather, little work, violent artillery fire

6/10 Memorable day for all. The storm of shells of all calibers all day, refuge in a little grotto. Work and building of a grotto under the grenades, fleeing, lives in danger on the road; passage impossible . . . I leave to go back, run into a horse trader running away with three horses I assume responsibility for him. 3 or 4 Italian airplanes rain down bombs and machine gun fire on us.

I keep on working on the grotto until noon. The reflectors shine on our work; artificial fires.

6/11 We have to stay, sad story macabre visions. The night in a grotto with Piero. Poison gas grenades.

6/13 Our artillery continues to rumble. At eight p.m. I go back fifteen steps to the post 30, the blow the lightning, the power of the air, the glance back at the ball.

6/15 In the night of the 14th an ugly quarter hour continuing anxiety. I and Pietro on the way to Assa followed by flares and reflectors while the cannon fired and the weapons firing . . .

This morning sick with neurasthenia and went to the doctor free day terrible anxiety waiting for the bombardment

3:30 p.m. the hellish music begins again and the enemy symphonies, the sphere of smoke the whistling directly above us

6/22 anxiety

6/30 Found the bad and destined for the interior

7/30 7 a.m. leaving for Salzburg.[9]

---

[9] In the hospital Tullio Nicoletti continues to write and to rewrite his experience at the front. In some pages (maybe less efficacious than the diary) he will tell in third person the onset of the "neurosis": "Strange however that evening our young man was more loquacious than ever; you would have thought him in the arms of the god Bacchus. An uncommon nerve ailment makes him start; he seems to have an unpleasant presentiment about something. Every so often he raises his voice and

Luigi Moresco was born in Spormaggiore (Trento) on October 20, 1897. A student at the diocesan seminary, he enlisted in May of 1915. In the summer of 1917 he was on Karst and found wandering semi-consciously around the field of battle.

Around the Isonzo June 22, June 30

This voyage too was, luckily, while I was on the train, similar to another. Having disembarked, we had to go up and down the mountains quickly, and they were high (not like the Alps, but high), and go up and down and walk through those valleys with a scorching sun, without even a drop of water. At least we had had water from the Polish pools! But nothing, nothing! Thirst, burning heat, nothing else. And even more, not even coffee could be found on that unlucky trip, in that horrid ungrateful land. We got a can of cold meat and a chunk of bread a day. We were hungry; usually, however, we didn't even eat that so as not to provoke even further the demon of thirst.

When will God let us reach the end after five days of a grueling march, and where? A nasty little place down down deep in one of the sink holes, with scarce water (for military use there was the famous voucher!) inhabited by semi- or quasi-barbarous Slovenes. We put up our tents: God who had helped us up to now, don't abandon us.

---

gesticulates, few sentences understandable, he was prey to a mysterious thing, a phantasm, one might say, he has one of those cases that only rarely succeed in life and he continued to repeat, in a guttural voice, the words tomorrow, the cable railway, the Italians, assaults, grenades, other things that couldn't be understood." And later on: "Throwing himself on the pallet our young man muttered between his teeth, 'It can't be me, it seems to be my spirit a kind of I-don't-know-what that's sinister and never felt it 'til now.' " Elsewhere he tries to describe by other means the experience of being bombed: "Suddenly an incredible racket mixed with yelling that seemed inhuman emanating from the valley followed at once by rolling whistle sounds and deep blunt blows that boomed repeatedly almost instantly transforming the valley into a great workshop where thousands of hammers beat on many anvils at the same time."

The 11ᵗʰ offensive on the Isonzo was June 30, 1917 to July 2.

Among those steep and difficult mountains, after having been run down by hunger and thirst for more than six weeks, after having almost turned into walking skeletons, after having struggled to bash those stones, to scale those slopes, there had to remain still one test, the greatest of the tests gone through until then, one of the most disastrous battles of the whole war.

On August 12 I had gone, with some others, to Trieste, to look to see if there were anything that could relieve the destitution of those mountains; I won't go at length into describing the beautiful and corrupt city, nor to tell of the meager results of that voyage. For me it was luck, the grace of heaven, for because of that I was removed from the fire pan of the days before the offensive. Upon returning to our mountains, we found the last train stations destroyed, where one was obliged to go along that long road on foot; we marched at first one day and one night, then, almost dead from fatigue, after about two hours of rest, a crossing place came up: the road was a long procession, slowly self-propelled by wounded of greater or lesser degrees, crossed and interrupted constantly by cars which went in loaded with munitions and came back out loaded with wounded.

Having reached the top, giving a glance to the sink hole that we had to traverse, it presented an indescribable spectacle: far far away on the opposite rim, a volcano, burst of dust, of stones, of smoke; a dull murmuring of sibilant grenades, whistling, exploding; a confused hustle of cars, fleeing fleeing of horses, oxen, cows, sheep, men; and the long, heavy procession of wounded who slowly advanced and the crazy running of other groups, again, of course maybe, who were running to the slaughter; and a stench of dust and gas, that tormented the nostrils and made the eyes water ; and a fog, a thick dust that confusingly enveloped everything, that made those figures look like fairy tales characters from a frightening dream. What to do? Forward! Going into that terrifying cataclysm, I lost my head; I no longer knew what I was doing; I was like a walking pole. Neither seeing at every step deformed corpses, wounded horribly torn apart, nor the hearing of grenades hissing overhead, falling a few feet from me, covering me with earth and with shrapnel shards, nor the yelling and crying, the running of everything that was around me, nor the general confusion in which I was and that was getting more and more confounding, nothing, all told, had the slightest influence on me; I didn't tremble, I didn't shudder, I wasn't afraid, I didn't scream, I didn't run, I didn't get lost. I went on my straight path. And after passing several hours in that terrible and ineffable confusion, without having found the location of the company, I calmly turned my shoulders to the enemy and, left on my own, I searched for more hours for the company, in the background woods. After much wandering, I found it.

Andrea Bertazzoni, dairy farmer, was born in San Bendetto Po (Mantua) on June 27, 1895. An autodidact, he cultivated from an early age a passion for literature and was drawn to the ideas of socialism. In January of 1915 he was called to the 3rd Regiment infantry. On May 16, 1917, after a series of clashes with military hierarchy, he came to the front at Hermada. Here he shot himself in the hand and goes before a military court.

I saw an artillery soldier standing and asked him in a low voice what news there was of us. "Within the hour," he said, "we have to open fire. You're the first to make assault on the enemy positions."

I thanked him and went off to think. The joy of finding myself safe from the two officials who wanted to eliminate me was disturbed by an anxious question: What would they make me do having figured out that I am not with their company and that I am on the front line unarmed?[10] I understood that every moment of hesitation could cost me my life.

Finally, in the disorder of my thoughts, a clear decision appeared: injure myself to get out of this hell. But how? On what part of my body? With what weapon, with what justification? It was a storm of questions and answers.

I decided to injure myself with a rifle, in my left hand, between the index and the middle finger. Cause: I bumped into a rifle that wasn't mine leaning against a protrusion in the trench. I grabbed the rifle of the soldier closest to me who was asleep, washed the bullet well to prevent infections, and sure of not being seen by anyone, aimed the shot at the target I'd selected. My left hand covered with blood, and the tension was so heavy that it felt like it didn't hurt.

The shot woke those closest to me. I called for help and gave my version of the accident to the guys around me. They quickly accompanied me to the closest aid station where they disinfected me and wrapped up my hand, bucking me up with a glass of vermouth. Then they hung my arm by my neck with a little card that read: accidental wound. I was quickly taken to the Red Cross ambulance that was to take me to one of the field hospitals behind the front line . . .

On August 22, 1917 my turn came. I was called along with two other comrades, before the war tribunal of the 13th Armed Corps.

The three of us sat down, one next to the other, before the judges, waiting for their verdicts. The process was of an

---

10 In earlier pages of his memoirs Bertazzoni tells of feeling threatened by two officials who had followed him since Hermada with the intent to kill him. We don't know if this was a real threat or an imagined one.

extreme simplicity and the same for everyone. After having read the particulars and the charges, the P.M. reads the closing speech. Then the president turns to the official lawyer with the one question that completes the parody: You, Attorney, what do you have to say in defense of the accused? And this one rises to say: "I leave the matter to the express judgment of Your Excellence. The court retires for ten or fifteen minutes and then reopens to pronounce the definitive sentence." The same thing happened for each one of the three of us. The first was sentenced to firing squad; the second to a life sentence in prison, and the third, who was me, after having heard a proposal in the closing arguments for my being executed by firing squad, in virtue of article 92 of the C.P.M. the sentence was commuted to the minimum, which is twenty years in military prison. . . .

The next morning we were wakened by the terrifying screams of the most wretched of the three, father of many offspring, who was condemned to die. Before sitting on his coffin to be conducted before the firing squad he had ceased to be a man. He was completely insane in his cell; he'd removed all his clothes and was naked, he was scraping and slashing himself as though he wanted to drown in his own blood. A horrendous scene and unforgettable, which we could see from the window.

After some days I left with a military convoy of prisoners to the prisons of Cervignano. And from there to the penitentiary in Padua where our names and surnames were changed into numbers.

Giuseppe Ruberti was born in Copertino (Lecce) June 14, 1890. After grade school he entered the seminary at Nardo, and then went to the seminary at Molfetta. He was almost at the end of his studies when he got drafted. In the fall of 1915 he left for the front at Karst as a doctor's assistant. The little camp hospital where he worked from November 1915 to September 1916 was located close to San Martino del Carso across from Gradisca. On December 4, 1917, he attended the execution of a soldier who deserted intending to return home.

December 4, 1917

Today is a memorable day for me. I attended the execution of a soldier from the 270th machine gunners. Poor young guy. Yesterday evening my chaplain told me that he had to go to Salicetto to attend a sentencing. He wanted me to go also. We left with the ambulance close to ten. Having gotten there, we were sent to the garrison. There was a police marshal: they told us to wait because it wasn't time yet. Around 11 that night with a Lt Adv of military tribunal we entered the cell of the condemned man, telling him the verdict that the gracious sovereign had not ruled in his favor.

"However," said the Lt. Advocate, " the chaplain is ordered here. Ask whatever you want and it will be given to you." The poor soldier didn't say anything; he only repeated a few words. "I understand," he said, "When do they have to shoot me, now?" "No," the lieutenant replied, "there's still some time." The commander behind the other lieutenant, the public minister, having ascertained that they had requested in a

public trial to condemn him to execution, said, "You, lieutenant sir . . ." At these words this person moved away. I wanted to cry. Everyone left. It was a small cell, with a bit of straw where the poor soldier had lain down. The marshal asked him if he wanted anything, he asked for wine and grappa and cigarettes. Everything was brought to him and drinking and smoking, so much that he got drunk, that he vomited. However he was calm, sometimes he wept, he wrote in his own hand a letter home. His hand wasn't shaking. The chaplain and I began to talk about religion; he was cursing the whole time.

At 2 o'clock he fell asleep and slept heavily until 5. At five he got up and, since the hour was approaching, he was trembling and was all excited. He made confession and took Holy Communion but after having drunk a bit too much he spilled it, so much so that I had to take the straw where he had spilled and burn it. I spoke to him a bit, I comforted him, I tied a medallion to his chest, I gave him my rosary and tied it to his right arm.

The hour was coming closer and he was trembling.

Finally the ambulance arrived, we took him out, we got into the car, I, the chaplain, two police officers, a friend of his, also a policeman, and the condemned.

When the ambulance encircled by armed mounted guard moved out, we heard our hearts pounding. I was shaking, we were all of us white as sheets. The condemned, yelling, requested to the driver, who was in the front with the doctor and a health-services soldier, to drive slowly, so he could live a few more minutes.

We finally got to a street where the appointed place was located. We got out of the ambulance, the poor man making sad gestures, we began to walk to the fields. Dio Dio, he kept saying, where's the chaplain, and he hugged him. You are my God, my mother. He embraced the captain several times, when he saw the blindfold he cried out, No no, a little longer! Finally they put the blindfold on him and after a few more steps he arrived at the spot. There were 300 soldiers with arms presented, reading, or rather hearing read the sentence of death, by a lieutenant.

The poor condemned man was tied seated to a chair. He was yelling, "My God, my God, where is the chaplain?" Here he is here. Courage. Can you shoot me in the chest and not in the back? It was not allowed. Everyone moved away, he understood. The chaplain moved away and the commander of the platoon who was to give the signal to fire, gave the sign with a twig. Six shots rang out and all of them hit his head. There was silence like in a tomb. The first six who shot quickly moved away to give their places to them in case their shots had not killed him. But he was already dead. I came closer, and the chaplain and the doctor did the same. There were rivers of blood. The soldiers began to go away, the poor dead man was unbound, two townsmen came with a coffin. They put him inside it with ropes. Then the chaplain gave him absolution and we left.

What a tragedy! And who can describe it! His name was Pietro Nannucci, from the class of 1889, a native of Florence, a soldier in the 270th machine-gun unit.

Sources

Amaduzzi Alessandro
Lettere in Verificato per censura. *Lettere e cartoline di soldati romagnoli nella prima guerra mondiale*, edited by G. Bellosi and M. Savini, Il Ponte Vecchio, Cesena 2002, pp. 137-138.

Animelli Filippo
The memoir is described and quoted in the essay by Giampiero Valoti, "Non piu nulla si calcolava la vita." *La memoria della Grande Guerra di Filippo Animelli*, in "Studi e ricerche di storia contemporanea," 1991, 35, pp. 28-46.

Ardizzone Mario
Diary (june 21-September 12 1916), manuscript, notes. *Diario Guerra Italo-Austriaca 1916 Memorie del Serg. Mario Ardizzone, aiutante medico della Squadra B della XX Sezione disindezione addetta al XX Corpo d'Armata*, in Museo Storico Italian della guerra, Rovereto.

Artel Umberto
Diary (September 9 1914- February 16, 1915), manuscript, in Fondazione Museo storico del Trentino, Archivio della scrittura popolare.

Aspesi Giuseppe
Diary (1916-1917), manuscript, in Museo storico Italiano della guerra, Rovereto.

Atzori Efisio
Correspondence edited with the title *Edelweiss per un alpino cagliaritano*, edited by J. Atzori, Cuec, Cagliari 2002.

Baccalaro Bartolomeo
Numerous excerpts of the diary in G. Romiti, *Uomini di Creta. I diari di un soldato novarese nella Grande Guerra*, Edizioni Helicon, Arezzo 2012.

Belli Battista
Letter in L. Fabi, *Notizie dal fronte. Soldati della Provincia di Cremona nelle trincee della Grande Guerra*, Persico, Cremona 2005, pp. 44-45.

Beltrami Giacomo
Autobigraphical memoir (August 2 1914-March 12 1916), manuscript, *La Vita Gueresca*, in Fondazione Museo storico del Trentino, Archivio della scrittura popolare.

Bertazzoni Andrea
Autobiographical memoir in A. Bertazzoni, *La "guerra" di un pacifista*, preface by I. Guerrini and M. Pluviano, Gaspari, Udine 2005.

Botteri Guerrino
Diary (October 2-18 1914) published in *Guerrino Botteri, Vigilio Caola, Giovanni Lorenzetti, Valentino Maestranzi, Giuseppe Scarazzini*, edited by Q. Antonelli, M. Broz, G. Pontalti, Museo storico in Trento-Museo storico italiano della guerra ("Scrittura di guerra," VIII), Trento-Rovereto 1998, pp. 11-43.

Bresciani Giuseppe
Diaries and letters in G. Bresciani, *Una generazione di confine. Cultura nazionale e Grande Guerra negli scritti di un barbiere rivano*, edited by G. Fait, Museo del Risorgimento e della Lotta per la Liberta-La Grafica, Trento 1991.

Bussi Giovanni
Autobiographical memoir published by G. Bussi, *Forse nessuno leggera queste parole. Diario della Grande Guerra*, edited by R. Grimaldi, Meltemi, Roma 2002.

Calderale Annibale
Memoir published in the volume *La gente e la guerra. Documenti*, edited by L. Fabi, Il Campo, Udine 1990, pp. 119-178. A copy of the manuscript is held at the Fondazione Museo storico del Trentino, Archivio della scrittura popolare.

Calosso Emanuele
Correspondence in *Le terre matte e il caro paese. Epistolario di guerra*

dell'alpino Emanuele Calosso (1915-1918), edited by F. Caffarena, Comune di Finale Ligure 2001.

Cantini Quintilio
Numerous citations from the diary in the essay of Manuela Maggini, *Diario di un fante toscano in Valsugana*, in "Protagonisti," 2008, 94, pp. 41-63.

Capacci Giuseppe
Autobiographical memoir published with the title *Diario di guerra di un contadino toscano*, edited by D. Priore, Cultura Editrice, Firenze 1982. New edition with another title: *Diario di un contadino alla "Grande Guerra,"* edited by D. Priore, Aska Edizioni, Firenze 2014. The page numbers refer to this later edition.

Cazzoli Alfonso
Autobiographical memoir, *Ricordi e Memorie durante il mio soggiorno in Russia – prigioniero di guerra – 8 giugno 1916-30 gennaio 1918*, published by C. Zadra in "Materiali di lavoro," 1986, 1-2, pp. 185-206.

Cella Antonio
Typewritten autobiographical memoir, *Memorie della Grande Guerra europea da Cella Antonio fu Antonio Paularo Villamezzo*, in Museo storico italiano della guerra, Rovereto.

Coppola Nunzio
Diaries and letters from prison published in N. Coppola, *Un professore al fronte. Diari e lettere di guerra e di prigionia*, edited by G. Coppola and M. Ermacora, Gaspari, Udine 2011.

Costantini Ottone
Correspondence published with the title *Un contabile alla guerra. Dall'epistolario del sergente di artiglieria Ottone Costantini (1915-1918)*, edited by C. Costantini, Scriptorium, Torino 1996.

Della Martera Augusto
Correspondence published in *Le pallottole sono matte e noi eravamo peggio degli uccelli. La guerra di Augusto Della Martera 1915-1916*,

edited by P. Sorcinelli Istituto pesarese per la storia del movimento di Liberazione, Clueb, Bologna 1990.

Di Nucci Luciano
The war diary of Luciano Di Nucci (Karst March 14- October 12, 1916) is published in *Scritti in onore di Raffaele Rossi*, edited by L. Brunelli and A. Sorbini, Isuc/Editorial Umbra, Citta di Castello 2003, pp. 125-156. A copy of the manuscript is housed at the Fondazione Museo storico del Trentino, Archivio della scrittura popolare.

Disacciati Primo
Diary)May 22, 1915-February 19, 1919) published with the title *Mio Diario di guerra, in "Passato Presente,"* 1988, 13, pp. 29-174; 1991, 19, pp. 23-119.

Dotta Francesco
Autobiographical memoir (1915-1918), manuscript, *Leggenda della mia vita dall'eta di diciannove a ventiquattro anni*, in Fondazione Museo storico del Trentino, Archivio della scrittura populare.

Farabegoli Primo
Letters in *Verificato per censura. Lettere e cartoline di soldati romagnoli nella prima guerra mondiale*, edited by G. Bellosi and M. Savini, Il Ponte Vecchio, Cesena 2002, pp. 274-288.

Faustinelli Duilio
Autobigraphical memoir published by Circolo culturale G. Ghislandi with the title *La "catastrofe." Diario di guerra di un pastore camoruno*, Tip. Valgrina, Esine 1982.

Ferrari Eugenio
Letters in T. Cavalli, *Isonzo infame. Soldati bresciani nella guerra '15-'18*, Edizioni del Moretto, Brescia 1983, pp. 195-199.

Ferrari Francesco
Correspondence published with the title *Scrivere per non morire. Lettere dalla Grande Guerra del soldato bresciano Francesco Ferrari*, edited by F. Croci, Marietti, Genova 1992.

Ferrari Pietro
Diary published with the title *Vita di guerra e di prigionia. Dall'Isonzo al carso. Diario 1915-1918*, edited by M.T. Aiolfi, Mursia, Milano 2004. A copy of the manuscript is housed in the Fondazione Museo storico del Trentino, Archivio della scrittura popolare.

Filippetta Giuseppe
Autobigraphical memoir published in G. Filippetta, *Memorie di un contadino poeta*, with support from the Biblioteca comunale di Moricone (Roma), Tip. C. Zirizzotti, Frosinone 1984.

Franzelli Carlo
Letter in T. Cavalli, *Isonzo infame. Soldati bresciani nella guerra '15-'18*, Edizioni del Moretto, Brescia 1983, pp. 298-299.

Fusari Emilio
Memoir-diary published in *Emilio Fusari, Giacinto Giacomolli, Fioravante Gottardi*, Museo storico in Trento-Museo storico italiano della guerra ("Scritture di guerra," III), Trento-Rovereto 1995, pp. 11-104.

Gabanini Secondo
Letters in *Verificato per censura. Lettere e cartoline di soldati romagnoli nella prima guerra mondiale*, edited by G. Bellosi and M. Savini, Il Ponte Vecchio, Cesena 2002, pp. 297-301.

Gaddo, Augusto
Autobiographical memoir (1914-1917), manuscript, in Fondazione Museo storico del Trentino, Archivio della scrittura popolare.

Gaggi Giovanni
Correspondence amply quoted in *"Noi avemo I pensieri incerti peggio dei carcerati ...," La Grande Guerra del bersagliere Giovanni Gaggi*, edited by V. Valeri, Istituto di storia politica e sociale Venanzio Gabriotto ("Quadrini," 2), Citta di Castello 2007.

Gandini Roberto
Diary (1915-1916) published by M. Gandini in *"Strada maestro. Quaderni della biblioteca comunale G. C. Croce di San Giovanni in Persiceto,"* 1979, 12, pp. 63-105.

Garzoni Giuseppe
Memoir published with the title *Diario della guerra del 1915* in *La gente e la guerra. Documenti*, edited by L. Fabi, Il Campo, Udine 1990, pp. 25-105.

Genga Mimo
Memoir published with the title *Ricordo dei disagi della guerra europea 1915-16-17-18*, edited by G. Pelosi and N. Tacchi, in *Filandaie, partigiani, portolotti tra storia e memoria. Note di storia contemporanea della Provincia di Pesaro-Urbino*, edited by G. Pedrocco and P. Sorcinelli, Sezioni di Pesaro dell-Anpi-Anppia-Irsmlm ("Quaderno 2,"). Pesaro 1981, pp. 9-36.

Giudici Romeo
Letter in L. Fabi, *Notizie dal fronte. Soldati della Provincia di Cremona nelle trincee della Grande Guerra*, Persico, Cremona 2005, p. 37.

Giuliani Francesco
Diary, correspondence, and poetry in F. Giuliani, *Diario della guerra 1915-18. Lettere dal fronte*, edited by P. Muzi, Japadre Editore, L'Aquila-Roma 2001.

Gottardi Fioravante
Diary published in *Emilio Fusari, Giacinto Giacomolli, Fioravante Gottardi*, edited by Q. Antonelli, Museo storico in Trento-Museo storico italiano della guerra ("scritture di guerra," III), Trento-Rovereto 1995, pp. 133-219.

Gottero Luigi
Correspondence in P. Nicola, *Voci da ina comunita Contadina piemontese durante la Grande Guerra*, PhD thesis, University degli Studi di Torino, Facolta di Lettere e Filosofia, a.a. 1981-1982, pp. 327-436.

Graziani, Antonio
The diary was published with the title *"Cera Cadorna..." Diary (1915-1917) della Grande Guerra del soldato Antonio Graziani*, edited by L. Mascanzoni, Longo ("I quaderni del Cardello," 8), Ravenna 1998, pp. 23-55.

Gazioli Antonio
Letter in L. Fabi, *Notizie dal fronte. Soldati della Provincia di Cremona nelle trincee della Grande Guerra*, Persico, Cremona 2005, p. 69.

Gregorich Ersilio
Correspondence (1915-16) partially published with the title *Un triestino sul "fronte delle pigne." Dall Isonzo al Tirolo (aprile 1915-giugno 1916)*, edited by M. Rossi and S. Ranchi, in "Qualestoria" April 1992, 1, pp. 95-116.

Laich Francesco
Memoir published in *Rodolfo Bolner, Giovanni Pederzolli, Francesco Laich*, edited by G. Fait, Museo storico in Trento-Museo storico italiano della guerra ("Scritture di guerra," X), Trento-Rovereto 2002, pp. 269-418.

La Scala Giuseppe
Diary published in G. La Scala, *Diario di guerra di up cappellano metodista durante la prima guerra mondiale*, edited by G. Vicentini, Cuadiana, Torino 1996.

Lorenzo Nello
The entire correspondence is published in N. Lorenzi, *Lettere ai famigliari (1913-1917). Epistolario di un giovane soldato valdarnese*, edited by C. Fabbri and D. Priore, Biblioteca comunale di Terranuova Bracciolini, San Giovanni Valdarno 1996.

Lucarini Alfonso
Correspondence in Fondazione Museo storico del Trentino, Archivio della scrittura popolare. A copy of the manuscript is housed at the Fondazione Museo storico del Trentino, Archivio della scrittura popolare.

Lunelli Giuseppe
Autobiographical memoir, June 28-August 1, 1914, manuscript, *La mobilitazione dell'Austria-Ungheria del 1914. La vita che passai io Giuseppe Lunelli addetto al IV Reggimento cacciatori Tirolesi nella mobilitazione e in tempo di g ...*, in Fondazione Museo storico del Trentino, Archivio della scrittura popolare.

Manclossi Stefano
Letter in L. Fabi, *Notizie dal fronte. Soldati della Provincia di Cremona nelle trincee della Grande Guerra*, Persico, Cremona 2005, p. 60.

Marchetti Vitaliano
Correspondence (1916-1918) partially published with the title "*Se avro la fortuna sempre di poter ritornare fra voi tutti . . .*" edited by R. Giacomini, in "Storia e problemi contemporanei," January-December 1988, 1-2, pp. 115-133.

Marzari Ezechiele
Diary *(Memorandum del Mobilizirun del 21 Maggio 1915 Giorno fatal Discrezione della mia vita passata nel Campo in Galizia e Lovinia)* published in *Ezechiele Marzari, Decimo Rizzoli, G.Z.*, edited by G. Fait, Museo storico in Trento-Museo storico italiano della guerra ("Scritture di guerra," II), Trento-Rovereto 1995, pp. 11-92.

Masera Giuseppe
Diary published in *Riccardo Malesardi, Giuseppe Masera, Rosina Fedrozzi Masera, Evaristo Masera Raffaelli*, edited by. G. Fait, Museo del Risorgimento e della lotta per la liberta-Museo storico italiano della guerra ("Scritture di guerra," I), Trento-Rovereto 1994, pp. 31-86.

Mazzera Giulio
Manuscript copy and a second typed copy (May 24-December 31, 1915) in Fondazione Museo storico del Trentino, Archivio della scrittura popolare.

Menapace Alessio
Memoir (May 10, 1915- January 1917), published with the title *Mia vita in guera*, edited by Q. Antonelli, Pro Cultura Centro Studi Nonesi, Cles 2012.

Menghi Cesare
Letters in *Verificato per censura. Lettere e cartoline di soldati romagnoli nella prima guerra mondiale*, edited by G. Bellosi and M. Savini, Il Ponte Vecchio, Cesena 2002, pp. 312-314.

Mich Eugenio
Diary (1914-1918), manuscript, in Fondazione Museo storico del Trentino, Archivio della scrittura popolare.

Moresco Luigi
Autobiographical memoir transcript, *Brevi ricordi de la mia vita militare*, in Fondazione Museo storico del Trentino, Archivio della scrittura popolare.

Nicoletti Tullio
Diary (1917), manuscript, in Fondazione Museo storico del Trentino, Archivio della scrittura popolare.

Opreni Giuseppe
Significant quotations from the diary in *A Sessant'anni da Caporetto. La guerra di un minatore*, edited by M. Massazza, in "Studi e ricerche di storia contemporanea," November 1977, 10, pp. 77-87.

Paoli Angelo
Memoir *(Mia vita in guerra)* and correspondence published in *Angelo Paoli, Celeste Paoli, Giuseppina Paoli, Luigia Paoli, Maria Paoli et alii*, edited by M. Paoli, Museo storico in Trento-Museo storico italiano della guerra ("Scritture di guerra," IX), Trento-Rovereto 2001, pp. 29-67.

Paoli Celeste
Diary and correspondence published in *Angelo Paoli, Celeste Paoli, Giuseppina Paoli, Luigia Paoli, Maria Paoli et alii*, edited by M. Paoli, Museo storico in Trento-Museo storico italiano della guerra ("Scritture di guerra," IX), Trento-Rovereto 2001, pp. 75-271.

Pasini Luigi
Letter in L. Fabi, *Notizie dal fronte. Soldati della Provincia di Cremona nelle trincee della Grande Guerra*, Persico, Cremona 2005, p. 71.

Passerini Giuseppe
Diary (1915-1919) and letters published edited by Diego Leoni in "*Materiali di lavoro,*" 1986, 1-2, pp. 153-173.
Pederzolli Giovanni

Autobiographical memoir, *Ricordo della guerra mondiale 1914-1916. Wienna 1 Agosto 1916*, published in Rodolfo Bolner, Giovanni Pederzolli, Francesco Laich ("Scritture di guerra," X), edited by G. Fait, Museo storico in Trento-Museo storico italiano della guerra, Trento-Rovereto 2002, pp. 201-267.

Pinelli Faustino
Letter in T. Cavalli, *Isonzo infame. Soldai bresciani nella guerra '15-'18*, Edizioni del Moretto, Brescia 1983, pp. 177-178.

Pisoni Biagio
Diary (September 20-October 20, 1915), manuscript, *Memorie del campo Austro-Italiano Anno 1915*, in Fondazione Museo storico del Trentino, Archivio della scrittura popolare.

Pistoia Andrea
Diary (August 1, 1914-November 27, 1918), typed manuscript, in Fondazione Museo storico del Trentino, Archivio della scrittura popolare.

Ruberti Giuseppe
Diary, *Note ed appunti militari*, typewritten, in Fondazione Museo storico del Trentino, Archivio della scrittura popolare.

Scarpocchi Bruno
Letter addressed to his parents, published in T. Cavalli, *Isonzo infame. Soldati bresciani nella guerra '15-'18*, Edizioni del Moretto, Brescia 1983, pp. 134-136.

Sommavilla Giacomo
Autobiographical memoir (Libro di guerra) in *Simone Chiocchetto, Viglio Iellico, Giacomo Sommavilla, Albino Soratroi*, edited by L. Palla. Museo storico in Trento-Museo storico italiano della guerra ("Scritture di guerra," VI), Trento-Rovereto 1997, pp. 129-168.

Spagnolini Carlo
Letter published in C. Stiaccini, *Trincee di carta. Lettere di soldati della prima guerra mondiale al parocco di Fara Novarese*, Interlinea, Novara 2005, p. 69.

Teoli Luigi
Letter published in T. Cavalli, *Isonzo infame. Soldati bresciani nella guerra '15-'18*, Edizioni del Moretto, Brescia 1983, pp. 214-215.

Tirel Callisto
Diary published with the title *Due contadini del Friuli orientale al fronte e in Russia. Le memorie di Callisto Tirel e Francesco Gri*, edited by T. Matta, in "Qualestoria," December 1992, 3, pp. 135-144.

Tirreni Mario
Correspondence in *Ta-Pum. Lettere dal fronte. Contributo Morubiano nella Grande Guerra*, edited by L. Beltrame Menini, Panda Edizioni, Padova 2001. Pp. 190-215.

Tonetto Agostino
Correspondence published in A. Tonetto, *Carisima moglie. lettere dal fronte della Grande Guerra da Ca' Savio a Caporetto 1916-1917*, edited by L. Bregantin, edizioni NovaCharta, Padova 2007.

Travostino Ettore
Copy of the entire war correspondence in Fondazione Museo storico del Trentino, Archivio della scrittura popolare.

Valenti Alfredo
The diary (1916-1917) was published with the title *"Tirava un forte vento." Diario della guerra Itala-Austro Ungarica di Alfredo Valenti*, edited by I. Pellicioli, Il filo di Arianna, Bergamo 1987.

Venturi Angelo
Letters in *Verificato per censura. Lettere e cartoline di soldati romagnoli nella prima guerra mondiale*, edited by G. Bellosi and M. Savini, Il Ponte Vecchio, Cesena 2002, pp. 403-405.

Zambelli Gabriele
Diary-memoir (August 17, 1914-May 3, 1925), manuscript in Fondazione Museo storico del Trentino, Archivio della scrittura popolare; partially published in *Ezechiele Marzari, Decimo Rizzoli, Gabriele Zambelli*, edited by G. Fait, Museo storico in Trento-Museo storico italiano della guerra ("Scritture di guerra," II), Trento-Rovereto 1995, pp. 143-230.

Zanni Giovanni
Letter in T. Cavalli, *Isonzo infame. Soldati bresciani nella guerra '15-'18*, Edizioni del Moretto, Brescia 1983, pp. 218-219.

Zanotti Giacomo
Letter in L. Fabi, *Notizie dal fronte. Soldati della Provincia di Cremona nelle trincee della Grande Guerra*, Persico, Cremona 2005, p.

Zaro Giovanni
Correspondence in P. Nicola, *Voci da una comunita Contadina piemontese durante la Grande Guerra*, PhD thesis, Universita degli Studi di Torino, Facolta di Letter e Filosofia, a.a. 1981-1982, pp. 488-491.

Index of Place Names

Abruzzo 62
Acquanegra sul Chiese 16
Acquileia 241
Ala 23
Albania xviii
Alexandria 38
Alsace-Lorraine 75
Altopiano dei Sette Comuni 291
Alzano Lombardo 143
Alzano Maggiore 143
Aquila 102, 133, 167, 231, 284
Arezzo 121, 188, 222, 268
Aris di Monfalcone 102
Asiago xviii, xix, 52, 60, 61, 63, 102, 134, 162, 167, 173, 182, 183, 205, 228, 231, 239, 256, 284, 301
Austria 25, 29, 30, 32, 36, 44, 48, 58, 59, 67, 69, 70, 71, 72, 78, 79, 92, 94, 95, 97, 98, 100, 104, 107, 112, 113, 114, 122, 123, 137, 141, 143, 147, 148, 152, 153, 156, 157, 160, 161, 162, 164, 167, 169, 173, 174, 176, 178, 179, 181, 182, 187, 190, 191, 193, 195, 196, 198, 202, 203, 204, 205, 207, 210, 219, 223, 227, 236, 243, 245, 246, 247, 254, 264, 268, 280, 283, 285, 293, 298, xii
Avio 97

Bagnolo Cremasco 275
Baricata 163
Bassano 48, 244
Belgrade xvi, xx
Belluno 48, 60, 244
Belprato 138
Belricetto 120, 185, 288
Bergamo 143, 153, 213, 321
Bibiana 258
Bocenago 89
Bonate Sopra 213
Borgo San Lorenzo 128
Brentonico 83

Brescia 39, 132, 138, 181, 210, 254, 314
Britain xiv
Bucovina xii, 69
Buia 105, 177
Busseto 107
Busto Arsizio 234

Ca' Tron 148, 149
Cadore 27
Cadorna 15, 49, 111
Cagliari 202
Cal Sugana 301
Calabria 26
Camaiore 42, 131
Camno 133
Campolongo 98, 101
Canada 244
Capella Slemme 275
Caporetto 25, 44, 54, 148, 196, 319, 321
Carnia 140, 226, 264
Carniche 219
Carzeto 110
Casa Dugo 275
Casale di Cesena 281
Castagnevizza 206
Castel del Monte 102, 133, 167, 231, 284
Castelnuovo 161
Cavallino 267
Celle (camp) 33
Cervignano 97, 101, 114, 308
Cesena 153, 279, 281
China xviii
Cividale 116
Cognola 73
Col Bricon 237
Col di Lana xvii
Colbordolo 115, 298
Condino 107, 108, 109
Copertino 158, 308
Cortina 14, 63, 219
Cortina D'Ampezzo 219
Cossano Belbo 145, 206
Crema 278

Cremona 21, 98, 129, 156, 191, 200, 278, 311
Cronsi 180
Cuneo 18, 19, 38, 145, 182, 206
Cusana 300
Denno 80, 228, 256
Doberdo 14, 161, 186
Dorson di Genova Lobia Alta 225

Eusebio Boroni 89

Fara Novarese 137, 212, 320
Ferrara 151, 279
Fiera di Primiero 235, 243, 244, 246
Finalborgo 226, 227
Finale Ligure 226
Florence 128, 135, 261, 310
Formigniano 151
Fossano 20
France xiv, 75, 79,
Friuli 57, 69, 72, 92, 95, 97, 152, 321

Galizia xii, xv, xvi, 69, 70, 71, 73, 75, 79, 80, 82, 83, 85, 86, 243,
Gallipoli xvi
Gattinara 140, 264, 266
Gemona 133
Genoa 38, 43
Germany xv, xvii, xviii, 40, 69, 105, 109, 177, 249,
Ginestreto di Pesaro 258
Giulie 219
Gradisca 158, 308
Grappa 14, 22
Greece xviii
Grodek 70

Isonzo xvi, xvii, xviii, xix, 22, 93, 94, 98, 99, 101, 106, 119, 128, 129, 133, 150, 152, 155, 186, 197, 212, 216, 258, 295, 299, 303, 304, 314, 315
Italy xii, xv, xvi, xvii, xx, 4, 15, 26, 29, 57, 58, 67, 72, 97, 115, 117, 119, 130, 149, 152, 164, 196, 199, 200, 201, 214, 219, 241, 242, 243, 244, 246, 247, 274, 280, 283, 298

Japan xv

Karst xii, xvii, 6, 23, 41, 60, 63, 114, 120, 132, 148, 151, 158, 160, 168, 169, 175, 177, 185, 188, 206, 212, 213, 241, 258, 269, 303, 308
Katzenau Camp 30
Kosana 93, 95
Krakow xv, 71

La Cella 268
Lagosin 163
Lake Garda 75, 79
Lavarone 301
Lecce 158, 308
Lemberg xv, 70, 71
Libya 99, 199
Livinallongo 59
Lombardy 15, 20, 21
Lucca 42, 131
Lugo di Romagna 120, 185, 288

Malga Cis 237
Malga Toraro 244
Malga Ziolera 234
Malo 183
Manchuria 57
Mantua 305
Marcesina 163
Margarita 20
Marmolada, Mt. 51, 221, 228, 231, 256
Marostica 244
Matera province 28
Mauthausen 30, 207
Miella Belbo 182
Milan 4, 234
Modena 205
Moena 82, 228
Molfetta 158, 308
Monopoli 169
Monte Coston 114
Monte Maggio 182, 184
Monte Nero 14
Monte Sabotino 182
Monte Santo 128, 300
Monte Sei Busi 185, 186
Monte Zugna 185
Monteforte D'Alpone 43
Montello 63
Montenegro xvii

Monterchi 121, 188, 222
Monticello 123, 223
Montichiari 254
Moresa 166
Moricone 244
Mt. Adamello 23, 132, 219, 221, 224, 225
Mt. Baldo 48, 120, 185, 228
Mt. Bisorte 223
Mt. Ermada 170, 193, 305, 306
Mt. Fin 164
Mt. Fortino 140
Mt. Mertzel
Mt. Nero 14, 117, 204, 267
Mt. Pizzac di Arabba 220
Mt. Zugna 120, 185, 202, 204, 288

Naples 169, 206,
Nardo 158, 308
Nave 197
Northern Austria 78
Novara 15, 38, 47, 212

Ombriano 278
Opacchiasella 258
Ortigara 14, 18, 20, 23, 63, 212, 214, 226
Ortles xii, 219
Osimo 116

Palermo 11
Palmanova 101, 266
Parma 107, 206
Passo Pordoi 220
Passo Rolle 237, 244
Pasubio 6, 7, 14, 190, 202, 219, 221, 233
Pavia 11, 281
Peri 48
Perugia 93
Pesaro 115, 258, 298
Petrograd
Pezzo 100, 299
Pian di Sco 268
Piave 15
Piedmont 15, 26, 127
Pietrarossa 192
Pinerolo 34, 100
Pistoia 261
Podgora 14, 128
Pomigliano d'Arco 206

Ponte di Legno 122, 123, 299
Portugal
Potosloki 57
Pozza 228, 231
Prescaglio 299
Primolano 244
Punta di Penia 222

Ravenna 49, 120, 185, 288
Rawa-Ruska 70, 71, 80, 83
Redipuglia 136, 168, 185
Reggio Emilia 113, 224
Riva 75
Roccafranca 181
Rochino 275
Rome 38, 116, 200, 201
Ronchi 134, 135, 168, 192, 293
Rosa 48
Rova del Garda 233
Rovereto 35, 36, 37, 40, 51, 59, 69, 263
Rudki 69

S. Lucia Under the Waters 150
S. Martino Quisca 94
S. Michele 161
S. Secondo 110
Sabotino 128, 139, 182, 299
Sacile 92
Salsa 174
Salzburg 77, 78, 303
Sambor 69
San Bendetto Po 305
San Daniele 140
San Giacomo 296
San Martino del Carso 158, 308
St. Martino di Castrozza 244
San Michele 5, 9, 20, 189
San Polo 168
San Vittore 190
Santa Maria 153, 155, 273
Sardegna/Sardinia 41, 175
Selz 160, 167, 168, 169, 192
Serbia xv, xvi
Serravalle 120
Siberia xix, 32
Sicily 43
Sigmundsherberg prison 226
Soresina 129

Southern Italy 243
Spormaggiore 303
St. Giovanni of the Tirol 76
St. Martino Hill 176
Starzava 79
Storo 295

Ternova d'Isonzo 106
Terranova 106
The Tofane 59
The Tonale 19
Theriesenstadt 30
Tizzana 261, 263
Tolmino 133, 156
Trentino xii, 22, 30, 35, 42, 45, 46, 50, 52, 53, 56, 57, 58, 67, 69, 72, 80, 85, 100, 107, 112, 120, 152, 182, 184, 185, 188, 200, 202, 219, 222, 226, 228, 234, 244, 261, 264, 288, 295, 301,
Trento 34, 38, 39, 45, 57, 73, 82, 83, 97, 175, 182, 185, 210, 214, 228, 233, 256, 293, 303
Trieste xx, 69, 85, 149, 153, 177, 210, 212, 260
Tuoro 93
Turin 38, 162, 163, 182
Turkey xv, xvi, xviii
Tuscany 24, 262

Udine 105, 140, 177, 182, 264, 277
Udine-Pontebba 140
United States 298

Vaiano Cremasco 156, 191
Val di Fassa 219
Val di Ledro 22
Val di Non 80
Val Lagarina 23, 120, 183, 288
Val Pellice 258
Val Pusteria 228, 256
Val Zanchetta 237
Valcamonica 60, 100, 299
Valle del Chiese 107
Valsulgana
Velechi Debeli 192
Venezia xii, 30, 267
Venezia Giulia vii
Vercelli 264

Verdun xvii, 160
Veronese 43, 48
Vezzena 301
Vicenza 27, 182
Vienna 40, 78, 79
Vigo di Fassa 228
Villa Poma 136
Villa Vicentina 101
Villach 153, 180
Villamontagna 73
Villesse 98, 99, 100
Vittorio Veneto xx, 21
Vodil 133
Volaria 133
Volinia xii

Ypres xvi

Zagara 298

Saggistica

Taking its name from the Italian word for essays, essay writing, or non-fiction, Saggistica is a referred book series dedicated to the study of all topics and cultural productions that fall under what we might consider that larger umbrella of all things Italian and Italian American.

Vito Zagarrio
The "Un-Happy Ending": Re-viewing The Cinema of Frank Capra. 2011. ISBN 978-1-59954-005-4. Volume 1.

Paolo A. Giordano, Editor
The Hyphenate Writer and The Legacy of Exile. 2010. ISBN 978-1-59954-007-8. Volume 2.

Dennis Barone
America/Trattabili. 2011. ISBN 978-1-59954-018-4. Volume 3.

Fred L. Gardaphè
The Art of Reading Italian Americana. 2011. ISBN 978-1-59954-019-1. Volume 4.

Anthony Julian Tamburri
Re-viewing Italian Americana: Generalities and Specificities on Cinema. 2011. ISBN 978-1-59954-020-7. Volume 5.

Sheryl Lynn Postman
An Italian Writer's Journey through American Realities: Giose Rimanelli's English Novels. "The most tormented decade of America: the 60s" 2012. ISBN 978-1-59954-034-4. Volume 6.

Luigi Fontanella
Migrating Words: Italian Writers in the United States. 2012. ISBN 978-1-59954-041-2. Volume 7.

Peter Covino & Dennis Barone, Editors
Essays on Italian American Literature and Culture. 2012. ISBN 978-1-59954-035-1. Volume 8.

Gianfranco Viesti
Italy at the Crossroads. 2012. ISBN 978-1-59954-071-9. Volume 9.

Peter Carravetta, Editor
Discourse Boundary Creation (LOGOS TOPOS POIESIS): A Festschrift in Honor of Paolo Valesio. 2012. ISBN 978-1-59954-036-8. Volume 10.

Antonio Vitti and Anthony Julian Tamburri, Editors
Europe, Italy, and the Mediterranean. 2012. ISBN 978-1-59954-073-3. Volume 11.

Vincenzo Scotti
Pax Mafiosa or War: Twenty Years after the Palermo Massacres. 2012. ISBN 978-1-59954-074-0. Volume 12.

Anthony Julian Tamburri, Editor
Meditations on Identity. Meditazioni su identità. 2014. ISBN 978-1-59954-082-5. Volume 13.

Peter Carravetta, Editor
Theater of the Mind, Stage of History. A Festschrift in Honor of Mario Mignone. 2014. ISBN 978-1-59954-083-2. Volume 14.

Lorenzo Del Boca
Italy's Lies. Debunk History's Lies So That Italy Might Become A "Normal Country". 2014. ISBN 978-1-59954-084-9. Volume 15.

George Guida
Spectacles of Themselves. Essays in Italian American Popular Culture and Literature. 2015. ISBN 978-1-59954-090-0. Volume 16.

Antonio Vitti and Anthony Julian Tamburri, Editors
Mare Nostrum: prospettive di un dialogo tra alterità e mediyrttsnrità. 2015. ISBN 978-1-59954-100-6. Volume 17.

Patrizia Salvetti
Rope and Soap. Lynchings of Italians in the United States. ISBN 978-1-59954-101-3. Volume 18.

Sheryl Lynn Postman and Anthony Julian Tamburri, Editors
Re-Reading Rimanelli in America: Six Decades in the Untied States. 2016. ISBN 978-1-59954-102-0. Volume 19.

Pasquale Verdicchio
Bound by Distance: Rethinking Nationalism through the Italian Diaspora. 2016. ISBN 978-1-59954-103-7. Volume 20.

Peter Carravetta
After Identity: Migration, Critique, Italian American Culture. 2016. ISBN 978-1-59954-072-6. Volume 21.

Antonio Vitti and Anthony Julian Tamburri, Editors
The Mediterranean as Seen by Insiders and Outsiders. 2016. ISBN 978-1-59954-107-5. Volume 22.

Eugenio Ragni
Giose 1959: un "suicido" annunciato. 2016. ISBN 978-1-59954-109-9. Volume 23.

www.ingramcontent.com/pod-product-compliance
Lightning Source LLC
Chambersburg PA
CBHW031754220426
43662CB00007B/406